Cognitive Modeling

This book is dedicated to the founding fathers of mathematical psychology and mathematical psychologists.

Cognitive Modeling

Jerome R. Busemeyer | **Adele Diederich**
Indiana University, Bloomington   *Jacobs University Bremen, Germany*

Los Angeles | London | New Delhi
Singapore | Washington DC

For information:

SAGE Publications, Inc.
2455 Teller Road
Thousand Oaks, California 91320
E-mail: order@sagepub.com

SAGE Publications India Pvt. Ltd.
B 1/I 1 Mohan Cooperative
 Industrial Area
Mathura Road, New Delhi 110 044
India

SAGE Publications Ltd.
1 Oliver's Yard
55 City Road
London EC1Y 1SP
United Kingdom

SAGE Publications
 Asia-Pacific Pte. Ltd.
33 Pekin Street #02-01
Far East Square
Singapore 048763

Printed in the United States of America

Library of Congress Cataloging-in-Publication Data

Busemeyer, Jerome R.
Cognitive modeling / Jerome R. Busemeyer; Adele Diederich.
 p. cm.
Includes bibliographical references and index.
ISBN 978-0-7619-2450-0 (pbk.: alk. paper)
 1. Psychometrics. 2. Scaling (Social sciences) 3. Psychology Mathematical models. 4. Cognitive psychology. I. Diederich, Adele. II. Title.

BF39.B84 2009
153.01′1—dc22   2008044866

This book is printed on acid-free paper.

09   10   11   12   13   10   9   8   7   6   5   4   3   2   1

Acquisitions Editor:	Erik Evans
Editorial Assistant:	Sarita Sarak
Production Editor:	Brittany Bauhaus
Copy Editor:	QuADS Prepress (P) Ltd.
Typesetter:	C&M Digitals (P) Ltd.
Proofreader:	Jenifer Kooiman
Indexer:	Rick Hurd
Cover Designer:	Edgar Abarca
Marketing Manager:	Stephanie Adams

Contents

Preface

Cognitive science is concerned with understanding the processes that the brain uses to accomplish tasks including perceiving, learning, thinking, problem solving, decision making, and moving in the environment. The goal of a cognitive model is to scientifically explain these basic cognitive processes, and how they interact. Models of cognitive processes are appearing in all fields of cognition at a rapidly increasing rate, and furthermore, applications are spilling over into other fields including human factors, clinical psychology, cognitive neuroscience, social psychology, agent based modeling in economics, and many more. Thus cognitive modeling is becoming an essential tool for Cognitive Science in particular and the Behavioral Sciences in general, and any serious student with an inclination toward theory development needs to learn these tools. But how can one learn these tools?

This book presents an elementary introduction to the basic methods used to develop and test cognitive models. It answers many of the questions that researchers face when beginning work on cognitive models: What makes a cognitive model different from conceptual or statistical models, and how do you develop such a model? How can you derive qualitatively different predictions between two cognitive models? How do you estimate the parameters to quantitatively test the predictions of these models, and how do you compare the performance of different models? This book provides an elementary presentation of the essential tools for solving these problems. It includes tutorial presentations of psychological, mathematical, statistical, and computational methods used in all areas of cognitive modeling. Detailed examples are provided showing how to use each of these tools in a variety of modeling areas including recognition, categorization, decision making, and learning.

Acknowledgments

We would like to acknowledge the comments provided by Colin Allen, Ken Malmburg, Roger Ratcliff, and John Kruschke. We also acknowledge help from Jay Myung and Mark Pitt to start this project.

SAGE Publications and the authors gratefully acknowledge the contributions of the following reviewers:

Stephen Blessing, *University of Tampa*

Paul M. Bronstein, *University of Michigan–Flint*

David Budescu, *University of Illinois, Champaign*

Michael R. W. Dawson, *University of Alberta*

Richard Gonzalez, *University of Michigan*

Catherine Harris, *Boston University*

Valerie James-Aldridge, *University of Texas–Pan American*

Victor Johnston, *New Mexico State University*

Koen Lamberts, *University of Warwick*

Zhong-Lin Lu, *University of Southern California*

Kevin MacDonald, *Cal State Long Beach*

Todd Maddox, *University of Texas at Austin*

Erik Nilsen, *Lewis and Clark*

Stellan Ohlsson, *University of Illinois at Chicago*

Thomas Palmeri, *Vanderbilt University*

David Peebles, *University of Huddersfield*

Thomas Wickens, *University of California–Los Angeles*

Jun Zhang, *University of Michigan*

1

Introduction to Cognitive Modeling

Cognitive science is concerned with understanding the processes that the brain, especially the human brain, uses to accomplish complex tasks, including perceiving, learning, remembering, thinking, predicting, inference, problem solving, decision making, planning, and moving around the environment. The goal of a cognitive model is to scientifically explain one or more of these basic cognitive processes, or explain how these processes interact.

Cognitive models are appearing in all fields of cognition at a rapidly increasing rate, ranging from perception to memory to problem solving and decision making. More than 80% of the articles appearing in major theoretical journals of cognitive science involve cognitive modeling.[1] Furthermore, applications of cognitive modeling are beginning to spill over into other fields, including human factors, clinical psychology, cognitive neuroscience, agent-based modeling in economics, and many more.[2] Thus, cognitive modeling is becoming an essential tool for cognitive science in particular and the social sciences in general; any serious student with an inclination toward theory development needs to become a competent reader and perhaps a user of these tools.

A Brief Example of a Cognitive Model

To get a quick idea about cognitive models, here is a briefly described example. One highly active area of cognitive modeling is concerned with the question of how we learn to categorize perceptual objects. For example, how does a radiologist learn to categorize whether an X-ray image contains a cancerous tumor, a benign tumor, or no tumor at all? How does a naturalist learn to categorize wild mushrooms as poisonous, edible, or harmless but inedible? How does an amateur art enthusiast learn to categorize paintings as belonging to the renaissance period, romantic period, modern period, or some other period?

One cognitive model is called the prototype model of categorization. According to this model, the learner estimates the central tendency from all the examples experienced from within each category during training. When a new target stimulus is presented, the similarity of this target to each category prototype is evaluated, and the category with the most similar prototype is chosen. Another cognitive model is called the exemplar model of categorization. According to this model, the learner memorizes all the examples that are experienced from each category during training. When a new target stimulus is presented, the similarity of the target to each stored example is computed for each category, and the category with the greatest total similarity is chosen.

Prototype and exemplar models (e.g., Medin & Schaffer, 1978) are just two examples of categorization models, and there are many more in the literature, including artificial neural network models, decision tree models, and production rule models of categorization. These models differ in terms of the assumptions they make regarding what is learned and how the category decision is made. But all these models must try to account for a common set of empirical laws or basic facts that have accumulated from experiments on categorization.

What Are Cognitive Models?

The above examples illustrate what we view as cognitive models. But what makes these models cognitive models as opposed to some other kind of models, such as conceptual models, statistical models, or neural models? Cognitive science is concerned with understanding the processes that the brain, especially the human brain, uses to accomplish complex tasks, including perceiving, learning, remembering, thinking, predicting, inference, problem solving, decision making, planning, and moving around the environment. The goal of a cognitive model is to scientifically explain one or more of these basic cognitive processes, or explain how these processes interact.

One hallmark of cognitive models is that they are described in formal mathematical or computer languages. Cognitive models differ from conceptual frameworks in that the latter are broadly stated, natural language (verbal) descriptions of the theoretical assumptions. For example, Craik and Lockhart's (1972) "levels of processing" hypothesis provides a conceptual framework for memory, whereas Shiffrin and Steyvers's (1997) REM model or Murdock's (1993) TODAM model, being mathematical, are examples of cognitive models of memory.

Another hallmark of cognitive models is that they are derived from basic principles of cognition (Anderson & Lebiere, 1998). This is what makes the cognitive models different from the generic statistical models or empirical curve-fitting models. For example, regression models, factor analysis models, structural equation models, and time series models are generally applicable to data from any field, as long as those data meet the statistical assumptions, such as normality and linearity. These statistical assumptions are not derived from any principles of cognition, and they may even be inconsistent with the known facts of cognition. For example, the normality and homogeneity assumptions of linear regression models are inconsistent with the fact that response time distributions are positively skewed and the variance increases with the mean. These basic facts are accommodated by cognitive models of response time, such as Link and Heath's (1975) random walk model or Ratcliff's (1978) diffusion model. It is possible to use statistical tools to analyze cognitive models. For example, the parameters of random walk or diffusion models can be estimated using maximum-likelihood methods, and the model can be evaluated by chi-square lack-of-fit tests.

Cognitive models are also different from neural models, although the two can be interrelated. Cognitive models serve to build a bridge between behavior and its neural underpinnings. Cognitive models describe human information processing at a more abstract and mathematical level of analysis. Ideally, we need to build bridges between the fine grain neural models and the more abstract cognitive models. To some extent, connectionist models strive to achieve this balance by building mathematical models that retain some of the properties of neural models (Rumelhart & McClelland, 1986).

What Are the Advantages of Cognitive Models?

The main advantage of cognitive models over conceptual frameworks is that, by using mathematical or computer languages, cognitive models are guaranteed to produce logically valid predictions. This is not true of conclusions based on intuitively based verbal reasoning. For example, early categorization researchers argued in favor of a prototype hypothesis over an exemplar hypothesis on the basis of the fact that a prototype stimulus, which was never experienced during training, was categorized more accurately than a training stimulus, on a subsequent delayed transfer test. However, to category researchers' surprise, once the exemplar model was mathematically developed and tested, it was shown that their logic was incorrect, and the exemplar model could easily account for superior performance to the prototype stimulus. In this case, reasoning from a conceptual framework led to incorrect conclusions about evidence for or against competing theories of category learning.

A second important reason for using mathematical or computer models is that they are capable of making precise quantitative predictions. This is not possible solely on the basis of a conceptual or verbal framework. Most researchers would reject a model whose predictions are an order of magnitude off the mark, even though the model makes the correct qualitative or ordinal prediction.[3] Thus, it is essential to examine both the qualitative and quantitative predictions of a model. Of course, it is always possible to convert a conceptual model into a cognitive model by formalizing the conceptual model (recasting the verbal statements into mathematical or computer language). In fact, this is a common method for developing cognitive models.

What are the advantages of cognitive models over generic statistical models or empirical curve-fitting models? Both use formal language and are capable of generating quantitative predictions. The answer is generalizability. For example, Newell (1990) reviewed a large number of studies of skill learning and formulated what he called the power law of practice—mean response time to perform a complex task decreases according to a power function of the number of training trials. The power function model provides a good quantitative fit and empirical summary of the findings, but it is not based on any cognitive principles. Logan (1988) formulated a cognitive model for the power law of practice, called the multiple-trace model. According to this model, a new memory trace is stored after each practice trial with a randomly determined retrieval time, and the observed response time is determined by the first trace to be retrieved from memory. Based on these cognitive principles, Logan mathematically derived and explained the power law of practice. The advantage of the multiple-trace model over the power function model is that the cognitive model can be used to derive new predictions for new relationships that go far beyond the original data. For example, the cognitive model can also be used to predict how the variance of the response time changes with practice, and how accuracy changes with practice, both of which happen not to follow a power law.

Finally, why not directly build neural models and skip over cognitive models? On the one hand, cognitive models provide an abstract level of analysis that makes it computationally feasible to derive precise predictions for complex tasks and multiple measures of behavior (such as choice accuracy, choice response time, and choice confidence), which is often computationally too difficult to do with fine grain neural models. On the other hand, neural models (e.g., Grossberg, 1982; O'Reilly & Munakata, 2000) describe the actual neural substrates and neural interconnections that implement these cognitive processes, and so they are better for inferring predictions for bold activation patterns from functional magnetic resonance images (fMRI) or neural activation patterns from multiple cell recording studies. However, the fine grain level of analysis required to build neural models (involving possibly thousands of neural interconnections) generally make them too difficult to scale up to address complex cognitive tasks. In sum, both types of models serve an important but somewhat different goal (with respect to measures that they try to predict), and so both are needed along with bridges that relate the two types of models (cf. Marr, 1982).

What Are the Practical Uses of Cognitive Models?

There are many practical uses for cognitive models in a wide variety of areas. Clinical psychologists use cognitive models to assess individual differences in cognitive processing between normal individuals and clinical patients (e.g., schizophrenics). Cognitive neuroscientists use cognitive models to understand the psychological function of different brain regions. Aging researchers use cognitive models to understand the aging process and the deterioration or slowdown of cognitive functioning with age. Human factors researchers use cognitive models to improve human-machine or human-computer interactions. Decision researchers use cognitive models of decision making to predict preferences for consumer products, investment portfolios for businesses, medical choices, and military strategies. Artificial intelligence and robotic researchers use cognitive models for automated detection of dangerous targets, automated recognition of handwriting, automated recognition of faces, or approach and avoidance movement behavior of robots. Researchers in social sciences such as economics and sociology use cognitive models to construct computerized agents in agent-based models of market behavior or social network working.

What Are the Steps
Involved in Cognitive Modeling?

The first step is to take a conceptual theoretical framework and reformulate its assumptions into a more rigorous mathematical or computer language description. Consider, for example, the prototype model that was briefly sketched earlier. We would need to formulate the prototype for each category as a vector of features, and write down formulas describing how to compute the distance between the target stimulus vectors and the prototype vectors. This first step uses the basic cognitive principles of the conceptual theory to construct the model.

Often the conceptual theory is insufficient or too weak to completely specify a model, or it is missing important details. In this case, the second step is to make additional detailed assumptions (called ad hoc assumptions) to complete the model. This is often necessary for generating precise quantitative predictions. For example, considering the prototype model, we would need to make detailed, but somewhat ad hoc, assumptions about what features should be used to represent the stimuli to be categorized. Theorists try to minimize the number of ad hoc assumptions, but this step is often unavoidable.

Models almost always contain parameters, or coefficients that are initially unknown, and the third step is to estimate these parameters from some of the observed data. For example, the prototype model may include weight parameters that determine the importance of each feature for the categorization problem. The importance weight assigned to each feature is a free parameter that is estimated from the choice response data (analogous to the problem of estimating regression coefficients in a linear regression model). Theorists try to minimize the number of model parameters, but this is usually a necessary and important step of modeling.

The fourth step is to compare the predictions of competing models with respect to their ability to explain the empirical results. It is meaningless to ask if a model can fit the data or not (Roberts & Pashler, 2000). In fact, all models are deliberately constructed to be simple representations that only capture the essentials of the cognitive systems. Thus, we know, a priori, that all models are wrong in some details, and a sufficient amount of data will always prove that a model is not true. The question we need to ask is "Which model provides a better representation of the cognitive system that we are trying to represent?" For example, we know from the beginning that both the prototype and the exemplar models are wrong in detail, but we want to know which of these two models provides a better explanation of how we categorize objects.

To empirically test competing models, researchers try to design experimental conditions that lead to opposite qualitative or ordinal predictions from the two models (e.g., the prototype model predicts that stimulus X is categorized in Category A most often, but the exemplar model predicts that stimulus X is categorized in Category B most often). These qualitative tests are designed to be parameter free in the sense that the models are forced to make these predictions for any value of the free parameters. However, it is not always possible to construct qualitative tests for deciding between the models, and we often need to resort to quantitative tests in which we compare the magnitude of the prediction errors produced by each model. Even if it is possible to construct qualitative tests, it is informative to examine the quantitative accuracy as well.

The last step is often to start all over and reformulate the theoretical framework and construct new models in light of the feedback obtained from new experimental results. Model development and testing is a never-ending process. New experimental findings are discovered all the time, posing new challenges to previous models. Previous models need to be modified or extended to account for these new results, or in some cases, we need to discard the old models and start all over. Thus, the modeling process produces an evolution of models that improve and become more powerful over time as the science in a field progresses.

Notes

1. Some examples are *Cognition, Cognitive Psychology, Cognitive Science, Neural Networks, Psychological Review, Psychonomic Bulletin and Review,* and *Journal of Mathematical Psychology.*

2. Examples are the special issues in *Psychological Assessment* (2002), *Human Factors* (2002), *Cognitive Science* (2008), and *Journal of Mathematical Psychology* (2009).

3. There is an interesting story by Galileo regarding his experiment of dropping a heavy and a light ball from the Leaning Tower of Pisa. The Jesuits, who believed in Aristotle's theory, predicted that the light ball would land after the heavy ball, whereas Galileo's theory predicted no difference in arrival times. In fact, the light ball did land a very tiny split second after the heavy ball (due to wind resistance). On the basis of the qualitative result, the Jesuits claimed that they were correct. But Galileo ironically pointed out that the error in Aristotle's prediction was several orders of magnitude larger than the prediction error from Galileo's theory. Science eventually sided with Galileo.

2

Qualitative Model Comparisons

Under ideal circumstances, researchers would like to base their comparison of models on empirical tests of their basic principles, free from dependence on any specific ad hoc assumptions. Furthermore, it is best if the models being compared make different predictions, which do not depend on any specific parameter values of the model, but rather hold true for any set of parameter values (see, e.g., Townsend, 1990, for further discussion of this important issue). This chapter examines mathematical and computational tools that can be used to perform these types of qualitative tests of cognitive models.

This chapter is organized as follows. First, we describe a (fictitious) experiment on category learning that examines performance of amnesic and normal participants on both categorization and recognition tasks, and we summarize the results of the experiment. Although the results are fictitious, they partly reflect the findings reported by Knowlton and Squire (1993). Second, two popular cognitive models of category learning are presented—one is a connectionist version of a prototype model and the other is a connectionist version of an exemplar model. Third, a qualitative comparison of the two models is presented that employs a test from fundamental measurement theory. In the final section, a qualitative analysis is used to determine whether it is possible to explain the experimental results using a single-memory system, or whether it is necessary to posit multiple-memory systems. This last analysis is based on Nosofsky and Zaki's (1998) reanalysis of the Knowlton and Squire (1993) data.[1]

U nder ideal circumstances, researchers would like to base their comparison of models on empirical tests of their basic principles, free from
dependence on any specific ad hoc assumptions. Furthermore, it is best if the
models being compared make different predictions that do not depend on
any specific parameter values, but rather hold true for any set of parameter
values. This chapter examines mathematical and computational tools that
can be used to perform these types of qualitative tests of cognitive models.

Several highly sophisticated methods have been developed for qualitatively testing models. Fundamental measurement theorists (Krantz, Luce,
Suppes, & Tversky, 1972) have derived basic axioms for testing judgment
and decision theories. Information processing theorists (Townsend, 1990)
have derived critical properties for distinguishing serial and parallel information processing systems. Stochastic choice theorists have derived general
conditions for comparing probabilistic models of preferential choice (Luce
& Suppes, 1965). This chapter will provide an example using a method from
fundamental measurement theory.

Category Learning Experiment

Stimuli

Category learning is a major topic in cognitive science, and human category learning has been studied in the experimental laboratory for almost a
century. A typical experiment consists of creating different sets of artificial
stimuli. One reason for using artificial rather than natural stimuli is that the
participants of the experiment have no prior knowledge or experience of the
categories. Another advantage of using artificial stimuli is that the experi-
menter gains a great deal of experimental control over the stimuli. As we
shall see later, this is crucial for the qualitative test of the models that we
wish to perform.

For our purposes, imagine that the stimuli are artificially generated X-ray
images showing a dangerous-looking node that may be cancerous or benign.
In many category experiments, the stimuli (e.g., X-ray images) are designed
to vary primarily as a function of two variables—for example, the diameter
and brightness of a node in an X-ray image. In this case, the stimuli can be
represented as points in a two-dimensional space. Figure 2.1 illustrates the
stimuli used in the fictitious experiment presented in this chapter. There are
two panels shown in Figure 2.1: The left represents stimuli presented during
training, and the right represents stimuli presented later during a transfer

test. The horizontal axis of each panel represents variation along the first stimulus dimension (e.g., diameter of a node), and the vertical axis represents the variation along the second dimension (e.g., brightness of a node). Each point represents a stimulus, with points marked by a plus sign representing stimuli belonging to Category A, and points marked by a circle representing stimuli belonging to Category B. Category A stimuli tend to be either low on the first dimension and high on the second dimension, or high on the first dimension and low on the second dimension. Category B stimuli tend to be either low on both dimensions, or high on both dimensions. This kind of arrangement between stimuli and categories is called an exclusive-or (XOR) problem (see Ashby & Maddox, 1993; Nosofsky, 1988, for a real study using these types of stimuli).

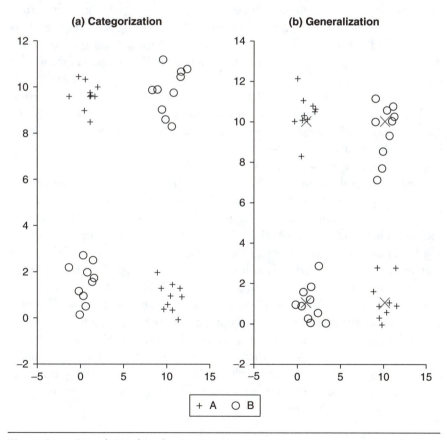

Figure 2.1   Stimuli Used in the Category Learning Experiment

Technically, the term *XOR* refers to a logical gate that has two binary inputs (on or off) and one binary output (on or off), and the gate only turns on when exactly one input unit is on. If no inputs are on, or if both inputs are on, then the output is off. This differs from an OR task, in which case the output is on if either one or both inputs are on. This also differs from an AND gate, in which case the output is on only if both inputs are on. This is a classic categorization task because it is much more difficult for people to learn the XOR problem as compared with the OR problem or the AND problem.

Procedure

Usually, there are two phases to a category learning experiment, a training phase followed by a transfer test phase. During the training phase of the experiment, each participant is presented a stimulus (e.g., X-ray image) and asked to categorize the stimulus into one of two categories: Category A (e.g., a cancerous node) versus Category B (e.g., a benign node). After making each category decision, the participant is given feedback indicating the correct category assignment. In a typical experiment, each participant is trained on the ensemble of stimuli for several replications. In this case, we simulated 10 repetitions, producing a total of 20 (stimuli) × 2 (categories) × 10 (repetitions) = 400 training trials per person.

Following this training, each participant is given one of two types of transfer tests—either a generalization test or a recognition test. No feedback is presented during the transfer phase, and this phase is designed to assess what has been learned after training is completed.

For the generalization test, the participant is asked to categorize all the stimuli shown in both panels. The stimuli in the right panel, which were not presented during training, are called generalization test stimuli. There are 20 such stimuli generated from each of the two categories. In addition, there are 4 special transfer stimuli marked by the red crosses shown in the right panel that were never presented in training. Note that these special transfer stimuli lie at the centroid of each stimulus cluster, and they are located at dimension values [1, 1], [1, 10], [10, 1], and [10, 10]. These special transfer stimuli are critical for the qualitative model comparison presented later.

The second type of transfer test is a recognition test. In this case, the participant is asked to decide whether the presented stimulus is a new transfer stimulus (never seen before) or an old stimulus experienced during training. In this condition, the participant makes an old versus new decision to all the stimuli shown in both panels.

Participants

Suppose that two different populations of participants are recruited for the experiment: One is a group of 50 amnesic individuals who suffer severe episodic memory deficits, and the second is a group of 50 individuals with normal memory. The amnesic group is expected to perform very poorly on the recognition test. The critical question is "How well does the amnesic group perform on the categorization task?" Assume that the groups are approximately matched with respect to age (see Knowlton & Squire, 1993, for a real study of these two populations).

Transfer Test Results

Figure 2.2 and Table 2.1 contain the (fictitious) probabilities of choosing Category A for the four special transfer stimuli (the crosses at the centroid of each stimulus cluster in the right panel of Figure 2.1), averaged across all participants. Note that Figure 2.2 reveals a crossover interaction effect: When the first dimension was fixed at a high value (first row), the probability of choosing Category A decreased as the value of the second dimension increased; however, when the first dimension was fixed at a low value (second row), the probability of choosing Category A increased as the value of the second dimension increased. Thus, the value of the second dimension had opposite effects on response probability, depending on the value of the first dimension. These results are exactly what one would expect if the participants accurately learned the category assignments for each cluster of stimuli. These results are critical for the model comparisons discussed later.

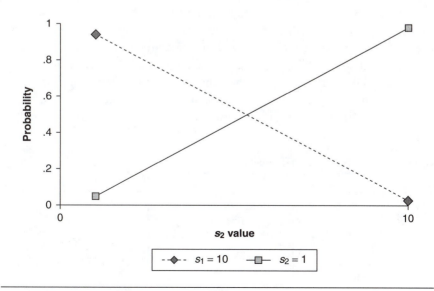

Figure 2.2 Fictitious Results for Transfer

Table 2.1   Probability of Choosing Category A for the Four Special Transfer Stimuli

	$s_2 = 1$	$s_2 = 10$
$s_1 = 10$	.94	.03
$s_1 = 1$	.05	.98

Table 2.2 presents the results for the transfer test stimuli broken down by type of transfer test and type of group. The column labeled "Proportion Correct Categorization" shows the proportion of the correctly categorized stimuli, pooled across the 40 generalization test stimuli (not including the four special transfer stimuli), and averaged across the participants within each group. The column labeled "d' Recognition" is a commonly used measure of recognition performance: If we define $h = $ Pr[respond old | training stimulus] and $f = $ Pr[respond old | transfer stimulus], then

$$d' = \ln[h/(1 - h)] - \ln[f/(1 - f)].$$

(The rationale behind this measure is explained in the next section after we describe the model for recognition responses.) The results shown in the table were obtained by first computing d' separately for each participant, and then averaging across participants within each group (see Malmberg & Xu, 2006, for a discussion of this point).

Table 2.2 shows a puzzling interaction effect—as expected, the normal group performed much better than the amnesic group on the recognition test, and in fact the recognition performance of the amnesic group is near zero. Surprisingly, the amnesic group performed about equal or slightly better than the normal group on the generalization test. The amnesic group seemed capable of performing the categorization task at transfer without being able to recognize the old training stimuli.

Table 2.2   Performance on Transfer Tasks

Group	Proportion Correct Categorization	d' Recognition
Normal group	.95	1.26
Amnesic group	.98	0.15

These results lead one to think that perhaps categorization and recognition are based on separate memory systems (see Knowlton & Squire, 1993). One is an implicit system (e.g., prototype learning) used for categorization, and another is an explicit system (e.g., exemplar learning) used for recognition. Both systems are effective for the individuals with normal memory. The implicit system remains intact but the explicit system is damaged for the amnesic individuals.

Two Models of Category Learning

There are a large number of sophisticated models for category learning in the literature (see, e.g., Ashby & Maddox, 1993; Gluck & Bower, 1988; Kruschke, 1992; Medin & Schaffer, 1978; Nosofsky, 1988). We will focus on two reasonably simple connectionist types of models to illustrate methods for qualitative comparisons of models. One model is called a connectionist version of a prototype model, and another model is called a connectionist version of an exemplar model. There has been a long debate about which of these two models (prototype vs. exemplar) best represents category learning, and some question whether it is possible to empirically distinguish between these two models. Below we show that the answer is yes if one uses the right design.

We will present a connectionist approach (Rumelhart & McClelland, 1986) to modeling the prototype and exemplar models. It is not necessary to do this for these two models, but the advantage is that a connectionist approach provides an elegant learning model that is worth understanding in its own right. Connectionist models assume that stimuli activate input nodes, and this input activation is passed along to output nodes representing the category responses. Many connectionist models also use a set of hidden nodes that transform the original stimulus into new codes or features, and then map these new codes into the category responses. Furthermore, a nonlinear activation function is used to map the inputs into the hidden nodes. However, these hidden units are not needed for the prototype and exemplar models that we develop here, and so we will simply use a two-layer network that connects inputs directly to outputs using linear mapping.

To present these models, we need to introduce some notation. The stimulus presented on training trial t is denoted as $S(t) = [s_1(t), s_2(t)]$, where $s_1(t)$ represents the value of the stimulus on the first dimension and $s_2(t)$ represents the value of the stimulus on the second dimension. For example, if the special transfer indicated by the red cross in the lower right-hand corner of Figure 2.1b is presented, then $S(t) = [10, 1]$. The target feedback is represented numerically by $F(t) = [f_1(t), f_2(t)]$, where $F(t) = [1, 0]$ if a stimulus from

Category A is presented on trial t, and $F(t) = [0, 1]$ if a stimulus from Category B is presented on trial t.

Prototype Model

The prototype model is illustrated in Figure 2.3. Briefly, this model is based on three sets of assumptions. First, there are two sets of inputs nodes: One set (labeled X) is activated by the value of the stimulus on the first dimension (s_1), and the other set (labeled Y) is activated by the value of the stimulus on the second dimension (s_2). Note that s_1 only connects to the X nodes, and s_2 only connects to the Y nodes. Second, these inputs are passed through a set of weighted connections to the output nodes corresponding to each category, which then generate the response. Note that X connects to both output nodes, and Y also connects to both output nodes. Finally, the connection weights are updated on the basis of feedback following each response during training. The details about the assumptions are presented next.

The prototype model assumes that two sets of input nodes are used to represent the stimulus, $S(t)$. The number of nodes in each set is denoted by m, and so there are a total of $2m$ nodes. The first set of nodes are designed to detect values of the stimulus on the first dimension, $s_1(t)$; and the second set of nodes are designed to detect values of the stimulus on the second dimension, $s_2(t)$. Each node within a set is designed to detect a particular stimulus value, which is called the ideal point of the node. The ith node in

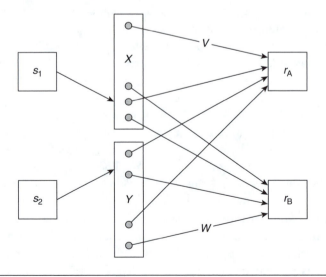

Figure 2.3   A Connectionist Version of a Prototype Model

the first set is designed to detect a stimulus value denoted as X_i, and the activation of this node, denoted as $x_i(t)$, is determined by the similarity of $s_1(t)$ to X_i. The ith node in the second set is designed to detect a stimulus value denoted as Y_i, and the activation of this node, denoted as $y_i(t)$, is determined by the similarity of $s_2(t)$ to Y_i. The similarity between the current stimulus value and the ideal point for each node is determined by a Gaussian type of generalization gradient

$$\text{sim}(X_i, s_1) = e^{-\left(\frac{|X_i - s_1|}{\sigma}\right)^2}, \tag{2.1a}$$

$$\text{sim}(Y_i, s_2) = e^{-\left(\frac{|Y_i - s_2|}{\sigma}\right)^2}. \tag{2.1b}$$

The parameter σ in the above equations is called the discriminability parameter, and it determines the width or spread of the activation around the ideal point. A low discriminability parameter (large σ) makes it hard to discriminate differences between stimulus values, and a high discriminability parameter (small σ) makes it easy to discriminate differences between stimulus values.

The input activation generated at the ith node is determined by the similarity of that node relative to the similarity of all the nodes:

$$x_i(t) = \frac{\text{sim}(X_i, s_1)}{\sum \text{sim}(X_i, s_1)},$$

$$y_i(t) = \frac{\text{sim}(Y_i, s_2)}{\sum \text{sim}(Y_i, s_2)}.$$

A stimulus produces a distribution of activation across the input nodes for each set, resulting in two separate distributions. The distribution for each set is centered on the stimulus value for the corresponding dimension. Figure 2.4 shows the two distributions produced by setting $S(t) = [3, 7]$. To generate this figure, we used $m = 121$ equally spaced nodes with ideal points covering the stimulus range from 0 to 12, and we set the discriminability parameter equal to $\sigma = 1$. Note that the distribution for the first set is centered on $s_1 = 3$ and the distribution for the second set is centered on $s_2 = 7$.

To see more concretely how this input activation function works, let us take a very simple example. Suppose that we use only $m = 3$ equally spaced input nodes to cover the range of our stimuli. One node is designed to detect

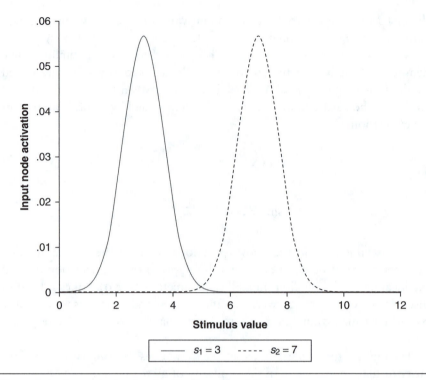

Figure 2.4   Input Activation for the Prototype Model

low stimuli, a second is designed to detect intermediate stimuli, and a third is designed to detect large stimuli. The stimuli range in value from 0 to 12, so we set ideal points for the three detectors equal to $X_1 = 0$, $X_2 = 6$, and $X_3 = 12$ for the first set; and $Y_1 = 0$, $Y_2 = 6$, and $Y_3 = 12$ for the second set. Suppose the discriminability parameter is equal to $\sigma = 3$. Also suppose that the stimulus $S(t) = [3, 7]$ is presented. First, we compute the similarity between the stimulus value $s_1(t) = 3$ and the three nodes for the first set of input nodes:

$$e^{-\left(\frac{|0-3|}{3}\right)^2} = 0.368, e^{-\left(\frac{|6-3|}{3}\right)^2} = 0.368, e^{-\left(\frac{|12-3|}{3}\right)^2} = 0.000.$$

These similarities sum up to $0.368 + 0.368 + 0.000 = 0.736$, and the resulting activations are

$$x_1(t) = 0.368/0.736 = 0.50,$$
$$x_2(t) = 0.368/0.736 = 0.50,$$
$$\text{and } x_3(t) = 0.000/0.736 = 0.00.$$

We do this again for the second set using the stimulus value $s_2(t) = 7$:

$$e^{-\left(\frac{[0-7]}{3}\right)^2} = 0.004, \, e^{-\left(\frac{[6-7]}{3}\right)^2} = 0.895, \, e^{-\left(\frac{[12-7]}{3}\right)^2} = 0.062.$$

The sum of similarities is 0.961 for the second set, and so the resulting activations are

$$y_1(t) = 0.004/0.961 = 0.004,$$
$$y_2(t) = 0.895/0.961 = 0.931,$$
$$\text{and } y_3(t) = 0.062/0.961 = 0.065.$$

This same procedure was used to generate Figure 2.4, except that we used 121 nodes rather than just 3 nodes.

The input nodes are connected to two category nodes, one for each category. The activation of the two category nodes are denoted as $r_A(t)$ and $r_B(t)$ for Categories A and B, respectively. The connection weight, $v_{ik}(t)$, connects the input activation $x_i(t)$ to the kth category output; the connection weight, $w_{ik}(t)$, connects the input activation $y_i(t)$ to the kth category output. The activation of the category nodes is based on the following linear input to output mapping:

$$r_k(t) = \sum_i v_{ik}(t) \cdot x_i(t) + \sum_i w_{ik}(t) \cdot y_i(t). \tag{2.2}$$

This model is called a prototype model because the set of weights $[v_{1A}, \ldots, v_{mA}; w_{1A}, \ldots, w_{mA}]$ connecting the inputs to the output for Category A forms a representation of the prototype pattern for Category A. The more similar the input activation pattern is to these weights, the more likely the stimulus matches the prototype for Category A. Likewise, the set of weights $[v_{1B}, \ldots, v_{mB}; w_{1B}, \ldots, w_{mB}]$ connecting the inputs to the output for Category B forms a representation of the prototype input pattern for Category B.

To be more concrete, reconsider the earlier example with only three input nodes for each stimulus dimension. In this case, there are three connection weights connecting the first set of nodes to Category A, and another three connection weights connecting the second set of nodes to Category A. The same holds for Category B, producing a total of 12 connection weights. Suppose after some amount of training, that the connection weights from the first set of nodes to Category A are $[v_{1A} = 1, v_{2A} = 0.02, v_{3A} = 0.01]$, and the connection weights from the second set of nodes to Category A are $[w_{1A} = 0.02, w_{2A} = 0.01, w_{3A} = 1]$. In this case, the prototype for Category A is a low value on the first dimension and a high value on the second dimension. Suppose the connection weights from the first set to Category B are $[v_{1B} = 0.02, v_{2B} = 1, v_{3B} = 0.01]$, and the connection weights from the second set of nodes to Category B are $[w_{1B} = 0.01, w_{2B} = 1 \ w_{3B} = 0.02]$. Then, the Category B prototype has intermediate values on both dimensions. If the stimulus $S(t) = [3, 7]$ is presented, then using the input activation values computed earlier, the output activation to Category A is

$$r_A = [(1)(0.500) + (0.02)(0.500) + (0.01)(0.000)] + \\ [(0.02)(0.004) + (0.01)(0.931) + (1)(0.065)] = 0.5844.$$

The output activation to Category B is

$$r_B = [(0.02)(0.500) + (1)(0.500) + (0.01)(0.000)] + \\ [(0.01)(0.004) + (1)(0.931) + (0.02)(0.065)] = 1.4423.$$

Therefore, the input activation pattern produced by $S(t) = [3, 7]$ matches the Category B prototype better than it matches the Category A prototype.

The connection weights are updated according to an error reduction or delta learning rule (see Rumelhart & McClelland, 1986, for further discussion):

$$v_{ik}(t + 1) = v_{ik}(t) + \alpha[f_k(t) - r_k(t)]x_i(t), \quad\quad (2.3a)$$

$$w_{ik}(t + 1) = w_{ik}(t) + \alpha[f_k(t) - r_k(t)]y_i(t). \quad\quad (2.3b)$$

The delta rule is based on the following simple idea. The difference $[f_k(t) - r_k(t)]$ is called the error signal because it equals the difference between the observed feedback and the prediction of that feedback. For example, if Category A is the correct stimulus so that $f_A = 1$, and if $r_A(t) = 0.5$, which is too low so that the error is positive, then the weight is increased, making the activation stronger on the next appearance of this stimulus.[2]

The whole learning process begins with some initial weights, and usually these are randomly assigned to represent a state of ignorance at the beginning of the learning process. Alternatively, if some prior knowledge or training exists, then the initial weights can be set to values that represent this prior knowledge or training.

To be more concrete, reconsider the earlier example where we computed the category outputs to the stimulus $S(t) = [3, 7]$. In that case, the Category A output was $r_A = 0.584$, and the Category B output was $r_B = 1.4423$. Suppose the correct category for this stimulus is B, in which case $f_2(t) = 1$ for this stimulus. In this case, the output response exceeds the feedback value, and so the error is negative, indicating that the weight needs to be decreased. Consider the change in the weight, $w_{2B}(t)$, connecting the activation, $x_2(t)$, to the Category B response. Recall that the connection weight used to compute the output in this example was $w_{2B}(t) = 1.00$. Suppose the learning rate is $\alpha = 0.25$ and recall that $x_2(t) = 0.50$ in this example. Then this weight is updated for the next trial as follows:

$$w_{2B}(t + 1) = 1.00 + (0.25)(1 - 1.4423)(0.50) = 0.9447,$$

which is a change in the appropriate direction. This same procedure is applied to all 12 connection weights after each feedback trial.

For a categorization task, the probability of choosing Category A is based on a ratio of strength of the output activations. After t trials of training,

$$\Pr[A|S(t)] = \frac{e^{b \cdot r_A(t)}}{e^{b \cdot r_A(t)} + e^{b \cdot r_B(t)}}. \tag{2.4}$$

The coefficient b is called a sensitivity parameter, which determines the sensitivity of choice probability to the activation of each category. Increasing the sensitivity parameter increases the slope of the function relating choice probability to the activation of a category. The ratio of strength choice rule is commonly used in connectionist models of choice.

Reconsidering the previous example, recall that when the stimulus $S(t) = [3, 7]$ was presented, then the outputs to Categories A and B were $r_A = 0.584$ and $r_B = 1.4423$. In this case, Category B is the favored response. If we set $b = 1$, then the probability of incorrectly choosing Category A equals

$$\frac{e^{(1)(.584)}}{e^{(1)(.584)} + e^{(1)(1.4423)}} = 0.2977,$$

which is low but there is still a fair chance for making an error. However, if we increase this to $b = 2$, then the probability of error drops to 0.1523. Thus, as the parameter b increases, the probability of error decreases.

For a recognition task, the probability of making an old recognition response is assumed to be an increasing function of the total amount of activation produced by the stimulus to both output nodes (cf. Nosofsky & Zaki, 1998). More specifically, a logistic function is used to relate total activation to old-new recognition response probability:

$$\Pr[\text{old}|S(t)] = \frac{e^{c[r_A(t) + r_B(t)]}}{\beta + e^{c[r_A(t) + r_B(t)]}}, \tag{2.5a}$$

$$\Pr[\text{new}|S(t)] = 1 - \frac{e^{c[r_A(t)+r_B(t)]}}{\beta + e^{c[r_A(t)+r_B(t)]}} = \frac{\beta}{\beta + e^{c[r_A(t)+r_B(t)]}}. \quad (2.5b)$$

The parameter c determines the sensitivity of the recognition probability to the category activations. Increasing the sensitivity parameter c causes the recognition probability to be more strongly influenced by the category activations.

The parameter β is used to represent the activation favoring a new response produced by the associations of the test stimulus with background context features. The background context is assumed to be constant across trials, and therefore unrelated to new or old stimuli, and so this parameter does not depend on whether the test stimulus is new or old. Thus, it is a response bias parameter representing the tendency to say new to any stimulus, and increasing β increases the tendency to respond new.

The d' index, commonly used to measure recognition performance, is designed to be insensitive to this response bias parameter. To see this, define $h = \Pr[\text{respond old} | \text{training stimulus}]$; and define r_{old} as the summed output, $r_A(t) + r_B(t)$, that is generated by an old training stimulus. Then, from Equation 2.5a, we find that

$$\frac{h}{1-h} = \frac{e^{c \cdot r_{\text{old}}}}{\beta} \text{ and } \ln\left(\frac{h}{1-h}\right) = c \cdot r_{\text{old}} - \beta.$$

In a similar manner, define $f = \Pr[\text{respond old} | \text{transfer stimulus}]$; and define r_{new} as the summed output, $r_A(t) + r_B(t)$, that is generated by a new transfer stimulus. Then, from Equation 2.5b, we find that

$$\frac{f}{1-f} = \frac{e^{c \cdot r_{\text{new}}}}{\beta} \text{ and } \ln\left(\frac{f}{1-f}\right) = c \cdot r_{\text{new}} - \beta.$$

The difference yields

$$d' = \ln\left(\frac{h}{1-h}\right) - \ln\left(\frac{f}{1-f}\right) = (c \cdot r_{\text{old}} - \beta) - (c \cdot r_{\text{new}} - \beta) = c \cdot (r_{\text{old}} - r_{\text{new}}).$$

Thus, d' directly measures the difference in activation by old and new stimuli.

In sum, the prototype model has five model parameters: the discriminability parameter σ, which determines the width of the generalization gradients;

the learning rate parameter α, for the delta learning rule; the sensitivity parameter *b*, for the categorization choice rule; and two parameters for the recognition response rule—a sensitivity parameter *c* and a response bias parameter β.

Exemplar Model

The exemplar model is illustrated in Figure 2.5. This model is also based on three sets of assumptions. First, the inputs to the network are assumed to form a square grid, with each point on the grid representing a single input node. The stimulus $S(t) = [s_1(t), s_2(t)]$ activates a circular receptive field of grid points. The centroid of the receptive field is located at the pair of stimulus values (s_1, s_2). The amount of activation of a nearby input node declines as a function of the distance of the node from this center. Second, these inputs are passed through a set of weighted connections to the output nodes corresponding to each category, which are used to generate the category response. Finally, the connection weights are updated on the basis of feedback following each response during training. The details about the assumptions are presented next.

The exemplar model assumes that the stimulus is represented by a square grid (or square table) of input nodes, with *m* rows and *m* columns. Each node on the grid (or cell of the table) is designed to detect a pair of stimulus values.

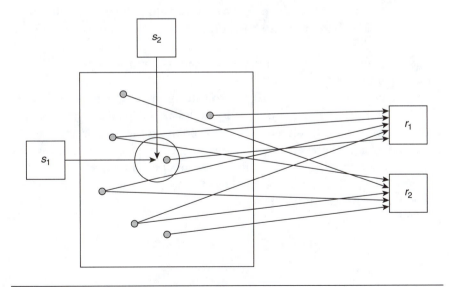

Figure 2.5   A Connectionist Version of an Exemplar Model

In particular, the node in the cell corresponding to row i and column j is designed to detect the value $X_{ij} = [X_i, X_j]$, which is called the ideal point for this node. The activation of this node, denoted as $x_{ij}(t)$, is determined by the similarity of the stimulus $S(t)$ to the ideal point X_{ij}, denoted as $\text{sim}(X_{ij}, S)$. A Gaussian type of generalization gradient is used to form the receptive field:

$$\text{sim}(X_{ij}, S) = e^{-\left(\frac{[X_i - s_i]}{\sigma}\right)^2} \cdot e^{-\left(\frac{[X_j - s_2]}{\sigma}\right)^2}. \tag{2.6a}$$

The parameter σ is the discriminability parameter, which determines the width of the generalization gradient of the receptive fields. Low discriminability (large values of σ) produce a large receptive field, which makes it hard to detect differences among stimuli. High discriminability (small values of σ) produce a small receptive field, which makes it easy to detect differences among stimuli.

The activation corresponding to the node in row i and column j of the grid, $x_{ij}(t)$, is determined by the similarity for this node relative to the sum of all the similarities in the grid or table:

$$x_{ij}(t) = \frac{\text{sim}(X_{ij}, S)}{\sum \sum \text{sim}(X_{ij}, S)}. \tag{2.6b}$$

A stimulus produces a bivariate distribution of input activations on the grid, which is centered on the pair of stimulus values. Figure 2.6 illustrates the bivariate distribution of activation produced by the stimulus $S(t) = [3, 7]$. To generate this figure, we used $m = 121$ equally spaced nodes with ideal points covering the stimulus range from 0 to 12, and we set the discriminability parameter $\sigma = 1$.

The input nodes are connected to two category nodes, one for each category. The activation of the two category nodes are denoted as $r_A(t)$ and $r_B(t)$ for Categories A and B, respectively. Each point on the grid or each cell of the table has a connection weight connecting an input node to a category. The connection weight, $w_{ij,k}(t)$, connects the input activation $x_{ij}(t)$ to the kth category output. The activation of the category nodes is based on the following linear input to output mapping:

$$r_k(t) = \sum_i \sum_j w_{ij,k}(t) \cdot x_{ij}(t). \tag{2.7}$$

In other words, we multiply the connection weight in each cell by the input activation for that cell, and sum across all the cells in the table of input nodes.

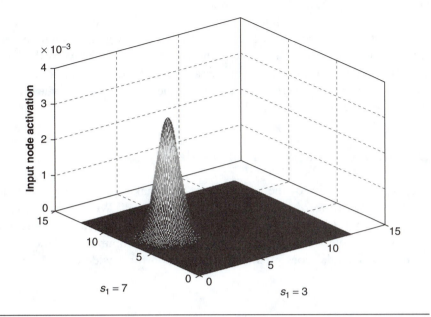

Figure 2.6 Input Activations Produced by the Exemplar Model

This model is called an exemplar model because each receptive field of a training stimulus is associated with the output category nodes through a separate set of connection weights. Thus, the model simply associates each region of the stimulus space with a response, and similar examples get mapped to similar responses.

The connection weights are updated according to an error reduction or delta learning rule:

$$w_{ij,k}(t + 1) = w_{ij,k}(t) + \alpha[f_k(t) - r_k(t)]x_{ij}(t). \tag{2.8}$$

This is the same learning model that was used for the prototype model.

For a categorization task, the probability of choosing Category A to a given stimulus is given by the ratio rule given earlier as Equation 2.4; and for a recognition task, the probability of responding old to a stimulus is determined by sum of activations as expressed in Equation 2.5a.

In sum, the exemplar model, like the prototype model, has four crucial model parameters: the discriminability parameter σ, which determines the width of the stimulus generalization gradients; the learning rate parameter α, for the delta learning rule; the sensitivity parameter b, for the categorization choice rule; and two parameters for the recognition response rule—a sensitivity parameter c and a response bias parameter β.

The two models share many assumptions, including the use of Gaussian generalization gradients for the input nodes, linear mappings from inputs to outputs, and choice response rules. The main difference between the two models is in terms of the input representation: In the first case, two univariate sets of input nodes were used, whereas in the second case, a single bivariate grid of input nodes was used.

Qualitative Comparison of Models

Despite the similarity of the two models, they make qualitatively different predictions with regard to the special transfer stimuli. We can mathematically prove that the prototype model cannot predict the crossover interaction observed in Table 2.1, and we can show through computer simulation that the exemplar model does predict this interaction for a wide range of parameter values.

Predictions of Prototype Model

First, we will prove that the prototype model cannot produce the crossover interaction shown in Table 2.1. To do this, it will be useful to rewrite Equation 2.4 in a more convenient form:

$$\Pr[A|S(t)] = \frac{e^{b \cdot r_A(t)}}{e^{b \cdot r_A(t)} + e^{b \cdot r_B(t)}} \cdot \frac{e^{-b \cdot r_A(t)}}{e^{-b \cdot r_A(t)}} = \frac{1}{1 + e^{b \cdot [r_B(t) - r_A(t)]}}. \quad (2.9)$$

This new expression makes it clear that the probability of choosing A is an increasing function of the difference

$$[r_A(t) - r_B(t)] = \left\{ \sum_i v_{iA} \cdot x_i(t) + \sum_i w_{iA} \cdot y_i(t) \right\}$$
$$- \left\{ \sum_i v_{iB} \cdot x_i(t) + \sum_i w_{iB} \cdot y_i(t) \right\} \quad (2.10)$$
$$= \sum_i (v_{iA} - v_{iB}) \cdot x_i(t) + \sum_i (w_{iA} - w_{iB}) \cdot y_i(t).$$

The time index has been dropped from the connection weights because the transfer tests in Table 2.1 occur after training, and no more feedback is provided. Thus, we assume that the connection weights are fixed at this point. We note that $x_i(t)$ is solely a function of $s_1(t)$ and so we can rewrite the first sum in Equation 2.10 more conveniently as

$$V[s_1(t)] = \sum_i (v_{iA} - v_{iB}) \cdot x_i(t).$$

Similarly, we note that $y_i(t)$ is solely a function of $s_2(t)$ and so we can rewrite the second sum in Equation 2.10 more conveniently as

$$W[s_1(t)] = \sum_i (w_{iA} - w_{iB}) \cdot y_i(t).$$

Using this new notation, when stimulus $S = (s_1, s_2)$ is presented for categorization, then

$$(r_A - r_B) = V[s_1] + W[s_2]. \tag{2.11}$$

In other words, the probability of choosing A is an increasing function of the additive effects of the first- and second-dimension values.

Fundamental measurement theorists (Krantz et al., 1972) call Equation 2.11 an additive conjoint measurement model, and this class of models must satisfy an ordinal property called the independence axiom. This axiom is derived below. We start by noting that the second row of Table 2.1 implies

$$\Pr[A|S = (1, 1)] < \Pr[A|S = (1, 10)]$$

$$\rightarrow V[s_1 = 1] + W[s_2 = 1] < V[s_1 = 1] + W[s_2 = 10].$$

Canceling the common term from the left- and right-hand side yields

$$\rightarrow W[s_2 = 1] < W[s_2 = 10],$$

and adding a common term to the left- and right-hand side yields

$$\rightarrow V[s_1 = 10] + W[s_2 = 1] < V[s_1 = 10] + W[s_2 = 10]$$

$$\rightarrow \Pr[A|S = (10, 1)] < \Pr[A|S = (10, 10)].$$

Thus, we have proved that the rank order of the columns observed in the first row of Table 2.1 must be the same as the rank order of the columns in the second row of Table 2.1. This is the independence axiom implied by additive conjoint measurement models. The crossover interaction violates this independence axiom, ruling out the additive conjoint measurement model, and thus disconfirming the predictions of the prototype model.

It is important to note that this test of the prototype model is very robust with respect to a number of ad hoc assumptions made regarding the prototype model. For example, suppose we changed the generalization gradient from the Gaussian activation function shown in Equation 2.1a to another activation function such as an exponential gradient. Changing this assumption has no effect on this test, because the prototype model must still satisfy the independence axiom. (Changing the number of input nodes, m, for each set also has no effect on this test.) Suppose we change the choice probability rule in Equation 2.4 to any other monotonically increasing function of the difference $(r_A - r_B)$. Once again, changing this assumption has no effect on this test because it is only sensitive to the ordinal relations among the choice probabilities. Suppose we change the learning rule from the delta rule to some other learning rule. Again this has no effect, and the independence axiom must still be satisfied by the prototype model. Finally, we note that this test of the prototype model does not depend on any specific values of the model parameters, and instead, it holds true for all parameter values.

Predictions of Exemplar Model

Turning to the exemplar model, how robustly does this model predict the crossover interaction effect shown in Table 2.1? It is difficult to prove that the exemplar model must predict the crossover interaction effect. An alternative method of analysis for this type of situation is to use computer simulation to examine a feasible range of the parameter space. This involves (1) selecting a set of parameter values; (2) looping through Equations 2.6a, 2.6b, 2.7, and 2.8 for the 400 training stimuli; (3) fixing the connection weights after training; (4) computing the predictions for the four special transfer test stimuli using Equations 2.6a, 2.6b, 2.7, and 2.8; (5) evaluating whether or not the predictions successfully reproduce the crossover interaction pattern; and (6) repeating this process with a new selection of parameter values until a wide range of values in the parameter space has been examined. This way, we can examine the extent to which the model supports a particular prediction across the entire parameter space.

For the categorization task, the exemplar model has three critical parameters: One is the discriminability parameter σ, which determines width of the generalization gradient for the receptive fields; a second is the learning rate α, for the delta learning rule; and a third is the sensitivity parameter b, for choice probability. A computer simulation of the model was conducted with σ ranging from 1 to 10 in unit steps, α ranging from 0.04 to 1.0 in 0.04 increments; and b ranging from 1 to 15 in unit steps. This generated $10 \times 25 \times 15 = 3,750$ simulations. For each simulation, we checked whether or not the model predicted a difference between the column proportions in the correct direction, separately for each row. Also, the difference had to exceed a cutoff equal to 0.20 in magnitude before it was counted as a success. (See the appendix to this chapter for the actual program used to compute these results.)

The results of these simulations can be summarized as follows. The model either reproduces the correct crossover interaction pattern or it predicts a difference that is too small to detect. Thus, it never predicted a pattern that satisfies the independence axiom for the parameter values that we examined. Whenever the discriminability parameter σ > 5, the correct pattern is successfully reproduced; after that the correct pattern occurs whenever the learning rate parameter α and sensitivity parameter b are sufficiently large. In all other cases, the correct pattern is predicted but the difference is below the cutoff. This is illustrated in Figure 2.7, which was generated by the exemplar model with σ = 5, producing 375 test points. The horizontal axis represents the 15 values of the sensitivity parameter, b, increasing from left to

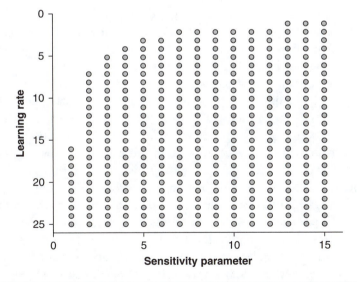

Figure 2.7   Points in the Parameter Space Where the Exemplar Model Predicts the Correct Pattern of Results for the Four Special Transfer Stimuli of Table 2.1

right; and the vertical axis represents the 25 values of the learning rate parameter α increasing from top to bottom. Each filled point indicates a combination of parameters that successfully reproduced the crossover interaction; and the filled points indicate parameters that failed to produce a detectable difference. The total number of combinations that reproduced the crossover turns out to be 337 out of 375 possibilities for $\sigma = 5$. As seen in Figure 2.7, the model successfully reproduces the crossover whenever all three parameters are sufficiently large.

As a check on our theory, we also ran the same computer simulation using the prototype model to generate the predictions rather than using the exemplar model. According to our theoretical test of independence, none of the parameters should be able to reproduce the interaction shown in Table 2.1. In fact, this is what we found when we checked the same 3,750 combinations of the parameters described above. Although computer simulation is never a substitute for a mathematical proof, it is useful to check the proof with computer simulation. Sometimes there is a hidden assumption in a proof that is not imposed on the computer simulation, and so the two methods could produce different results.

Experimental Design

The importance of using a well-controlled experiment with carefully designed transfer stimuli for comparing the models needs to be emphasized. The independence property that we established for the prototype model depends on manipulating one stimulus dimension while holding the other dimension constant in Table 2.1. Suppose we were not so careful with the design of the four special transfer stimuli located at the center of each cluster in Figure 2.1. Suppose that the four clusters are slightly perturbed and they are centered at positions [1, 1], [2, 10], [9, 1], and [10, 9] instead. Furthermore, suppose we observed a similar pattern of results as shown in Table 2.1 for these four new conditions. In this case, we cannot perform the test of independence—these stimuli fail to satisfy the criteria of holding one dimension constant while manipulating the other. With this design, we would have to resort to computer simulation to test whether or not the prototype model predicts the pattern of results, just as we did for the exemplar model. In fact, if we compute the predictions from the prototype model using the same 375 combination of parameters that we examined with the exemplar model (with $\sigma = 5$), then we obtain the results shown in Figure 2.8. This figure shows that more than 70% of the parameters succeed in reproducing the correct pattern. In sum, without the proper experimental design, it is very difficult to discriminate the prototype from the exemplar model.

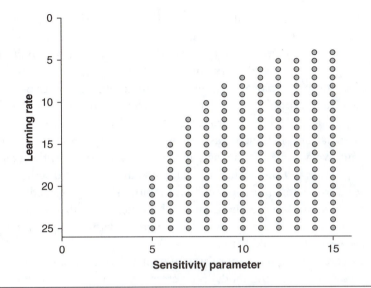

Figure 2.8   Points in the Parameter Space Where the Prototype Model Predicts the Correct Pattern When the Four Transfer Stimuli in Table 2.1 Are not Properly Controlled

One or Two Memory Systems?

Next, we turn to a qualitative analysis of a theoretical issue raised by the findings shown in Table 2.2. Recall that the amnesic participants performed slightly better than the normal controls on the categorization task; but the amnesic participants performed much worse than the normal controls on the recognition task. It seems that the amnesic participants could categorize the stimuli without recognizing them. These results suggest that an explicit memory system, used for recognition, is damaged in the amnesic participants; while the implicit memory system, used for categorization, remains intact. This raises an important theoretical question: Can these results be explained by a single-memory system (e.g., the exemplar model), or must we resort to a dual-memory model to account for these results?

The first step in this analysis is to start out by examining the predictions of a single exemplar-based memory system for both the categorization and the recognition performance. To account for the differences between the amnesic and normal individuals, we assume that some model parameters differ across these two types of populations. At this point, we need to state some plausible assumptions that relate the parameters of the exemplar model to the individual differences between the normal and amnesic populations.

The hypothesis that we will examine is that the discriminability parameter differs across amnesic and normal individuals (see Nosofsky & Zaki, 1998, for the original version of this hypothesis). The discriminability parameter is a plausible candidate because it reflects the distinctiveness of the stimulus-response associations. A low discriminability parameter produces a diffuse set of associations, making it difficult to discriminate representations in memory, whereas a high discriminability parameter produces highly distinctive associations, making it easy to discriminate representations in memory. In sum, we assume that a single-memory system—that is, the exemplar model—operates, but the normal participants have a higher discriminability parameter (producing more distinctive memories) as compared with the amnesic individuals. So the question now becomes "Can this simple change in this single parameter across the two types of individuals explain the interaction shown in Table 2.2?"

To evaluate this single-memory system explanation, we can use computer simulations to examine the model predictions for categorization and recognition across a wide range of model parameters. For this analysis, the learning rate and the response sensitivity parameters were not critical to the results, and so they were simply fixed to the same values for both the normal and the amnesic populations for all the simulations. The critical discriminability parameter σ was varied from 0.5 to 3.5 in 0.125 increments.

The results of these simulations are shown in Figure 2.9. The left panel shows the predicted results for categorization of the generalization test stimuli, and the right panel shows the predicted results for recognition of old training from new transfer stimuli. The horizontal axis on each panel represents the values of the discriminability parameter, and the vertical axis represents performance on each task. Recall that small values of σ produce high levels of discriminability, and large values of σ produce low levels of discriminability. The predictions turn out to be highly nonlinear and very counterintuitive. On the one hand, categorization performance is a nonmonotonic function of discriminability—it increases and then decreases as a function of σ. On the other hand, recognition performance is a monotonically decreasing function of σ.

What are the implications of these predictions for a single- versus dual-memory system explanation of the findings in Table 2.2? Suppose that normal subjects tend to have a high level of discriminability (e.g., $\sigma = 1$), whereas the amnesic subjects tend to have a low level of discriminability (e.g., $\sigma = 3$). Then, the single-memory model successfully reproduces the puzzling pattern of findings in Table 2.2. If we choose these values of discriminability for the normal and amnesic groups, then the amnesic group

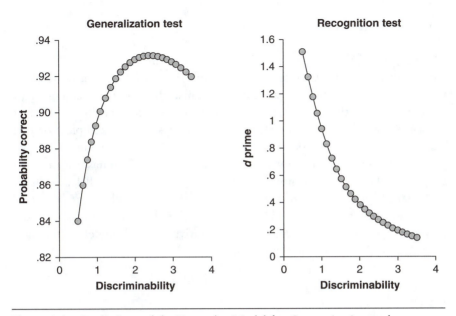

Figure 2.9   Predictions of the Exemplar Model for Categorization and
Recognition

performs slightly better than the normal group on categorization, whereas
the normal group greatly exceeds the amnesic group in terms of recognition
performance. In fact, recognition performance for the amnesic groups is predicted to be close to zero, even though categorization performance for this
same group is predicted to be close to perfect.

In summary, an intuitively appealing explanation for the puzzling results
of Table 2.2 is that a dual-memory system is operating. However, a more
rigorous cognitive modeling analysis indicates that this conclusion is pre-
mature. The data can be easily explained by a single-memory system. This
example shows the importance of examining explanations at a more rigorous level of analysis rather than relying on intuitive reasoning. The above
analysis was inspired by Nosofsky and Zaki's (1998) reanalysis of the
Knowlton and Squire (1993) data. Nosofsky and Zaki (1998) demon-
strated that a single-memory system model, in particular, an exemplar
model, could account for both the categorization and recognition performance of the amnesic and normal group data reported by Knowlton and
Squire. This is a very good example of the use of cognitive models for evaluating basic theoretical issues.

Conclusion

The purpose of this chapter was to provide a detailed example of how one can perform a qualitative test of two cognitive models. A qualitative test pits the ordinal predictions of one model against the ordinal predictions of another, where these predictions do not depend on specific parameter values. We used the prototype and exemplar models as examples for this demonstration, and we derived a test of additivity to distinguish the two models. However, as we noted in the introduction, this idea has been applied to many other cognitive models (e.g., testing serial vs. parallel models of information processing), and it is a powerful method whenever it can be used. Unfortunately, it is often difficult to derive these parameter-free tests, and so we often need to resort to quantitative tests of models, which are described in the subsequent chapters.

Appendix

This appendix has two purposes. One is to reformulate the exemplar model using matrix algebra. This is important for speeding up the computational process, shortening the length of the code, and simplifying the program. Furthermore, matrix operators are quite useful for other topics covered in this book. The second purpose is to describe the computer program that was used to qualitatively analyze the predictions of the exemplar model (i.e., the program used to compute Figure 2.6).

Review of Matrix Algebra

Matrix algebra is a mathematical formalism that is based on objects called column vectors, row vectors, and matrices, and matrix operators such as transpose, matrix sum, scalar multiplication, inner product, matrix product, Kronecker product, and matrix inverse (see Strang, 1988). For our purposes, an n by m matrix is just a table of values that has n rows and m columns, and the entire table is denoted by a boldface letter such as $\mathbf{X}$. An example of a 2 (row) by 3 (column) matrix is shown below.

$$\mathbf{X} = \begin{bmatrix} 1 & 0 & 3 \\ 2 & 1 & 4 \end{bmatrix}.$$

The transpose of a matrix, symbolized by $\mathbf{X}^{\mathrm{T}}$, simply means that we change the columns into rows.

$$\mathbf{X}^{T} = \begin{bmatrix} 1 & 2 \\ 0 & 1 \\ 3 & 4 \end{bmatrix}.$$

A column vector is just a matrix with only one column, such as

$$\mathbf{B} = \begin{bmatrix} 1 \\ 0 \\ 2 \end{bmatrix}.$$

A row vector is just a matrix with one row, or it can be viewed as the transpose of a column vector.

$$\mathbf{C}^{T} = \begin{bmatrix} 3 & 1 & -1 \end{bmatrix}.$$

It is often more convenient to use row vectors inside the text of a document.

Two matrices can be summed if they have the same dimensions, and the matrix sum is obtained by summing the corresponding elements. For example, if we use the $\mathbf{X}$ matrix defined above and define another matrix as

$$\mathbf{D} = \begin{bmatrix} 1 & 2 & 1 \\ 2 & 1 & 2 \end{bmatrix}, \text{then } \mathbf{X} + \mathbf{D} = \begin{bmatrix} 1 & 0 & 3 \\ 2 & 1 & 4 \end{bmatrix} + \begin{bmatrix} 1 & 2 & 1 \\ 2 & 1 & 2 \end{bmatrix} = \begin{bmatrix} 2 & 2 & 4 \\ 4 & 2 & 6 \end{bmatrix}.$$

Scalar multiplication means we multiply a single number times each element of a matrix:

$$2 \cdot \mathbf{X} = \begin{bmatrix} 2 \cdot 1 & 2 \cdot 0 & 2 \cdot 3 \\ 2 \cdot 2 & 2 \cdot 1 & 2 \cdot 4 \end{bmatrix} = \begin{bmatrix} 2 & 0 & 6 \\ 4 & 2 & 8 \end{bmatrix}$$

An inner product is performed on row and column vectors of the same dimension, and this operation is denoted by $\mathbf{C}^{T}\mathbf{B}$. The inner product is defined as the sum of the cross products of the coordinates for the two vectors. For example, using the definitions of $\mathbf{C}^{T}$ and $\mathbf{B}$ given above,

$$\mathbf{C}^{T}\mathbf{B} = \begin{bmatrix} 3 & 1 & -1 \end{bmatrix} \cdot \begin{bmatrix} 1 \\ 0 \\ 2 \end{bmatrix} = (3)(1) + (1)(0) + (-1)(2) = 1.$$

A matrix product between two matrices is defined by a matrix of inner products. If we multiply an n by m matrix $\mathbf{X}$ times an m by p matrix $\mathbf{Y}$ then the answer is an n by p matrix $\mathbf{Z}$. The element in the ith row and jth column of $\mathbf{Z}$ is the inner product of the ith row of $\mathbf{X}$ with the jth column of $\mathbf{Y}$. For example,

$$
\mathbf{X} \cdot \mathbf{B} = \begin{bmatrix} 1 & 0 & 3 \\ 2 & 1 & 4 \end{bmatrix} \cdot \begin{bmatrix} 1 \\ 0 \\ 2 \end{bmatrix} = \begin{bmatrix} (1)(1)+(0)(0)+(3)(2) \\ (2)(1)+(1)(0)+(4)(2) \end{bmatrix} = \begin{bmatrix} 7 \\ 10 \end{bmatrix}.
$$

The Kronecker product between an n by m matrix and a p by q matrix is denoted as $\mathbf{X} \otimes \mathbf{B}$, which forms a new matrix with $n \cdot p$ by $m \cdot q$ elements. Each element of the new matrix is formed by scalar multiplying each cell entry of the matrix $\mathbf{X}$ by the entire matrix $\mathbf{B}$. Consider, for example, the previous definitions of $\mathbf{X}$ and $\mathbf{B}$:

$$
\mathbf{X} \otimes \mathbf{B} = \begin{bmatrix} 1 & 0 & 3 \\ 2 & 1 & 4 \end{bmatrix} \otimes \begin{bmatrix} 1 \\ 0 \\ 2 \end{bmatrix} = \begin{bmatrix} (1)\begin{bmatrix}1\\0\\2\end{bmatrix} & (0)\begin{bmatrix}1\\0\\2\end{bmatrix} & (3)\begin{bmatrix}1\\0\\2\end{bmatrix} \\ (2)\begin{bmatrix}1\\0\\2\end{bmatrix} & (1)\begin{bmatrix}1\\0\\2\end{bmatrix} & (4)\begin{bmatrix}1\\0\\2\end{bmatrix} \end{bmatrix} = \begin{bmatrix} 1 & 0 & 3 \\ 0 & 0 & 0 \\ 2 & 0 & 6 \\ 2 & 1 & 4 \\ 0 & 0 & 0 \\ 4 & 2 & 8 \end{bmatrix}.
$$

We can define an elementwise function of a matrix as simply applying the function to each element of the matrix. (The elementwise function of a matrix needs to be distinguished from a *matrix function*, which is not covered here.) For example, the elementwise exponential function of the matrix $\mathbf{B}$ is defined as

$$
e^{\mathbf{B}} = \begin{bmatrix} e^1 \\ e^0 \\ e^2 \end{bmatrix}.
$$

The elementwise square of the matrix $\mathbf{B}$ is defined as

$$
\mathbf{B}^2 = \begin{bmatrix} 1^2 \\ 0^2 \\ 2^2 \end{bmatrix}.
$$

Finally, there are two special types of matrices that often appear in matrix calculations. One is a vector filled with all ones, denoted by $\mathbf{J}$. For example,

$$
\mathbf{J} = \begin{bmatrix} 1 \\ 1 \\ 1 \end{bmatrix}.
$$

This is useful for turning a scalar into a vector:

$$s \cdot J = \begin{bmatrix} s \\ s \\ s \end{bmatrix}$$

or for summing a vector, $J^T B = (1 \cdot 1 + 1 \cdot 0 + 1 \cdot 2) = 3$. Another matrix, called the identity matrix and denoted as I, has ones in the diagonal entries and zeros in all the off-diagonal entries. For example,

$$I = \begin{bmatrix} 1 & 0 & 0 \\ 0 & 1 & 0 \\ 0 & 0 & 1 \end{bmatrix}.$$

This matrix has the following special property: $X \cdot I = X$; in other words, it leaves X unchanged.

The inverse of a matrix is used to perform matrix division. The inverse of the square matrix Y is another square matrix, which we denote as Y^{-1}. The matrix inverse is defined by the property that $YY^{-1} = I = Y^{-1}Y$. For example, if we define Y as

$$Y = \begin{bmatrix} 2 & 1 \\ 5 & 5 \end{bmatrix} \text{then } Y^{-1} = \begin{bmatrix} 1 & -.2 \\ -1 & .4 \end{bmatrix}, \text{because} \begin{bmatrix} 2 & 1 \\ 5 & 5 \end{bmatrix} \cdot \begin{bmatrix} 1 & -.2 \\ -1 & .4 \end{bmatrix}$$
$$= \begin{bmatrix} 1 & 0 \\ 0 & 1 \end{bmatrix}.$$

As can be seen from this example, finding the inverse is not intuitively simple, but fortunately, inverse operators are available in mathematical programming languages. It can be used to perform matrix division as follows. Suppose Z and Y are known, and we wish to solve for W in the linear equation $Y = Z \cdot W$, then the solution is

$$Z^{-1}Y = Z^{-1}Z \cdot W = I \cdot W = W.$$

Now let us briefly introduce the concepts of eigenvectors and eigenvalues. Consider a square $n \times n$ matrix X that has the same number of rows and columns. An $n \times 1$ vector V_j is an eigenvector of this matrix if and only if $X \cdot V_j = \lambda_j \cdot X$, where λ_j is a scalar called the eigenvalue corresponding to the eigenvector V_j. The matrix X can have at most n linearly independent eigenvectors. Suppose these eigenvalues are all unique. Then, we can decompose the original matrix by $X = V \cdot \Lambda \cdot V^{-1}$, where V is an $n \times n$ matrix with each column representing an eigenvector, and $\Lambda = \text{diag}[\lambda_1, \ldots, \lambda_j, \ldots, \lambda_n]$ is a diagonal matrix with a unique eigenvalue in a column corresponding to each eigenvector. This decomposition is useful for defining a matrix function. Consider the matrix square function: $X^2 = (V \cdot \Lambda \cdot V^{-1}) \cdot (V \cdot \Lambda \cdot V^{-1}) = V \cdot \Lambda^2 \cdot V^{-1}$. More generally, the matrix function $f(X)$ is defined by $f(X) = V \cdot f(\Lambda) \cdot V^{-1}$, where $f(\Lambda) = \text{diag}[f(\lambda_1), \ldots, f(\lambda_j), \ldots, f(\lambda_n)]$. Note that this definition of a matrix function is different from the elementwise definition provided above. Both definitions are useful, but we must be careful to be clear about which one is being used. Matrix programming uses syntax that distinguishes these two definitions.

Exemplar Model

Now, we shall use some of these concepts to rewrite the exemplar model in matrix terms. First, we will compute all the input activations for the exemplar model using matrix operators. Define X as a column vector of ideal points. To be concrete, the stimuli range from 0 to 12, and we will use 13 equally spaced points defined by $X^T = [0\ 1\ 2\ 3 \ldots 11\ 12]$. The deviations between the ideal points and the stimulus values on each dimension can be represented by the two vectors

$$D_1 = \frac{1}{\sigma}[X - s_1(t) \cdot J] \text{ and } D_2 = \frac{1}{\sigma}[X - s_2(t) \cdot J], \qquad (A2.1a)$$

where J is a 13×1 vector with all ones. We can compute the similarities for these deviations using the elementwise matrix functions

$$Sim_1 = e^{-D_1^2}, Sim_2 = e^{-D_2^2}. \qquad (A2.1b)$$

Note that Sim_1 and Sim_2 are both 13×1 vectors. Then, all the elements contained in the square 13×13 grid of input nodes can be computed by the Kronecker product:

$$Sim = Sim_1 \otimes Sim_2. \qquad (A2.2a)$$

Sim is a column vector with 13^2 similarities, and each element corresponds to Equation 2.6a. The sum of all these similarities is obtained from the inner product $J^T Sim$, where J is a $13^2 \times 1$ vector containing all ones.

Finally, the input activations for all the input nodes contained in the 13×13 grid are defined by

$$x = \frac{1}{\mathbf{J}^{\mathsf{T}}\mathbf{Sim}}\mathbf{Sim}, \tag{A2.2b}$$

where x is a column vector containing the 13^2 input activations, and each element corresponds to Equation 2.6b.

The connection weights connecting the two outputs to each of the 13^2 input nodes are represented as a 2×13^2 matrix denoted as $\mathbf{W}$. When a stimulus is presented, the inputs are transformed into two output activations, one for each category, which is represented by the row vector $\mathbf{R}^{\mathsf{T}} = [r_A, r_B]$, and $\mathbf{R}$ is the column vector form for this. The matrix equation for the output activations is simply the matrix product

$$\mathbf{R}(t) = \mathbf{W}(t) \cdot x(t). \tag{A2.3}$$

The row vector $\mathbf{F}^{\mathsf{T}} = [f_1(t), f_2(t)]$ represents the correct feedback on trial t, and $\mathbf{F}$ is the column form for this. The matrix form for the delta learning rule is

$$\mathbf{W}(t + 1) = \mathbf{W}(t) + \alpha \cdot [\mathbf{F}(t) - \mathbf{R}(t)] \cdot x(t). \tag{A2.4}$$

This completes the matrix reformulation of the exemplar model.

These matrix formulas greatly speed up the computations for this model. In this example, we used only $m = 13$ ideal points to detect stimulus values, which is a relatively small number. Suppose $m = 121$ as it was in the example displayed in Figure 2.5. Then, this increase in computational speed makes a huge difference. For example, rather than writing a series of m^2 loops ($13^2 = 169$ but $121^2 = 14,641$) to compute the outputs from all the input activations for each trial, only a single matrix operation is required. Matrix programming languages are extremely efficient at computing these matrix operations. In addition, the code is simpler and easier to read and debug.

MATLAB Computer Program

The *main* program is very simple. It simply sets some initial values, loads the stimuli, loops through all the decay rate and initial strength parameters on which we wish to perform the model tests, stores all these results in a large table called MT, and finally plots these values. The rows in the matrix MT represent different levels of decay rate, the columns represent different levels of initial strength, and the cell values are 1 or 0 depending on whether the prediction from Line 8 was successful or not, respectively. The function *spy* in MATLAB is a function that plots a point corresponding to each positive value of the matrix MT. This program is shown in Figure A2.1.

```
% main program
nr = 10; % (1) sets no. of rep's
load stimuli ; % (2) loads a file containing the
stimuli in XAC XBC and P
aa = 25; AV = ((1:aa)./aa); % (3) set learning rate values
bb = 15; BV = (1:bb); % (4) set sensitivity values
MT=[]; % (5) Initializes test result matrix
sig = 5; % (6) Set discriminability
for i = 1:aa % (7) loop through predictions
for j = 1:bb for each learning rate and
alf = AV(i) sensitivity
b = BV(j)
T = exemplar(alf,b,sig,XAC,XBC,P,nr,cutoff); % (8) generate prediction
MT(i,j) = T; % (9) store result
end
end
spy(MT) % (10) plot results
```

Figure A2.1   Main MATLAB Program for Exemplar Model

The *exemplar* function is the heart of the program (see Figure A2.2). First, the initial values are set for variables. The constant *ns* represents the number of stimuli, which is 20 in this case. Then Line 2 finds the maximum stimulus value, which happens to be Max = 12. Then, the program generates the 13 ideal points. The MATLAB code 0:Max generates a row vector [1 2 . . . 12]. Line 3 is used to construct a 2 × 13 initial weight matrix filled with zeros. The next statement just initializes two matrices that are later used to store results. Lines 4 to 10 perform the training for the model across all the stimuli and all the replications. Lines 6 and 8 generate the input and output activations by a function described later. The delta learning rule is applied in Lines 7 and 9, according to Equation A2.4. Lines 11 to 15 perform the transfer test on the critical transfer stimuli. Lines 13 and 15 compute the choice probabilities using Equation 2.4. The last line in this program performs the check to see whether the model correctly predicts the crossover interaction pattern.

The function *InOut* performs two basic matrix operations (see Figure A2.3). One is to construct the input node activations that we labeled **Sim** in Equation A2.2b above, and the other is to compute the output activations labeled **R** in Equation A2.3 above. Lines 1 and 2 perform the computations shown in Equations A2.1a and A2.1b, and Line 3 performs the Kronecker product shown in Equation A2.2a and A2.2b. The last line computes the output using Equation A2.3.

```
function mT = exemplar(alf,b,sig,XAC,XBC,P,nr,cutoff)
ns = size(XAC,1);   % (1) number of stimuli
Max = round(max(max(XAC))); % (2) defines the set of ideal points
I1 = 0:Max; I2 = 0:Max;
W = zeros(2,(Max+1)); % (3) Initial connection wgts
TA = []; TB = [];
for rep = 1:nr % (4) loop for replication
for st = 1:ns % (5) loop for stimuli
[In Out] = InOut(I1,I2,XAC,W,sig,st); % (6) Generate input and output
WA = alf*([1 0]'–Out)*In'; % (7) delta rule
[In Out] = InOut(I1,I2,XBC,W,sig,st); % (8) Generate input and output
WB = alf*([0 1]'–Out)*In'; % (9) delta rule
W = W + WA + WB; % (10) store wgt changes
end
end
for st = 1:4 % (11) loop for transfer test
if st == 2 | st == 3 % (12) test stim from cat A
[In Out] = InOut(I1,I2,P,W,sig,st);
pa = exp(b*Out); pa = pa(1)./(sum(pa)); % (13) prob choose A given cat A
TA = [TA ; pa];
else
[In Out] = InOut(I1,I2,P,W,sig,st); % (14) test stim from cat B
pb = exp(b*Out); pb = pb(1)./(sum(pb)); % (15) prob choose A given cat B
TB = [TB ; pb];
end
end
mT = ((TA(1) – TB(1)) > cutoff)*((TA(2) – TB(2)) > cutoff); % (16) Perform test of prediction
```

Figure A2.2   Exemplar Function

```
function [In Out] = InOut(I1,I2,X,W,sig,st)
in1 = 1./exp(((I1–X(st,1))/sig).^2); % (1) Sim for s1
in2 = 1./exp(((I2–X(st,2))/sig).^2); % (2) Sim for s2
In = kron(in1,in2); In = (In./sum(In))'; % (3) Grid of input activations
Out = W*In; % (4) Input – Output Activations
```

Figure A2.3   InOut Function

This program could have been written just as easily using another programming language such as Mathematica, GAUSS, or SAS.

Notes

1. The design of the fictitious experiment described here was inspired by Knowlton and Squire's (1993) research, and the analysis of single- versus dual-memory systems was inspired by the work of Nosofsky and Zaki (1998). However, the design and results presented here were modified to meet the pedagogical needs of this chapter.

2. The delta learning rule can be derived from the gradient of the sum of squared prediction errors with respect to the connection weights (see Rumelhart & McClelland, 1986).

3

Nonlinear Parameter Estimation

It is not always possible to establish a qualitative comparison of models. If the predictions overlap to some extent, or if the predictions vary depending on parameters, then we need to resort to a quantitative comparison of the models. Even when a qualitative test is possible, examining the quantitative predictions would still prove to be informative. It is not sufficient for a model to predict the correct qualitative ordering of performance across two conditions. It is also necessary for a model to make quantitative predictions that are more accurate than its competitors.

When the quantitative predictions of a model are to be evaluated, the test must be performed on the basis of an optimal selection of parameters. Otherwise, one could reject a perfectly good model simply because the researcher happened to select a poor set of parameters to evaluate the model. This implies that the quantitative comparison of the two models would depend completely on the researcher's arbitrary selection of parameters.

The purpose of this chapter is to review some of the technical issues involved in estimating parameters for cognitive models. First, we introduce a very simple experiment and its (fictitious) results to provide a concrete example for this chapter. Second, we present a correspondingly simple cognitive model for the example. In this section, we also introduce the distinction between linear and nonlinear models. This distinction is important because cognitive models usually fall into the latter class. Third, we introduce some alternative methods for measuring the quantitative accuracy of a model, including sum of squared errors and maximum-likelihood methods. Fourth, we review some properties of the parameters obtained by these methods, which provide a rationale for selecting an estimation method. Fifth, we discuss some of the technical details concerning the parameter search methods and try to indicate the most appropriate conditions for using each method. Finally, we present the results of using these methods on the cognitive model applied to the experimental data of our example.

The primary purpose of this chapter is to review some of the technical issues involved in estimating parameters for cognitive models. This chapter does not address the important problem of quantitative model comparisons, which is a complex topic that is discussed in detail in later chapters. First, we introduce a very simple experiment and its (fictitious) results to provide a concrete example for this chapter. The example data and model used in this chapter are based on a similar research that has been published by Ruben and Wenzel (1996).

Retention Experiment

Stimuli and Procedure

Suppose 5 amnesic participants and 5 control participants are initially trained on a category learning experiment in which they are trained to categorize mushrooms as edible or inedible. For the experiment, the stimuli are more complex, being characterized by four dimensions, namely, length of stem, width of rim, lightness, and texture. The participants are trained on the two categories for 400 trials, and then they are tested on new transfer stimuli. For the experiment analyzed in this chapter, the results are based on a new set of 200 transfer test stimuli that are presented at each of 11 different delay conditions: immediately after training, after 1 week, after 2 weeks, and so on, and finally after 10 weeks.

Figure 3.1 shows the percentage correct categorization as a function of delay, averaged over the 200 transfer stimuli, and averaged across the 5 participants within each group. The points plotted in the figure represent the (fictitious) data, and the lines connecting the points are predictions (discussed later). The amnesic group performed almost as well as the controls after a single-week delay. But after the first week, the control participants retained their memory for the categories longer than the amnesic group.

Retention Model

Now we will develop a simple model for this retention performance based on the connectionist version of the exemplar model discussed in the previous chapter. First, we need to introduce an assumption about the effect of delay for the exemplar model. A simple hypothesis is that the connection weights decay back toward zero with each delay period.

The exemplar model assumes that there exists a list of input nodes that are activated by the stimulus presented on trial t, and the activations of these

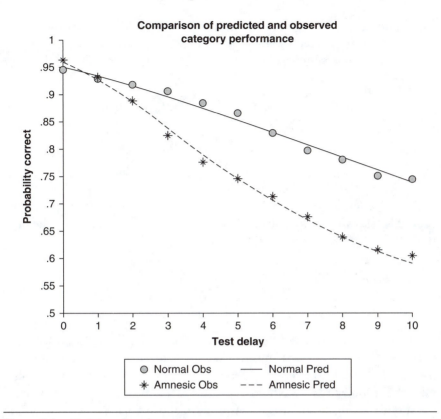

Figure 3.1 Fictitious Results

nodes are represented by the variables $\{x_1(t), x_2(t), \ldots, x_j(t), \ldots, x_J(t)\}$. The connection weight connecting an input node j to a response category k immediately after training is denoted as $w_{j,k}$. The connection weight that remains after waiting a time period equal to d weeks is denoted as $w_{j,k}(d)$, where $d = 0, \ldots, 10$ weeks. Note that $w_{j,k}(0) = w_{j,k}$, which is just the connection weight immediately after training. The decay hypothesis states that

$$w_{j,k}(d + 1) = \gamma \cdot w_{j,k}(d), \text{ for } d = 0, 1, \ldots, 10.$$

For example, $w_{j,k}(1) = \gamma \cdot w_{j,k}(0) = \gamma^1 \cdot w_{j,k}$, and $w_{j,k}(2) = \gamma \cdot w_{j,k}(1) = \gamma^2 \cdot w_{j,k}$, and $w_{j,k}(3) = \gamma \cdot w_{j,k}(2) = \gamma^3 \cdot w_{j,k}$; and inductively we have $w_{j,k}(d) = \gamma^d \cdot w_{j,k}$. The parameter γ is a decay rate that ranges between 0 and 1, and faster decay or forgetting is produced by smaller values of the decay parameter.

Next, consider how this delay affects the output activations after a delay. The output activation for kth category evoked by the stimulus presented on trial t after a delay of d weeks is denoted as $r_k(t, d)$. Recall that the output activation for each category equals the sum of the products of the input activations and connection weights. After a delay of d weeks, this equals

$$r_k(t,d) = \sum_j w_{j,k}(d) \cdot x_j(t) = \sum_j (\gamma^d \cdot w_{j,k}) \cdot x_j(t)$$
$$= \gamma^d \cdot \sum_j w_{j,k} \cdot x_j(t) = \gamma^d \cdot r_k(t,0) = \gamma^d \cdot r_k(t),$$

where $r_k(t)$ is the output activation immediately after training.

Finally, consider the probability of categorizing a stimulus into Category A after a delay of d weeks, denoted as $\Pr[A|S(t), d]$. This is given by the ratio of the strengths of the output activations

$$\Pr[A|S(t), d] = \frac{e^{b \cdot r_A(t) \cdot \gamma^d}}{e^{b \cdot r_A(t) \cdot \gamma^d} + e^{b \cdot r_B(t) \cdot \gamma^d}}. \tag{3.1}$$

Note that in the original formulation of the exemplar model presented in Chapter 2, the output activations, $r_k(t)$, depend on the particular stimulus presented on trial t. Here, we will make a simplifying assumption to minimize the complexity of the model for this chapter. We will assume that all the stimuli belonging to Category A produce approximately the same output activations for Categories A and B, denoted as r_C and r_I for correct and incorrect, respectively. Similarly, we will assume that all the stimuli belonging to Category B produce approximately the same output activations for Categories B and A, which also equal r_C and r_I for correct and incorrect, respectively. Using this simplifying assumption, the probability of making a correct categorization is only a function of the delay:

$$P(d) = \frac{e^{b \cdot r_C \cdot \gamma^d}}{e^{b \cdot r_C \cdot \gamma^d} + e^{b \cdot r_I \cdot \gamma^d}}. \tag{3.2}$$

Equation 3.2 is a simple model of retention, which expresses the performance measure on the left-hand side as a function of a single independent variable, denoted as d, for the delay, on the right-hand side. In this form, the model has four parameters $\{b, r_C, r_I, \text{and } \gamma\}$.

This simplifying assumption needs some justification. First, as we mentioned above, we want to focus on parameter estimation, and so we want to keep the model as simple as possible for pedagogical reasons. Beyond that, simplifying assumptions help us see mathematical properties that are not apparent in the more complex model. Also, if the simplifying assumption is approximately correct, then we can make nearly the same predictions using a much simpler equation, and this greatly facilitates later analyses.

Statistical Models

It is difficult to evaluate a model in an absolute sense. No model is perfect, so how can one say a model is good without comparing it with other competitors? Therefore, we will compare this cognitive model with two other purely statistical models—the saturated model and the null model, which provide the upper and lower bounds for fit indices. These models are not derived from any cognitive principles, but they are helpful for evaluating the fit of the cognitive model.

The saturated model uses a new free parameter to predict the probability correct at each delay condition. (It is called the saturated model because it has the same number of free parameters as the number of data points.) This model perfectly reproduces the observed proportions, because it simply makes a prediction for each condition that is equal to the observed relative frequency for that condition. Thus, the prediction for condition d is simply: $p_d = (n_{Cd}/n)$, where n_{Cd} equals the frequency of correct choices, n_{Id} equals the frequency of incorrect choices, and $n = (n_{Cd} + n_{Id})$ the total number of trials for condition d ($n = 200$ observations per condition for each person in our example). The saturated model provides an upper bound for measuring model fit. Obviously, this model has no explanatory power, but it is useful in measuring how far the fit of the retention model is below the upper bound.

The null model assumes that probability correct remains constant across all conditions, that is, there is no true effect of the delay on performance. Any deviation from constant performance is assumed to be sampling error. This model has only one free parameter, which is estimated by the mean proportion correct, averaged across all the 11 conditions: ($\Sigma p_d/11$). This mean is used as the prediction for all the 11 conditions. The null model is the simplest possible model, and it provides a lower bound for measuring model fit. Obviously, this model is wrong, but it is useful for measuring how far the fit of the retention model is above the lower bound.

The improvement in fit of the cognitive model over the null model indicates the amount of the treatment effect that is predicted by the cognitive model, and improvement of the saturated model over the cognitive model indicates the amount of the treatment effect left unexplained by the cognitive model.

Linear Versus Nonlinear Models

Estimating the parameters of the cognitive model is analogous to estimating the regression coefficients of the linear model. The basic idea is to search for the set of parameter values that produces the best fit to the data. However, there is an important technical difference between estimating parameters for the linear and cognitive models. The former is a special case of a statistical class of models called the general linear class, whereas the latter is in the nonlinear class.

A linear model can be recognized by its simple form: Each unknown parameter is multiplied by a known number (the known score on a predictor variable), and these products are summed to produce the prediction: $y' = \Sigma \beta_j \cdot x_j$. The xs in the equation are treated as known numbers, and the parameters β_j are the unknown variables. The xs in this equation can be anything: For example, setting $x_1 = d^1$ and $x_2 = d^2$, where d is the value of the independent variable, still produces a linear model; so does setting $x_1 = \sin d$, $x_2 = \cos d$. Estimating the parameters of a linear model can usually be done with a single-step algorithm that is guaranteed to produce an optimal solution. Linear models satisfy a special condition: The average of the predictions from two different sets of parameters equals the prediction produced by the average of the two sets of parameters. Nonlinear models do not satisfy this property. (This distinction between linear and nonlinear models is presented in the appendix to this chapter.)

The retention model (Equation 3.2) is a nonlinear model, and this has important implications for the estimation of parameters—there are no known single-step solutions for estimating the parameters. Instead, an iterative process (a sequence of steps where the next step in the process depends on the earlier steps) must be used to search the parameter space for the optimal solution, and there is no guarantee that the optimal solution will be found. The later sections of this chapter treat these issues in more depth. But first we need to address several other important issues.

Parameter Identification

Before we charge ahead and try to estimate the parameters of a model, we need to check and make sure that it is indeed possible to obtain a unique optimal solution. One condition that is usually necessary for the parameters to be identifiable is that there are more data points than parameters. The difference between the number of data points and parameters is called the degrees of freedom (denoted as df), and this should generally be greater than zero. However, this is only a necessary condition, and it is not a sufficient condition for all the parameters to be identified.

Referring back to our retention model, we have four parameters $\{b, r_C, r_I, \gamma\}$, but it is not possible to estimate all these parameters with the present experimental design. To understand this issue better, it will help to rewrite Equation 3.2 in its alternative form:

$$P(d) = \frac{e^{b \cdot r_C \cdot \gamma^d}}{e^{b \cdot r_C \cdot \gamma^d} + e^{b \cdot r_I \cdot \gamma^d}} \cdot \frac{e^{-b \cdot r_C \cdot \gamma^d}}{e^{-b \cdot r_C \cdot \gamma^d}} = \frac{1}{1 + e^{-b \cdot (r_C - r_I) \cdot \gamma^d}}. \qquad (3.3)$$

Suppose we generated artificial data with the parameters $b = 3$ and $(r_C - r_I) = 2$, so that the product in the exponent of Equation 3.3 equals $-6\gamma^d$. Then, suppose we try to fit the same artificial data, but we mistakenly set $b = 1$ during the fitting process. Can we still exactly reproduce the artificial data? The answer is yes, provided that we adjust $(r_C - r_I)$ by multiplying the original value by 3 so that it equals $(r_C - r_I) = 2 \cdot 3 = 6$. Then, exactly the same predictions are produced because the product in the exponent of Equation 3.3 remains the same. More generally, we can set the parameter b to any arbitrary nonzero value (e.g., $b = 1$) and then adjust the parameters r_C and r_I into $r_C \times b$ and $r_I \times b$ to accommodate this arbitrary selection. Only the product of $b \times (r_C - r_I)$ is needed. Therefore, we can eliminate the parameter b without any loss in predictive power of the model. Thus, the parameter b cannot be identified in this application, and we simply fix it to some easily interpretable value such as $b = 1$.

A similar problem of identification occurs with the two parameters r_C and r_I. Suppose, we generated the data setting $r_C = 10$ and $r_I = 5$. Then, suppose we tried to exactly fit the same data after arbitrarily setting $r_I = 0$. We could adjust r_C so that $r_C = (10 - 5) = 5$ and exactly reproduce the same results. Only the difference $(r_C - r_I)$ is important, and so we can replace the two parameters with a single parameter $r = (r_C - r_I)$, without any loss in generality. We would then interpret this estimate of r as the original difference.

What about the parameter γ? Can this be set to some arbitrary value without losing any generality? The answer is no because there is no way to adjust any other parameter in the model to compensate for changes in this parameter. This parameter is an exponential function of the independent variable, the delay d, and hence no other parameter can compensate for this feature. Thus, the decay rate is an identifiable parameter.

In sum, our retention model has only two identifiable parameters, the initial connection strength parameter r and the decay rate parameter γ that need to be estimated from the data, and so we have $11 - 2 = 9$ df, where 11 comes from the number of data points from our 11 experimental conditions. Therefore, we can rewrite the retention model in the reduced form without any loss in generality:

$$P(d) = \frac{1}{1 + e^{-r \cdot \gamma^d}} \qquad (3.4)$$

Hereafter, this form of the retention model will be used in all the remaining analyses.

There is one last comment that needs to be given about parameter identification. This issue depends on the design of the experiment. For some experimental designs, a set of parameters may not be identified, but if we changed the design, then they can be identified. For example, in the present experimental design, the parameter b is not identified because it is not manipulated. However, if we manipulated this parameter by some experimental factor at K different levels, then this parameter is not identified for the first level, but it is identified for the other $K - 1$ levels (i.e., this parameter is identified up to a ratio scale). For example, we could manipulate b across three levels by emphasizing the speed versus the accuracy of the decisions (low-, medium-, and high-speed stress). Then, this parameter would not be identified for the low-stress level, but it would be identified for the other two levels. (A general mathematical method for determining parameter identification is discussed in the appendix.)

Data Representation

Before we can estimate the parameters from the data, we need to be clear about the data to be used in the estimation procedure. At first, this may seem like a trivial step, but there are several important issues that must be decided. Consider the example from this chapter, where we have data from 5 participants within each group, and proportions from 11 delayed test conditions for each participant, with 200 observations per proportion.

Aggregate Modeling

The first approach is the aggregate data-fitting approach. Using this approach, we fit the choice proportions separately for each group, pooled across participants within each group. In this case, the data set would consist of the 11 choice proportions, per group, corresponding to the 11 delay conditions, per group, as seen in Figure 3.1. One set of parameters would be estimated from the normal group, and a second set would be estimated from the amnesic group. However, this approach implicitly assumes that there are no important individual differences within each group. More technically, this approach assumes that there is no variance in the model parameters within each group. For example, this approach would require one to assume that all individuals within a group have exactly the same decay rates, or that all individuals within a group have exactly the same initial association strengths.

Many cognitive researchers consider individual differences to be very important and therefore reject the aggregate data approach (see Cohen, Sanborn, & Shiffrin, in press; Estes & Maddox, 2005). If individual differences are strong, and usually they are, then fitting the model to the aggregate data, averaged across individuals, can be very misleading. Consider the following well-known example from early learning theory. Early concept learning theorists were interested in comparing all-or-none learning models with incremental strength learning models. At the individual level, the all-or-none model produces a learning curve that starts at chance performance and jumps suddenly to a solution that produces perfect performance. In contrast, the incremental learning model produces a smooth and gradually increasing learning curve for each individual. Now suppose we generate a fictitious data set containing 100 simulated subjects from the all-or-none learning model, but we allow large individual differences in the amount of training required to find the correct solution to the problem. In this case, the true model is known to be the all-or-none model, and all the individual learning curves reveal a jump from chance to perfect performance, but the jump occurs at a different point in training for each person. Next, suppose we average the data across subjects. This average would generate a smooth and gradually increasing learning curve for proportion correct, consistent with the incremental learning model. Furthermore, if we compare the fits of the two models, the incremental model could produce a superior fit, even though we know for sure that it is the wrong model. The final section in this chapter provides a concrete example of this problem.

Individual Modeling

The second approach is the individual data-fitting approach. Using this approach, we fit the model to the 11 proportions from each individual separately, allowing separate parameters and even separate models to be best fit for each person. This approach requires a large amount of data from each individual. Figure 3.2 is an example of a (fictitious) data set from one of the individuals taken from each group. Comparing this with the average data shown in Figure 3.1, it is obvious that the individual data are noisier.

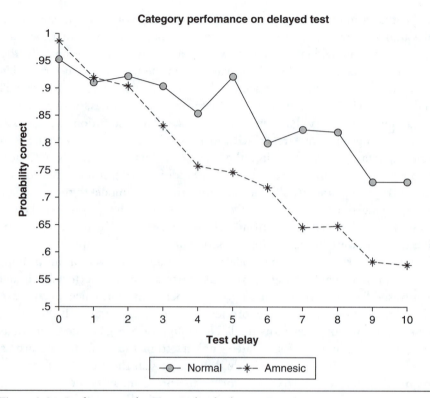

Figure 3.2   Performance for Two Individuals

One important advantage of the individual modeling approach is that it allows one to determine which model best fits each person from a set of competing cognitive models. In other words, this method allows for individual differences in the best-fitting type of model, and the percentage of individuals best fit by each cognitive model can be examined. Obviously, another advantage of the individual modeling approach is that it allows for any type of individual differences in parameters. Using this approach, one can estimate the distribution of parameters separately for the amnesic and control groups. Furthermore, one can compute the means of the parameters for each group as well as perform statistical tests on these means to determine whether the differences between groups are statistically significant. For example, after estimating the five sets of parameters for the normal and amnesic groups, we can compute the mean decay rate for each group and test whether the mean decay rate is significantly different for the two groups.

Hierarchical Modeling

There is a third approach, called the hierarchical data-fitting approach (see Lee, 2008; Rouder & Lu, 2005), which is a compromise between the first two. The idea is to fit a single probability mixture model to all the data from all the participants. The mixture model incorporates an extra, higher-level set of assumptions regarding the distribution of the parameters across individuals within each group. For example, to formulate a hierarchical version of the retention model, we would need to postulate a bivariate density function for each group that represents the distribution of the two model parameters within each group. Thus, we do not estimate the parameters for any individual, and instead we estimate the parameters of the bivariate density function of each group. This approach requires a large number of participants to obtain accurate estimates of the mixture density.

The hierarchical modeling approach has an advantage over the aggregate modeling approach because it allows for a distribution of parameters across individual differences. It also has an advantage over the individual modeling approach because it avoids fitting separate parameters to each person. If we assume that the hypothesized mixture density for the distribution of parameters is true, then the hierarchical model provides more precise estimates of the distribution of parameters as compared with the individual model fitting approach. However, if the wrong mixture density function is assumed for the distribution of parameters, then the hierarchical modeling approach could produce poorer estimates of the distribution of parameters than the individual modeling approach.

The hierarchical data-fitting approach is an attractive approach, but there remain some important advantages for the individual modeling approach. First, the latter does not require any extra assumptions about the distribution of parameters across individuals. Second, individual modeling allows one to compare the fits of the competing models separately for each person. A third advantage of the individual modeling approach is that it allows one to examine correlations between model parameters and other individual difference assessments. For example, after fitting the retention model to each participant from the amnesic group, one could examine the correlation between the retention parameter and brain images produced by functional MRI techniques.

Recommendations

In summary, the individual modeling approach is ideal for cognitive experiments involving a small number of participants and a large amount of data per person. In this case, one can obtain precise estimates from each person, and no assumptions must be made about the distribution of parameters across individuals. The hierarchical approach is difficult to apply with a small number of participants because it is difficult to estimate the density function of the parameters from a small number of individuals. The hierarchical approach is ideal for studies with a large number of participants and a small amount of data per person. In this case, the parameter estimates obtained from the individual modeling approach are poorly estimated, and the density function of the parameters for the hierarchical approach can be estimated more precisely. Most cognitive modeling applications employ a small number of participants across a large number of trials, and so most of our examples will use the individual modeling approach. However, the last chapter in this book presents an example of using the hierarchical approach. The aggregate approach may be justified only when there is too little data per person to use the individual modeling approach and the model is too complex to use the hierarchical approach (Cohen et al., in press).

Objective Functions

There are various measures, or *objective functions*, that have been used to assess the fit of predictions to data. Objective functions map parameters into fit indices: For each combination of parameter values, the predictions are computed, and the fit to the data is measured. We will review the three most commonly used objective functions: the least-squares objective, the weighted least-squares objective, and the likelihood objective.

We will initially consider fitting the results from the normal participant shown in Figure 3.2. The data from this person are reproduced in Table 3.1. For example, at delay $d = 2$, the observed proportion for this person is $p_2 = .9204$.

The first step for all these objectives is to generate the predicted probabilities from a model for each delay condition using a specific set of parameter values. To illustrate the process, we will initially evaluate the predictions of

Table 3.1   Results for the Control Participant Shown in Figure 3.2

Delay	0	1	2	3	4	5	6	7	8	9	10
Observed	.9538	.9107	.9204	.9029	.8515	.9197	.7970	.8228	.8191	.7277	.7276
Predicted	.9526	.9168	.8721	.8229	.7736	.7277	.6871	.6523	.6232	.5993	.5798

the retention model (using Equation 3.4) generated by setting $r = 3$ and $\gamma = .80$. These are not the optimal parameters, and they should be considered as only an initial guess. We will show how to find the optimal parameters later. Table 3.1 above also shows the predicted probabilities from Equation 3.4 with $r = 3$ and $\gamma = .80$. Considering the first delay condition, $d = 0$, the prediction is $P(0) = 1/\{1 + \exp[-3 \cdot (.80)^0]\} = .9526$, and the probability of an incorrect response is $1 - (.9526) = .0474$. Skipping up to the delay condition $d = 2$, the predicted probability is $P(2) = 1/\{1 + \exp[-3 \cdot (.80)^2]\} = .8721$, and the incorrect probability is $1 - .8721 = .1279$. Finally, moving down to the final delay condition, $d = 10$, the predicted probability is $P(10) = 1/\{1 + \exp[3 \cdot (.80)^{10}]\} = .5798$, and the probability incorrect is $1 - .5798 = .4202$.

Least-Squares Objective

Perhaps the most commonly used method for measuring fit is to sum the squared deviations between the observed and predicted values. For example, at delay $d = 2$, the observed proportion equals $p_2 = .9204$, the prediction for this condition was $P(2) = .8721$, and so the error is $[p_2 - P(2)] = (.9204 - .8721) = .0483$. Squaring this error produces $[p_2 - P(2)]^2 = (.0483)^2 = .0023$. This computation is performed on all 11 proportions to yield the sum of squared errors (SSE):

$$SSE = \Sigma[p_d - P(d)]^2,$$

which in this case is $SSE = 0.1695$.

One problem with the SSE measure of fit is that it penalizes all errors the same. However, some errors may be considered more serious than others, depending on the precision of the estimated proportion $p_d = (n_{Cd}/n)$, where n_{Cd} is the number correct and n is the total number of trials per condition. Suppose that the retention model is the true model. Then, the variance of the sample proportion is given by

$$\text{Var}[p_d] = \sigma^2(d) = \frac{P(d) \cdot Q(d)}{n},$$

where $Q(d) = [1 - P(d)]$. For example, $\sigma^2(0) = (.9526)(.0474)/200 = .00023$ and $\sigma^2(10) = (.5798)(.4202)/200 = .00122$. As can be seen from this formula, the variance is a quadratic function of probability: This quadratic has an inverted U-shaped form with a maximum at $P(d) = .50$ and a minimum at the extremes of 1.0 and 0.0. Based on this sampling distribution, we expect smaller estimation errors at short delay conditions, where the probability is closer to 1.0, and we expect larger estimation errors at longer delay conditions, where the probability is closer to .50. Thus, errors at the longer delays should be given less weight because they are likely to be the result of estimation error. The least-squares criterion gives all errors equal weight. As we shall discuss later, this failure to take the variance of the estimation error into account causes the least-squares method to be an inefficient method for estimating parameters.

Weighted Least-Squares Objective

The next criterion is closely related to the least-squares method. The weighted least-squares method (denoted as *WSSE*) is computed from the squared deviations between the predicted and observed data points, but these deviations are weighted by the inverse of the variance of the prediction.

$$WSSE = \sum \left(\frac{[p_d - P(d)]}{\sigma_d} \right)^2 = \sum \frac{1}{\sigma_d^2} \cdot [p_d - P(d)]^2$$

which in this case is $WSSE = 158.4059$. The *WSSE* statistic is mathematically equivalent to the Pearson chi-square statistic:

$$\chi^2 = n \cdot \sum \left(\frac{[p_d - P(d)]^2}{P(d)} \right) + \left(\frac{[q_d - Q(d)]^2}{Q(d)} \right),$$

where $q_d = (1 - p_d)$ and $Q(d) = [1 - P(d)]$. The proof is simple if we examine each term being summed. First, we note that $[q_d - Q(d)]^2 = \{(1 - p_d) - [1 - P(d)]\}^2 = [p_d - P(d)]^2$. Then, using a common denominator, we combine the two terms within the Pearson chi-square statistic as follows:

$$n \cdot \frac{Q(d)[p_d - P(d)]^2 + P(d)[q_d - Q(d)]^2}{P(d) \cdot Q(d)}$$

$$= n \cdot \frac{[Q(d) + P(d)] \cdot [p_d - P(d)]^2}{P(d) \cdot Q(d)}$$

$$= n \cdot \frac{1 \cdot [p_d - P(d)]^2}{P(d) \cdot Q(d)} = \frac{[p_d - P(d)]^2}{\sigma^2(d)}.$$

Comparing the left- and the right-hand sides, we see that each term in the Pearson chi-square sum is exactly equal to each term in the *WSSE* sum. Thus, the two statistics are equivalent.

Likelihood Objective

The last method computes the likelihood that a model would have generated the observed data, given a fixed set of parameter values. Once again, we will illustrate this method using the retention model with the parameters set equal to $r = 3$ and $\gamma = .80$.

To compute this likelihood, it is useful to list all the 2,200 trials in the exact order of presentation. Part of these data is shown below in Table 3.2, which is from the same data that were summarized in Table 3.1. The first column indicates the trial number, the second column indicates the observed response on each trial (in this case, whether the choice was correct or incorrect), the next column indicates the experimental delay condition, and the last column shows the predicted probability of being correct for that person on that trial.

To compute the likelihood, we need to make an important assumption. We must assume that the response on any trial is *statistically independent* of

Table 3.2 List of Data That Were Summarized in Table 3.1

Trial	Choice	Delay	Prediction
1	C	0	.9526
2	I	0	.0474
3	C	0	.9526
4	C	0	.9526
5	C	0	.9526
. . .			
310	C	2	.8721
320	C	2	.8721
330	I	2	.1279
340	I	2	.1279
. . .			
2,190	C	10	.5798
2,200	I	10	.4202

the response on any other trial. A statistically independent sequence of binary responses is called a Bernoulli process. This assumption is probably false because of temporally extended factors such as fatigue, drifting attention, or response alternation tendencies; but it is often made for simplicity. Violations of statistical independence can be checked by statistically testing the autocorrelations at various lags, or testing the spectral density for deviations from white noise. However, for the purposes of this chapter, we will simply assume that the process is a Bernoulli process (in fact, it is true, because the data were artificially generated that way). This assumption is commonly made in cognitive modeling research, but caution about this assumption must always be kept in mind.[1] In a later chapter, we will relax this assumption and allow for statistical dependencies across trials.

Assuming statistical independence across trials, the joint probability of the responses across all trials is simply the product of the probabilities from each trial. (A general form for the likelihood function is given in the appendix to this chapter.) Referring to Table 3.2, the likelihood for the retention model, denoted as L_R, is computed by multiplying all the probabilities under the predicted column:

$$L_R = (.9526)(.0474)(.9526)(.9526)(.9526) \ldots (.8721)$$
$$(.8721)(.1279)(.1279) \ldots (.5798)(.4202).$$

As you might expect, this product turns out to be a very small number, and so it is more convenient to work on the log scale by taking the natural logarithm of the product, which is called the log likelihood. (Recall that the log of a product equals the sum of the logs.) In this case, we obtain

$$\ln(L_R) = \ln(.9526) + \ln(.0474) + \ln(.9526) + \ln(.9526) + \ln(.9526) + \ldots$$
$$+ \ln(.8721) + \ln(.8721) + \ln(.1274) + \ln(.1274) + \ldots$$
$$+ \ln(.5798) + \ln(.4202)$$
$$= -969.9514.$$

We can simplify this log-likelihood expression by counting the number of correct responses for each condition, n_{Cd}, and counting the number of incorrect responses for each condition, n_{Id}. By combining all the terms contributed by the correct responses for each condition and also combining all the terms contributed by the incorrect responses to each condition, we obtain a much shorter formula:

$$\ln(L_R) = \sum_{d=1,\ldots,11} n_{C,d} \cdot \ln[P(d)] + n_{I,d} \cdot \ln[Q(d)] = -969.9514. \quad (3.5a)$$

This is the standard formula for the log likelihood of a Bernoulli process, and it is closely related to the formula for the binomial distribution.[2]

It is difficult to judge whether this likelihood produced by this model is good or bad without having some idea about the maximum that can possibly be obtained for any model and any set of parameters. Assuming statistically independent observations, this maximum can be determined by evaluating the log likelihood of the saturated model. Recall that the saturated model simply uses the observed relative frequencies as the prediction for each delay condition:

$$\ln(L_S) = \sum n_{C,d} \cdot \ln[p_d] + n_{1d} \cdot \ln[q_d]. \qquad (3.5b)$$

Using the observed relative frequencies shown in Table 3.1 to compute the log likelihood for the saturated model produces the result $\ln(L_S) =$ -879.9013. Note that the saturated model has higher log likelihood as compared with that produced by the retention model. This must always be true.

When maximum likelihood is used to estimate parameters, the lack of fit is usually measured by a statistic called G^2. This is computed as follows. First, the difference between the log likelihoods of the saturated model and the retention model is computed: $\ln(L_S) - \ln(L_R) = (-879.9013) -$ $(-969.9514) = 90.0501$. This difference is called the log-likelihood ratio because $\ln(L_S/L_R) = \ln(L_S) - \ln(L_R)$. The G^2 statistic is defined as twice the difference in the log-likelihood ratio:

$$G^2 = 2[\ln(L_S) - \ln(L_R)], \qquad (3.6)$$

and in this case $G^2 = (2)(90.0501) = 180.1002$. This measures the lack of fit between the cognitive model and the saturated model. The parameters that maximize the likelihood objective are equivalent to the parameters that minimize G^2. Hereafter, when we refer to the maximum-likelihood objective, we will actually be minimizing G^2.

Relations Among Objectives

Here, we briefly point out some of the mathematical relationships among the three objective functions that we have reviewed. First, consider least squares and weighted least squares. If the variance does not change across conditions so that the weight is constant, then the weighted least-squares objective is equivalent to the least-squares objective. For example, linear regression models usually assume homogeneous variance (constant variance across conditions), and in that case the two objectives are identical. But as we noted earlier, choice probabilities do not satisfy the homogeneous variance assumption. Neither does choice response time—the variance of response time for each condition tends to increase with the mean response time for each condition. Thus, it is unsafe to assume homogenous variance across conditions. (However, in the appendix, we present a method for transforming the dependent variable so that a weighted least-squares problem can be solved using least-squares methods.)

Next, consider the relation between weighted least squares and maximum likelihood. If we assume that the model is true, then the G^2 statistic, which is used with the maximum-likelihood objective, has the same asymptotic distribution as the *WSSE* statistic—both are asymptotically chi-square distributed (Rao, 1965). Furthermore, these two methods produce parameter estimates that have the same asymptotic normal distribution (see the appendix for more details about this point). Therefore, with large sample sizes, these two objectives produce very similar results.

Finally, consider the relation between least squares and maximum likelihood. This relation depends on the performance measure. In the present case, we are considering proportion correct as the performance measure, which has a binomial distribution. However, if the performance measure was normally distributed, and we assumed homogenous variance across conditions, then G^2 is linearly related to the sum of squared errors. Under these special conditions, minimizing sum of squared error is equivalent to maximizing the likelihood function (see the appendix).

Efficiency of Estimators

We have presented three methods for estimating parameters, and this naturally leads one to a question: How do we choose an objective for estimating parameters? This is usually decided on the basis of the statistical properties of the estimates produced by each method. There are two important properties of estimators: consistency and efficiency. Suppose the model we are fitting is the true model that actually generated the data. Then, the parameter values that minimize lack of fit to the sample data are sample estimates of the true parameters. A method for estimating parameters is consistent if the parameter estimates that it produces converge (in distribution) to the true values as the sample size for each condition increases to infinity. The method is efficient if, among all the consistent estimators, it produces estimates that have minimum variance. All three methods generally satisfy the consistency property, so this does not lead to a basis for preference. However, the methods differ with respect to the efficiency property. If homogeneity of variance is not satisfied, then the least-squares method is not efficient. This is an important reason for using either the weighted least squares or the maximum-likelihood objectives. Mathematically, it has been proven that parameter estimates obtained from minimizing weighted least squares or maximum likelihood are consistent and efficient (Rao, 1965).

Searching for Optimal Parameters

Recall that the retention model produced a $G^2 = 180.1002$ using the specific parameter values $\gamma = .8$ and $r = 3$. But this is not necessarily the best or worst choice. In fact, if we set $\gamma = .8$ and $r = 2$ we obtain a much worse fit, $G^2 = 359.913$; and we shall see later that the optimal parameters are obtained by setting $\gamma = .9042$ and $r = 2.9166$, which produces a $G^2 = 15.8077$. How we found this will be discussed below.

Grid Search

To glean some idea about how computer search programs work, we will analyze the search problem in a bit more detail. Consider forming a two-dimensional grid by crossing 151 values for γ (.80, .51, .52, . . . , .95) with 201 values for r (2, 1.01, 1.02, . . . , 4.0) producing $151 \cdot 201 = 30,351$ points on the grid. Suppose we compute a G^2 fit statistic for the data from Table 3.2 at each of these points on the grid, and then plot the G^2 values above each point on the grid. This produces the response surface plot shown in Figure 3.3. The left horizontal axis represents the 201 values of the association strength parameter r; the right horizontal axis represents the 151 values of the decay parameter γ; and the vertical axis represents the value of G^2 above each grid point. The surface produced by this looks like a curved sheet of paper. Our task is to find the grid point that lies at the bottom of this curved sheet. If we start from one of the corners and move step by step in the direction downhill, we will eventually reach the bottom where a move in any direction takes us back uphill. This is the minimum point for which we are looking, and in this case, it happens to be located at ($\gamma = .9042$, $r = 2.9166$). This is called hill climbing (downhill).

The curves shown in the horizontal plane at the bottom of the response surface are contour curves. Each contour curve indicates the set of grid points that produce exactly the same G^2 lack of fit. The outer contour curves show the points that produce a large G^2 or poor lack of fit, and the inner contour curves that surround the minimum point produce small G^2 or good fit. Notice that the inner contour curve that surrounds the minimum is elliptical with the major axis aligned with the negative correlation between the strength and decay parameters. This shows that changes in the parameters along this line produce only small changes in fit.

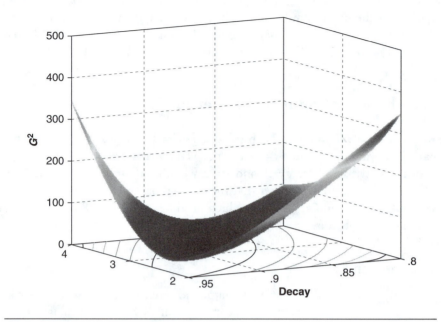

Figure 3.3   Response Surface Analysis

The graphical analysis described above is not really practical in most model-fitting applications. There are two reasons for this. One is that the graphical analysis can only be used with one or two parameters and the other is that most applications have more than two parameters. A grid search can be used with any number of parameters to find a rough idea of where the maximum is located, but this solution is usually too crude, and more precise estimates are usually required. Grid searches are useful for finding a starting point for a more precise analysis. Parameter optimization for models with many parameters requires the use of sophisticated search processes on a computer. Mathematical programming languages such as MATLAB, Mathematica, GAUSS, or SAS provide programs for performing search of parameters for nonlinear models.

Below we sketch the basic idea of a steepest-descent algorithm.

Steepest-Descent Search

Computer search programs are designed to find the parameters that produce the minimum of an objective function, G^2 in our case. Some of these programs use a form of steepest descent, which can be roughly described as follows. We can start at any point, say, for example, the point $(\gamma = .8, r = 4)$ in the back corner of Figure 3.3. From here, we can consider moving a small step to a nearby grid point, say the point ($\gamma = .801$, $r = 3.99$). The line connecting these two points forms a direction. If we compute the change in the G^2 statistic produced by moving in this direction, we would find that it produces a decrease in G^2. But this may not be the direction producing the maximum decrease. Alternatively, we could consider moving a small step to another adjacent grid point such as ($\gamma = .8$, $r = 3.99$) or ($\gamma = .801$, $r = 4$), and compute the change in G^2 produced by this direction. By checking all the possible small moves at adjacent grid points in every direction, we could find the move that produces the largest decrease in G^2, which is the direction of steepest descent. The program takes a very small step in the direction of steepest descent. After making this move to this new position, we have a new set of parameters that are better than the starting values. This completes the first iteration of the search process, and the whole procedure is repeated. For the second iteration, we start from the current point after the first iteration, find the direction of steepest-descent from this new point, and take a second small step in the direction of the gradient at this point to produce the second position after the second iteration. This process continues until we reach a point where a move in any direction fails to decrease the objective, our G^2 statistic. At this minimum point, the surface becomes perfectly flat, and all directions lead uphill (which is at $\gamma = .9042$ and $r = 2.9166$ in this case).

Mathematically, the direction of steepest descent is found by computing the *gradient* of the objective function at current point of search in the parameter space. The gradient is equal to the partial derivative of the objective function with respect to each parameter. Steepest-descent search programs move downhill in the direction of the gradient until the gradient reaches zero. Steepest-descent programs do not require the user to supply the gradient; instead the program uses finite difference methods to estimate the gradient automatically for the user. In the appendix to this chapter, we provide more details about the steepest-descent search methods, as well as an example program.

Constraints on Parameters

Often the parameter estimates for a cognitive model need to be constrained so that they fall within theoretical boundaries. For example, the decay rate should range from 0 (complete forgetting) to 1 (no forgetting), and the initial strength should be nonnegative. Sometimes, however, an unconstrained search algorithm will explore parameter values that fall outside the boundaries. When this happens, it may be a signal that the model is not fitting very well or the data are too noisy. In this case, it may be necessary to force the parameter search to stay within the theoretical boundaries. There are a couple of ways to do this.

Constrained steepest-descent programs are designed to satisfy what are known as the Kuhn Tucker conditions, which are necessary conditions for optimality under nonlinear constraints. These programs incorporate the information about the Kuhn Tucker conditions directly into a modification of the objective function, called the Lagrangian function, and the search is based on this modified objective. This method provides the most effective way to deal with the parameter constraint problem.

Other search programs (described below) cannot incorporate information about the Kuhn Tucker conditions into the search process. These alternative search algorithms require another method for incorporating constraints. Another way to do this is to reparameterize the model using new parameters that have no constraints. For example, if we wish to impose the constraint $r > 0$, we could define the initial strength as $r = e^u$, and search for the parameter u instead of r; and if we wish to constrain the decay rate γ to range from 0 to 1, then we could define the decay rate as $\gamma = 1/(1 + e^{-v})$, and estimate v instead of γ. Using this method, the search program searches for the pair of parameters (u, v), which are then used to compute the two cognitive parameters r and γ, and finally, the latter are inserted into the retention model to make predictions. Although this method of imposing constraints works, it is less than ideal because it adds extra complications to the search process.

Flat Minimum Problem

Several problems can occur with the parameter search process. If the response surface is very flat, then the steepest-descent search process may terminate prematurely because the changes in the objective function are too small to detect improvements. Notice in Figure 3.3 that the surface is steep along the line formed by connecting the left corner point (.95, 4) with the front corner point (.95, 2). Changes in parameters along this line produce a very large change in the lack-of-fit measure. But the surface is very flat along the line connecting (.95, 2) to (.90, 3). In other words, near the minimum point, decreasing the decay parameter γ can be compensated by increases in the strength parameter r to produce almost the same fit. If we start at the point where the function is the minimum, and move along this negatively correlated line where the function is flat, then substantial changes in parameter values produce small changes in the lack of fit. This insensitivity of the objective function to changes in parameter values causes instability in the parameter estimates. More precisely, the curvature of the objective function near minimum determines the variance of the parameter estimates. Flatness near the minimum produces parameter estimates with large standard errors.

Local Minima Problem

There is an important limitation with steepest-descent search algorithms called the local minimum problem. Note that the objective function plotted in Figure 3.3 has only one minimum. In fact, the surface can be well approximated by a bowl-shaped quadratic function near the minimum. This is a desirable situation but there is no guarantee that this will occur. Consider, for example, the search for a maximum problem illustrated in Figure 3.4. In this example, a grid of points for a single parameter is plotted on the horizontal axis, and the objective function is plotted on the vertical axis. If the steepest-ascent search program began its search on the far left side, then it would succeed in finding the global maximum, which is the desired point. However, if the program started on the far right side, then it would get stuck at the local maximum and never find the global maximum. The only way to avoid getting stuck at the local maximum in this case is to try out several starting positions.

As the number of parameters increases, the possibility of more than one local minimum increases and this becomes a serious problem. When several local minima are possible, it is important to try out a grid of starting positions

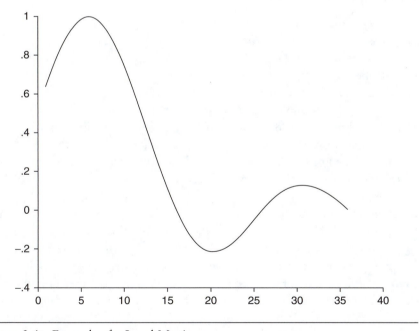

Figure 3.4   Example of a Local Maximum

or a random sample of starting positions. If two different starting positions produce different search results, then of course, you choose the search result that yields the smallest value for our objective function. But this would also serve as a warning that local minima are a problem.

For very difficult search problems, such as highly nonlinear problems involving a large number of parameters, many local minima may be present, and then it may be advantageous to use a stochastic search called simulated annealing to avoid getting stuck in a local minimum (Ingber, 1993; Kirkpatrick, Gelatt, & Vecchi, 1983). Briefly, the simulating annealing algorithm works as follows. From a given starting position, the program randomly selects a new position and evaluates this new position compared with the old position. With probability p, the algorithm selects the superior of these two points, and with probability $(1 - p)$ it selects the inferior. This procedure is repeated for many iterations; however, with each iteration the value of p gradually increases. The rationale behind this method is the following. Early in the search, the procedure bounces up and down a lot so that it can escape out of a local minimum; but later in the search, the procedure converges toward the global minimum.

Discontinuities

Steepest-descent algorithms require computing the gradient, and this is only feasible for objective functions that are smooth and continuous. When discontinuities, such as breaks, jumps, or kinks, exist in the objective function, then steepest-descent is no longer applicable, and some other non-derivative-based search process must be employed.

The most commonly used direct search method is the Nelder-Mead simplex algorithm (Nelder & Mead, 1965). To briefly describe this algorithm, consider the problem of searching the parameter space for the best-fitting two parameters of the retention model. The parameter space is represented by the rectangular horizontal plane shown in Figure 3.3. Each point on this plane represents a pair of parameters. This program starts by taking three points in this parameter space (three pairs of parameters), forming a small triangle (called the simplex), and evaluating these three points with respect to the objective function. Then, a new fourth point is generated, either within or nearby the edge of the triangle, from the original three points. For example, the new point may be formed by averaging the three points, producing a fourth point. Finally, the best three out of these four points is retained, and the worst point is dropped. This procedure is repeated until no new point can be generated that improves the objective function.

Many cognitive models encounter this problem of discontinuity. In particular, this problem occurs whenever the predictions of the model involve random elements. For example, a neural network model may use randomly selected initial connection weights prior to category learning. If this were the case, then the predictions from this neural network model would vary randomly even when the model parameters are held constant. If the predictions vary randomly, then so does the measure of fit. The result is that the objective function is no longer a simple function of the parameters. Even when the model parameters are held constant, the objective function will change abruptly due to the random elements. At one stage of the search process, one point in the parameter space may produce a better fit than another, but at the next stage, the order could reverse simply due to the random elements. For these types of models, involving random elements, derivative-based search methods cannot work, and a direct search algorithm is required.

Discrete-Valued Parameters

Some cognitive models involve integer- as well as continuous-valued parameters (e.g., the number of items that can be stored in a short-term store). One way to deal with this type of problem is to use a steepest-descent algorithm to minimize the continuously valued parameters for a specific value of the integer parameter. Then, repeat this process for each value of the discrete parameter producing a finite set of search results. Finally, select the discrete parameter value that results in the minimum of all these searches. However, if there are very many values of the discrete parameters to check, then this method becomes too difficult to employ.

Under these conditions, it may be advantageous to use a genetic algorithm to search for the optimal combination of discrete and continuous parameters. Genetic algorithms were invented by John Holland (1975) and are based on concepts from biological evolution. This method maintains a population of candidates (called genes), where each candidate is a binary coded representation of a combination of parameter values. Then genetic principles of random crossovers and mutations are used to generate new candidates, and evolutionary principles of fitness and selection are used for reproduction of candidates.

Results From Each of the Estimation Methods

What happens when we use different objective functions to estimate the parameters for the same data shown in Table 3.1? Will we obtain the same parameter estimates? In general, the answer is no. To illustrate, we used a modified steepest-descent algorithm to minimize SSE, $WSSE$, and G^2 for the data shown in Figure 3.2, separately for the normal participant (see Table 3.3a) and the amnesic participant (see Table 3.3b). This table shows the solutions for the best-fitting parameters produced by each method. As can be seen in this table, although the results are not exactly the same, they turn out to be very similar in this case. All three methods produce an estimate of the decay rate that is faster for the amnesic participant as compared with the normal participant. However, there is no guarantee that the results will always turn out this similar.

The parameters that minimized the G^2 criterion were found for all 5 participants from each of the two groups, and the results, averaged across participants, are shown in Table 3.4. Each cell shows the mean for each group, and the standard deviation is shown in parentheses. Once again, we observe a faster decay rate for the amnesic group. These data were artificially generated from the retention model using the following population parameters: ($\gamma = .90$, $r = 3.0$) for the normal population and ($\gamma = .80$, $r = 3.2$) for the amnesic population. Thus, the estimation procedure did a good job of recovering the true parameter values in this example.

Table 3.3a   Parameter Estimates Obtained From the Normal Person Shown in Figure 3.2

	Decay, γ	Strength, r	Fit Index
SSE	.8997	3.0046	SSE = 0.0095
WSSE	.9040	2.8863	WSSE = 14.81
Likelihood	.9042	2.9166	G^2 = 15.8077

Table 3.3b   Parameter Estimates Obtained From the Amnesic Person Shown in Figure 3.2

	Decay, γ	Strength, r	Fit Index
SSE	0.7902	3.3222	SSE = 0.0031
WSSE	0.7850	3.4042	WSSE = 5.4033
Likelihood	0.7820	3.4744	G^2 = 5.6596

Table 3.4   Means and Standard Deviations Averaged Across Participants Within Each Group

Group	Mean Decay	Mean Strength	Mean G^2
Normal ($N = 5$)	.9022 (.0135)	2.9373 (.1898)	10.8018 (5.0029)
Amnesic ($N = 5$)	.8062 (.0171)	3.1550 (.2145)	7.5540 (2.1606)

Variance of the Parameter Estimates

The standard deviations shown in Table 3.4 represent the variation in the estimated parameters across individuals within each group. There appears to be more variation in the strength parameter as compared with the decay parameter. It is important to note, however, that the variance of each parameter is influenced by two sources: One is variation caused by individual differences in the parameter across people within the same group; but another source is estimation error variance caused by noisy sample data.

In this example, the data were actually simulated with no variance in the true parameters across individuals within a group—all 5 participants within each group were generated using exactly the same parameter values. Therefore, the variation in parameter estimates across individuals for this artificial example is entirely attributed to estimation error. The standard error for the strength parameter is larger than that for the decay parameter.

It is possible to compute the standard errors of the parameters for each individual when steepest-descent algorithms are used with the weighted least squares or likelihood objectives. At the completion of the parameter search for the minimum, the steepest-descent algorithms can compute a matrix called the inverse Hessian matrix (see the appendix to this chapter for more details about this matrix). For large sample sizes, the element located in the ith diagonal position of this matrix provides an estimate of the variance of the ith parameter, and the square root of this element gives the standard error of this parameter. For example, the retention model has two parameters, and so the inverse Hessian is a 2×2 matrix with two diagonal elements. The first diagonal element provides an estimate of the variance of the decay rate, and the second diagonal element provides an estimate of the variance of the initial strength. In particular, for the normal participant shown in Table 3.1, the inverse Hessian matrix is

$$\begin{pmatrix} .0001 & -.0008 \\ -.0008 & .0160 \end{pmatrix}.$$

Therefore, an estimate of the standard error for this person on the decay rate equals $(.0001)^{.5} = .01$, and an estimate of the standard error for the initial strength is $(.0160)^{.5} = .1265$. These results reflect the sample estimates of the standard deviations (based on the estimate from 5 participants) shown in Table 3.4.

The off-diagonal elements of the inverse Hessian matrix are also informative. These indicate the covariance between a pair of parameters. For example, using the data from the normal participant shown in Table 3.1, the estimate of the covariance between the parameters equals $-.0008$, and the corresponding correlation is $(-.0008)/(.01)(.1265) = -.8187$, which is highly negative. This negative covariance reflects the parameter trade-off that we observed near the minimum in Figure 3.3.

For large sample sizes, when the weighted least squares or the likelihood objectives are used, the parameters are asymptotically normally distributed. Therefore, one can compute 95% confidence interval estimates of the parameters using a z table. Consider, for example, the data from the amnesic participant shown in Table 3.3b. The estimate of the decay rate for this person shown in Table 3.3b is .782. Using the methods discussed above, we find that the standard error of this estimate equals .1818. Finally, the 95% confidence interval is $.782 \pm (1.96)(.1818)$, which produces the interval [.4257, 1.1383]. The upper bound is too high, because it does not make sense to have decay rates greater than 1. A Bayesian method (see Chapter 6) that builds in this prior probability would produce a better estimate in this case.

Model Evaluation

Chi-Square Lack-of-Fit Test

Both the weighted least squares and the maximum-likelihood methods provide a statistical test of deviations between the cognitive model and the saturated model. If the sample size is sufficiently large, then both statistics, χ^2 and G^2, are approximately chi-square distributed. If we wish to test the null hypothesis of no difference between the cognitive model and the saturated model, then we can refer the computed χ^2 or G^2 statistic to a standard chi-square table with df equal to the number of data points minus the number of parameters in the cognitive model. If the statistic exceeds the table value at a specified significance level, then the null hypothesis can be rejected, which means that there are some significant deviations in fit of the model to the data.

The sample size was $n = 200$ per condition for each person, which is fairly large, and so these chi-square tests are reasonable in this case. The degrees of freedom for this problem is $df = 11 - 2 = 9$ (11 data points minus 2 parameters), and the table chi-square at the .05 significance level is 16.92. Comparing this with the WSSE and G^2 statistics shown in Table 3.3, we fail to reject the null hypothesis. In other words, we conclude that there are no statistically significant deviations from the model predictions. (This is the correct decision in this case, because the data were in fact artificially generated from the model.)

These statistical tests of lack of fit are of limited scientific use for the following reasons. First, we know a priori that our cognitive model is imperfect, and so we are bound to have deviations between it and the real cognitive system generating the empirical data. Second, statistical tests of lack of fit are only valid for large sample sizes, and as the sample size gets large, the power to reject the incorrect null hypothesis increases toward 1.0, even on the basis of small deviations. Therefore, with a sufficiently large sample size, we are almost guaranteed to reject the null hypothesis as a result of deviations that are certain to exist between the model and the true generating process. In short, failure to reject the null hypothesis only tells us that the sample size is too small to detect the imperfections that must exist, and rejection of the null hypothesis only tells us that the model is imperfect, which we knew from the beginning.

R^2 Index of Model Fit

It is difficult to judge whether the SSE statistic is good or bad, so we need to compare it with that produced by the saturated and null models. The sum of squared errors produced by the saturated model is obviously zero, because it exactly reproduces the observed choice proportions. The sum of squared errors produced by the null model is equal to the sum of squared deviations around the mean (denoted as TSS). An index of fit, called R^2, is defined as

$$R^2 = 1 - (SSE/TSS) = TSS/TSS - SSE/TSS = (TSS - SSE)/TSS = SSP/TSS,$$

where SSE is the sum of squared *errors* produced by the cognitive model, and SSP is the sum of squares *predicted* by the model. Thus, R^2 is the ratio of the predicted sum of squares to the total sum of squares, that is, the proportion predicted by the model. If $R^2 = 0$, the cognitive model is no better than the null model, and if $R^2 = 1$, the cognitive model is equal to the saturated model.[3]

The mean for the normal participant (the data shown in Table 3.1), equals 0.8503, which produces a TSS = 0.0615; the SSE for this individual (shown in Table 3.3a) is $SSE = 0.0095$. Therefore, $R^2 = 1 - (.0095/.0615) = .8455$, which is a mediocre fit. For the amnesic participant, the $R^2 = 1 - (.0031/.0615) = .9841$, which is much better. Note that SSE is a measure of badness of fit, whereas R^2 is a measure of goodness of fit. These two indices are linearly related to each other, so whatever parameters happen to minimize SSE will also maximize R^2.

Aggregate Versus Individual Modeling

To illustrate some of the problems that can be encountered by fitting average rather than individual data, two sets of predictions were generated from the retention model. One set was generated by setting $\gamma = .80$ and $r = 3.00$ (with no sampling error), which we will call the Person A data set; a second set was generated by setting $\gamma = .40$ and $r = 3.20$ (with no sampling error), which we will call the Person B data set. A third data set was constructed from the first two by averaging the corresponding values of the first two data sets, which we will call the Average Person data set. All three data sets are graphed in Figure 3.5 below, with Person A as the top curve, Person B as the bottom curve, and the Average Person is the middle curve.

The retention model was fit to all three data sets, solving for γ and r that minimized the SSE criterion.[4] The retention model perfectly fits the Person A data set with $R^2 = 1.0$; it also perfectly fits the Person B data set with $R^2 = 1.0$. This is exactly what we expect because this model generated these data. However, it did not generate the Average Person data set, and it cannot perfectly fit these data. In this third case, we find $R^2 = .9756$. This failure to fit the Average Person data is a direct consequence of the nonlinearity of the model.

Suppose we try fitting another model, called the power function model, to these same three data sets:

$$P(d) = r \cdot (d + 1)^\gamma.$$

This model also has two parameters, γ and r, that must be estimated from each data set. The power function model was fit to all three data sets, solving for γ and r that minimized the SSE criterion. The power function model cannot perfectly fit the Person A data set, and we find $R^2 = .8938$ for this case. It cannot perfectly fit the Person B data set either, and we find $R^2 = .9335$ for this case. Both these results are expected because the two individual data sets were not generated by the power function—they were generated by the retention model. However, when we fit the power function

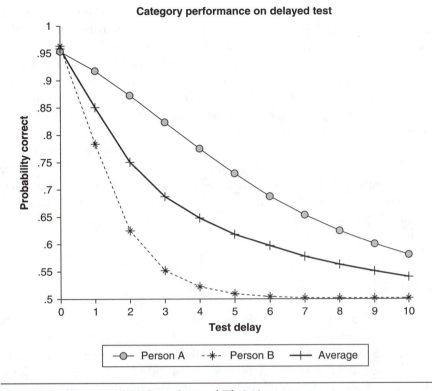

Figure 3.5   Two Fictitious Data Sets and Their Average

to the Average Person data set, we find $R^2 = .9924$, almost a perfect fit, and clearly superior to the retention model.

In this example, the retention model is the true model, and the power model is the false model, for the two individual data sets. When we compare the true model with the false model using the average data, the false model fits better. But if we compare the models using the individual data sets, the true model fits better in both cases. This example was based on earlier analyses of this problem by Myung, Kim, and Pitt (2000). This illustrates how aggregating data can mislead researchers, and it points out the importance of comparing models at the individual level of analysis.

Conclusion

Often a researcher wishes to compare the quantitative predictions between two cognitive models. In this case, it is necessary to obtain optimal estimates of the parameters from both models to give each model the best chance of predicting the data. We don't want to reject a model simply because we arbitrarily chose poor parameters. Furthermore, the parameter estimates themselves can be of great interest to the researcher, because they provide measures of important underlying cognitive processes. For example, in a memory retention model, we may be interested in estimating the difference in the decay rate parameter for amnesic and control subjects. We cannot extract this decay rate by simply looking at the raw data. Instead, we need to estimate the decay rate using the cognitive model. Cognitive models are usually nonlinear and this makes the parameter estimation process more complex than it is for linear models such as a regression model. However, with the availability of nonlinear search programs commonly available in mathematical programming languages, this process is becoming easier and more practical.

Appendix

This appendix provides more technical details about several of the topics concerning nonlinear parameter estimation. First, we present more general statements of both the least squares and the likelihood objectives. Then, we describe two of the most commonly used steepest-descent types of algorithms: the quasi–Newton-Raphson algorithm and the modified Gauss-Newton algorithm.

Generalized Least Squares

Weighted and unweighted least-squares methods require one to write the cognitive model as a nonlinear function, here denoted as M, that maps the independent variables and the parameters into a set of predictions. Define $\mathbf{Y}$ as a column vector of observations, $\mathbf{X}$ is a matrix of known independent variables, θ is a vector of parameters, and $\mathbf{E}$ is a column vector of errors. Mathematically, the cognitive model is represented by the following nonlinear model:

$$\mathbf{Y} = M(\mathbf{X}, \theta) + \mathbf{E},$$

where $\mathrm{Var}[\mathbf{E}] = \Sigma$ is the variance-covariance matrix of the errors.

Parameters that minimize the least-squares criterion, $SSE = \mathbf{E}^T\mathbf{E}$, are efficient if we assume that $\Sigma = \sigma^2\mathbf{I}$. When this assumption is not valid, we need to find parameters that minimize $WSSE = \mathbf{E}^T\mathbf{\Sigma}^{-1}\mathbf{E}$ to obtain efficient estimates. However, any weighted least-squares minimization problem can be linearly transformed into a least-squares minimization problem as follows.

First, we express the variance-covariance matrix of $\mathbf{E}$ in terms of its eigenvectors and eigenvalues: $\mathbf{\Sigma} = \mathbf{V}\mathbf{\Lambda}\mathbf{V}^T = \mathbf{V}\mathbf{\Lambda}^{1/2}\mathbf{\Lambda}^{1/2}\mathbf{V}^T$, where $\mathbf{V}$ is the orthonormal matrix of eigenvectors of $\mathbf{\Sigma}$, $\mathbf{\Lambda}$ is the diagonal matrix of eigenvalues of $\mathbf{\Sigma}$, and $\mathbf{\Lambda}^{1/2}$ contains the square roots of the eigenvalues. The inverse also can be expressed in terms of eigenvectors and eigenvalues as

$$\mathbf{\Sigma}^{-1} = \mathbf{V}\mathbf{\Lambda}^{-1}\mathbf{V}^T = (\mathbf{V}\mathbf{\Lambda}^{-1/2})(\mathbf{\Lambda}^{-1/2}\mathbf{V}^T),$$

where $\mathbf{\Lambda}^{-1/2}$ is the inverse of $\mathbf{\Lambda}^{1/2}$. Then, the weighted sums of squares can be rewritten as

$$WSSE = \mathbf{E}^T\mathbf{\Sigma}^{-1}\mathbf{E} = \mathbf{E}^T\mathbf{V}\mathbf{\Lambda}^{-1}\mathbf{V}^T\mathbf{E} = (\mathbf{E}^T\mathbf{V}\mathbf{\Lambda}^{-1/2})(\mathbf{\Lambda}^{-1/2}\mathbf{V}^T\mathbf{E}) = (\mathbf{E}^*)^T\mathbf{E}^*,$$

where $\mathbf{E}^* = (\mathbf{\Lambda}^{-1/2}\mathbf{V}^T)\mathbf{E}$. Note that the variance-covariance matrix of $\mathbf{E}^*$ is

$$\text{Var}[\mathbf{E}^*] = (\mathbf{\Lambda}^{-1/2}\mathbf{V}^T)\text{Var}[\mathbf{E}](\mathbf{V}\mathbf{\Lambda}^{-1/2}) = \mathbf{\Lambda}^{-1/2}\mathbf{V}^T \cdot \mathbf{V}\mathbf{\Lambda}^{1/2}\mathbf{\Lambda}^{1/2}\mathbf{V}^T \cdot \mathbf{V}\mathbf{\Lambda}^{-1/2} = \mathbf{I},$$

and so $\mathbf{E}^*$ satisfies the assumption required for least squares to produce efficient estimates. Now, we replace the original model with a new model:

$$\begin{aligned}\mathbf{Y}^* = (\mathbf{\Lambda}^{-1/2}\mathbf{V}^T)\mathbf{Y} &= (\mathbf{\Lambda}^{-1/2}\mathbf{V}^T)M(\mathbf{X}, \boldsymbol{\theta}) + (\mathbf{\Lambda}^{-1/2}\mathbf{V}^T)\mathbf{E} \\ &= M^*(\mathbf{X}, \boldsymbol{\theta}) + \mathbf{E}^*,\end{aligned} \tag{A3.1}$$

where $\mathbf{Y}^* = (\mathbf{\Lambda}^{-1/2}\mathbf{V}^T)\mathbf{Y}$ and $M^*(\mathbf{X}, \boldsymbol{\theta}) = (\mathbf{\Lambda}^{-1/2}\mathbf{V}^T)M(\mathbf{X}, \boldsymbol{\theta})$. In essence, we estimate the parameters that minimize the sum of squared error for the new model $\mathbf{Y}^* = M^*(\mathbf{X}, \boldsymbol{\theta}) + \mathbf{E}^*$. Finding the parameter vector $\boldsymbol{\theta}$ that minimizes $SSE = (\mathbf{E}^*)^T\mathbf{E}^*$ also minimizes $WSSE = \mathbf{E}^T\mathbf{\Sigma}^{-1}\mathbf{E}$. Later, if we wish to recover the predictions on the original scale, we apply the inverse transformation

$$(\mathbf{V}\mathbf{\Lambda}^{1/2})M^*(\mathbf{X}, \boldsymbol{\theta}) = (\mathbf{V}\mathbf{\Lambda}^{1/2})(\mathbf{\Lambda}^{-1/2}\mathbf{V}^T)M(\mathbf{X}, \boldsymbol{\theta}) = M(\mathbf{X}, \boldsymbol{\theta}).$$

In summary, we can always transform a weighted least-squares problem into a least-squares problem using the transformation shown above. The parameters obtained by minimizing the SSE of the transformed dependent variable will be exactly the same as the parameters obtained by minimizing the $WSSE$ of the original dependent variable. Furthermore, these parameters will have the same asymptotic distribution as the maximum-likelihood estimates.

The Generalized Likelihood Function

Suppose we observe a sequence of N ordered observations from an individual denoted as $(y_1, y_2, \ldots, y_t, \ldots, y_N)$, where each y_t has a discrete distribution.[5] In general, this sequence may be generated by any type of statistically dependent stochastic process. In this chapter, each observation indicated the choice made on each trial; but more generally, this could be any discrete measure, such as confidence ratings. The joint probability of these N observations is given by

$$\begin{aligned}
&\Pr[y_1 \cap y_2 \cap \ldots \cap y_t \cap \ldots \cap y_N] \\
&= \Pr[y_1] \cdot \Pr[y_2|y_1] \cdot \Pr[y_3|y_1 \cap y_2] \cdot \ldots \\
&\cdot \Pr[y_N|y_1 \cap y_2 \cap \ldots \cap y_{N-1}].
\end{aligned} \qquad \text{(A3.2)}$$

For convenience, define $\Pr[y_t|t - 1] = \Pr[y_t|y_1 \cap y_2 \cap \ldots \cap y_{t-1}]$ as the probability of observing the observation y_t, given all the preceding observations. Then, the log-likelihood statistic is defined as the natural log of Equation A3.1:

$$\ln(L) = \Sigma \ln(\Pr[y_t|t - 1]). \qquad \text{(A3.3)}$$

If we assume statistical independence, then $\Pr[y_t|t - 1] = \Pr[y_t]$, and the stochastic process reduces to what is called an independent process. The product rule for computing the likelihood is only valid for an independent process, which is a very specialized case of the more general likelihood function (see Anderson, 1971).

The G^2 statistic for comparing the cognitive model with the saturated model is defined as twice the difference in log likelihoods of the two models:

$$G^2 = 2[\ln(L_S) - \ln(L_R)]. \qquad \text{(A3.4)}$$

The G^2 statistic is the primary measure used to compare two models when using the maximum-likelihood method. When we search for parameters that maximize the likelihood function, or minimize the G^2 function, then these parameters are called maximum-likelihood estimates.

Newton-Raphson Search

This search method is applicable to any of the three objective functions that are presented in this chapter (Fletcher, 1987). For generality, define F as the objective function, where we could set $F = SSE$, or $F = WSSE$, or $F = G^2$.

Define θ as a column vector containing all the parameters of the cognitive model. For example, in the previous chapter, $\theta = [\gamma\ r]^T$, which is a 2×1 vector containing the decay rate and initial strength parameters. We insert θ into the cognitive model to generate predictions, and then the objective function F evaluates these predictions. Mathematically, F is a function that maps θ into a real-valued measure of fit. Our goal is to try to find an iterative scheme that changes the parameter vector at each step from θ to $(\theta + \delta)$ to produce a reduction in the objective function from $F(\theta)$ to $F(\theta + \delta)$.

Originally, Isaac Newton invented a procedure based on the following idea. First, we approximate the objective function by a second-order Taylor series expansion:

$$F(\theta + \delta) = F(\theta) + \delta^T \cdot \frac{\partial F(\theta)}{\partial \theta} + \frac{1}{2} \cdot \delta^T \cdot \frac{\partial^2 F(\theta)}{\partial \theta \cdot \partial \theta^T} \cdot \delta + \text{residual}.$$

This quadratic approximation to the objective function is accurate as long as the change, δ, is small in magnitude. This expression has two terms involving δ. The first term contains the first-order partial derivative of $F(\theta)$ with respect to the parameter vector, denoted $\nabla = \frac{\partial F(\theta)}{\partial \theta}$ with $\nabla_i = \frac{\partial F(\theta)}{\partial \theta_i}$, which is the gradient, and this provides the direction of steepest ascent (the negative of the gradient provides the direction of steepest descent). The second term contains the second-order partial derivative of $F(\theta)$ with respect to the parameter vector, denoted as $\mathbf{H} = \frac{\partial^2 F(\theta)}{\partial \theta \cdot \partial \theta^T}$ with $H_{ij} = \frac{\partial^2 F(\theta)}{\partial \theta_i \partial \theta_j}$, which is called the Hessian matrix, and its importance will be discussed later. Using this new notation, we can rewrite the Taylor series expansion as

$$F(\theta + \delta) = F(\theta) + \delta^T \cdot \nabla + (1/2)\delta^T \cdot \mathbf{H} \cdot \delta + \text{residual}.$$

Now we try to find the direction vector δ that minimizes this approximation (ignoring the residual). To do this, we take the first derivative of the approximation with respect to the direction vector δ, and set it equal to zero, which yields

$$(\partial/\partial\delta)[F(\theta) + \delta^T \cdot \nabla + (1/2)\delta^T \cdot \mathbf{H} \cdot \delta] = \nabla + \mathbf{H} \cdot \delta = 0.$$

Solving the last equation for δ, we obtain

$$\delta = \mathbf{H}^{-1} \cdot (-\nabla),$$

which provides the direction for minimizing our approximation to the objective function. But stepping from δ to $(\theta + \delta)$ minimizes the approximation, and not the original objective function. Therefore, we need to repeat this procedure. With each repetition, our approximation gets better, and we get closer to the minimum of the true objective function. Thus, we obtain a new estimate on iteration $\theta(n)$, from the old estimate, $\theta(n - 1)$, by the following updating rule:

$$\theta(n) = \theta(n - 1) + s \cdot \delta = \theta(n - 1) + s \cdot \mathbf{H}^{-1} \cdot (-\nabla), \qquad (A3.5)$$

where s is called the step size for the change. Another line search routine is used to find the step size s, which makes the improvement in the direction δ as large as possible. The whole process starts with the selection of an initial guess $\theta(0)$, which may come from a grid search. The iterations continue until the magnitude of the direction for change $|\delta|$ falls below some criterion. Equation A3.4 is called the Newton-Raphson search procedure.

The Hessian matrix $\mathbf{H}$, evaluated at the minimum, is very important for evaluating the precision of the parameter estimates of the cognitive model. The programs used to implement the quasi-Newton methods have options for computing and displaying this matrix and its inverse.

First of all, the rank of the Hessian matrix can be used to determine whether or not the parameters of the model are identified. If Hessian matrix is full rank, then the parameters are identified, and if it is less than full rank, then they are not identified. Note that if the Hessian matrix is not full rank, then the inverse does not exist, and one cannot use the quasi-Newton search methods. Consequently, if the parameters are not identified, the some parameters need to be eliminated or redefined to achieve identification.

Second, the diagonal elements of the inverse of the Hessian matrix provide information about the precision of the parameter estimates. If it is assumed that the cognitive model is the true model that generated the data, then the following theorem holds for the weighted least-squares and likelihood objectives: The parameter estimates are asymptotically normally distributed, with a mean equal to the true parameter values, and with a variance-covariance matrix equal to the inverse of the Hessian matrix. Thus, the diagonal elements of $\mathbf{H}^{-1}$ are used to estimate the variances of the parameters, and the off-diagonal elements are used to estimate the covariances between parameter estimates. To be more concrete, define h_{ii}^* as the diagonal element of $\mathbf{H}^{-1}$ in the ith row, then we estimate the standard error of θ_i by $\sqrt{h_{ii}^*}$.

Application to Linear Models

It is informative to apply these ideas to the standard linear model. Define **Y** as a vector of observations, **X** is a matrix of known independent variables, **θ** is a vector of parameters, and **E** is a vector of errors. The linear model is

$$\mathbf{Y} = M(\mathbf{X}, \boldsymbol{\theta}) + \mathbf{E} = \mathbf{X} \cdot \boldsymbol{\theta} + \mathbf{E}.$$

Linear models satisfy the following important property:

$$M(\mathbf{X}, a\boldsymbol{\theta}_1 + b\boldsymbol{\theta}_2) = \mathbf{X}(a\boldsymbol{\theta}_1 + b\boldsymbol{\theta}_2) = a\mathbf{X}\boldsymbol{\theta}_1 + b\mathbf{X}\boldsymbol{\theta}_2$$
$$= aM(\mathbf{X}, \boldsymbol{\theta}_1) + bM(\mathbf{X}, \boldsymbol{\theta}_2). \tag{A3.6}$$

Nonlinear models fail to satisfy this property.

If we make the standard homogeneous variance assumption, then the variance-covariance matrix for these errors is simply $\mathrm{Var}[\mathbf{E}] = \sigma^2\mathbf{I}$. In this case, the log likelihood can be expressed as (see Rao, 1965; or Wasserman, 2000)

$$\ln(L) = -\left\{ \frac{SSE}{2\sigma^2} + \left(\frac{N}{2}\right) \cdot [\ln(2\pi) + \ln(\sigma^2)] \right\}.$$

Maximizing this likelihood for **θ** is equivalent to minimizing the sum of squared error:

$$F = \frac{1}{\sigma^2}(\mathbf{Y} - \mathbf{X}\boldsymbol{\theta})^{\mathrm{T}}(\mathbf{Y} - \mathbf{X}\boldsymbol{\theta}) = \frac{1}{2\sigma^2}(\mathbf{Y}^{\mathrm{T}}\mathbf{Y} - 2\boldsymbol{\theta}^{\mathrm{T}}\mathbf{X}^{\mathrm{T}}\mathbf{Y} + \boldsymbol{\theta}^{\mathrm{T}}\mathbf{X}^{\mathrm{T}}\mathbf{X}\boldsymbol{\theta}).$$

Thus, for linear models, the sum of squared error function is exactly a quadratic function.

The gradient is equal to

$$\nabla = (1/2\sigma^2)(-\mathbf{X}^{\mathrm{T}}\mathbf{Y} + \mathbf{X}^{\mathrm{T}}\mathbf{X}\boldsymbol{\theta}) = (-1/\sigma^2)\mathbf{X}^{\mathrm{T}}(\mathbf{Y} - \mathbf{X}\boldsymbol{\theta}).$$

The minimum of the objective function lies at the point where the gradient is zero:

$$-\mathbf{X}^{\mathrm{T}}\mathbf{Y} + \mathbf{X}^{\mathrm{T}}\mathbf{X}\boldsymbol{\theta} = 0 \rightarrow \mathbf{X}^{\mathrm{T}}\mathbf{Y} = \mathbf{X}^{\mathrm{T}}\mathbf{X}\boldsymbol{\theta},$$

producing the set of normal equations for the linear model. In this case, the optimal parameters can be found by solving the normal equations in a single step:

$$\boldsymbol{\theta} = (\mathbf{X}^{\mathrm{T}}\mathbf{X})^{-1}(\mathbf{X}^{\mathrm{T}}\mathbf{Y}). \tag{A3.7}$$

The Hessian of F and its inverse are equal to

$$\mathbf{H} = \frac{1}{\sigma^2} \mathbf{X}^T\mathbf{X} \text{ and } \mathbf{H}^{-1} = \sigma^2(\mathbf{X}^T\mathbf{X})^{-1}.$$

The latter expression is the familiar formula for the variance-covariance matrix of the parameters for a linear model. The maximum-likelihood estimate of σ^2 is SSE/N. Substituting these estimates into the log likelihood yields the maximum log likelihood:

$$\ln(L) = -\left(\frac{N}{2}\right) \cdot \left[\ln\left(\frac{SSE}{N}\right) + \ln(2\pi) + 1\right]$$

and

$$G^2 = N \cdot \left[\ln\left(\frac{SSE}{N}\right) + \ln(2\pi) + 1\right].$$

Quasi-Newton Methods

In many cases, it is computationally intensive to determine the inverse of the Hessian matrix, $\mathbf{H}^{-1}$, for each iteration. To speed up the computations, procedures have been developed that build up an approximation to this inverse in an iterative fashion. These procedures start by setting $\mathbf{H} = \mathbf{I}$, the identity matrix, and in this case δ is simply proportional to the gradient. This initial value for the inverse reduces the computations, but searching for the minimum using only the gradient is very slow. Thus, after each step, the $\mathbf{H}^{-1}$ matrix is updated to more closely approximate its true value, and using this estimate of the inverse improves the speed of the search and convergence to minimum. This revision of the algorithm is called the Broyden-Fletcher-Powell modification of the Newton-Raphson method. This is the most commonly used gradient search approach, and it is available in mathematical programming languages such as MATLAB, Mathematica, GAUSS, or SAS.

Gauss-Newton Search Methods

This search method is only applicable to least-squares or weighted least-squares objectives (Gallant, 1986). Given that we can always transform a *WSSE* problem into a *SSE* problem, we will only present the least-squares version of the Gauss-Newton search algorithm.

The Gauss-Newton approach differs from the Newton-Raphson approach in the following way. The Newton-Raphson approach uses a second-order Taylor series to approximate the objective function F, whereas the Gauss-Newton approach relies on a first-order approximation to the nonlinear function M that generates the model predictions. Once again, the general idea is to find an iterative procedure to change from θ to $(\theta + \delta)$, so then we reduce the objective function from $SSE(\theta)$ to $SSE(\theta + \delta)$.

This method begins by approximating the nonlinear model by a first-order Taylor series expansion:

$$M(\mathbf{X}, \theta + \delta) = M(\mathbf{X}, \theta) + \frac{\partial M(\mathbf{X}, \theta)}{\partial \theta^T} \delta + \text{residual}.$$

The term involving δ, denoted as $\mathbf{J} = (\partial/\partial\theta)M(\mathbf{X}, \theta)$ with $J_{ij} = (\partial/\partial\theta_j) M_i(\mathbf{X}, \theta)$, is called the Jacobian matrix. This approximation to M will be accurate for small $|\delta|$. Given a previous evaluation of the model at the parameter vector θ, we can approximate the predictions at a new parameter vector $(\theta + \delta)$ by using the above approximation:

$$\mathbf{Y} = M(\mathbf{X}, \theta) + \mathbf{J} \cdot \delta + \mathbf{E}$$

$$\rightarrow \mathbf{Y} - M(\mathbf{X}, \theta) = \mathbf{J} \cdot \delta + \mathbf{E},$$

where $\mathbf{E}$ is a vector of residuals. Now we wish to find the direction of change δ that minimizes $SSE = \mathbf{E}^T\mathbf{E}$ in the above equation. Note that the last equation is a linear equation with respect to δ. The solution for minimizing SSE with linear equations was presented earlier as Equation A3.7. To adapt the earlier solution to this problem, we treat $\mathbf{Z} = \mathbf{Y} - M(\mathbf{X}, \theta)$ as the new transformed dependent variable, and we treat the Jacobian matrix $\mathbf{J}$ as the matrix of independent variables. Then, we obtain the least-squares solution:

$$\delta = (\mathbf{J}^T\mathbf{J})^{-1}(\mathbf{J}^T\mathbf{Z}).$$

This is the solution for the direction to change the parameter, and the new parameter vector is chosen to be a step in this direction:

$$\theta(n) = \theta(n - 1) + s \cdot \delta = \theta(n - 1) + s \cdot (\mathbf{J}^T\mathbf{J})^{-1}(\mathbf{J}^T\mathbf{Z}). \qquad (A3.8)$$

The step size, s, is chosen to produce the largest possible reduction in SSE in the direction given by δ.

The Gauss-Newton method is related to the Newton-Raphson method. The first term $\mathbf{J}^T\mathbf{J}$ is asymptotically equal to the Hessian matrix, and the second term $\mathbf{J}^T\mathbf{Z}$ is the negative of the gradient for the SSE objective function:

$$-\nabla = -(\partial/\partial\theta^T)SSE = -(\partial/\partial\theta^T)\mathbf{E}^T\mathbf{E}$$
$$= -(\partial/\partial\theta^T)[\mathbf{Y} - M(\mathbf{X}, \theta)]^T[\mathbf{Y} - M(\mathbf{X}, \theta)] = 2\mathbf{J}^T\mathbf{Z}.$$

Modified Gauss-Newton Method

If the initial starting position is far from the minimum, then the standard Gauss-Newton search encounters difficulty. In this case, it is better to start with a simple gradient search and gradually shift to the Gauss-Newton direction after the approximation starts to improve. This is called the Levenberg-Marquardt modification of the Gauss-Newton method. The modification is accomplished by adjusting the direction of search in the following manner:

$$\delta = (J^T J + \lambda_n I)^{-1}(J^T Z).$$

The coefficient λ_n determines the influence of $J^T J$. Initially, this coefficient is set to a large value so that $J^T J$ has little influence, and most of the weight is placed on the gradient. Later in the iterations, this coefficient is set to a small value so that $J^T J$ has more influence on the direction. The modified Gauss-Newton method is closely related to the method of ridge regression sometimes used to obtain more robust estimates from linear models.

Example Program

Although the technical aspects of nonlinear parameter estimation can become quite complex, easy-to-use programs are available to perform this task from mathematical programming languages such as MATLAB, Mathematica, GAUSS, or SAS. The example program described below is a MATLAB program for estimating the parameters of the retention model presented in Chapter 3. The program has two parts: a "main" program and a function called "Fitr" (see Figure A3.1).

```
% main fitting program              function G = Fitr(X)
global P;                           global P
load P; % load data                 a = X(1); r = X(2); % param's
oldopts = optimset('fminunc');      n = 200; % sample size
options =optimset(oldopts,'Display,"iter');   na = n*P; nb = n*(1-P);
% initial values                    t = (0:10)'; % time delays
a = .8; r = 3; X0 = [a r]           p = 1./(1+exp(-r.*(a.^t))); % predictions
"Initial Results'                   GR = na'*log(p) + nb'*log(1-p);
G = Fitr(X0)                        GC = na'*log(P) + nb'*log(1-P);
'Final Results'                     G = 2*(GC - GR); % G - Square
[X G] = fminunc('Fitr,' X0,0ptions)
```

Figure A3.1   Example Parameter Estimation Program

The "main" program first loads the data stored in a vector called **P**. The "options" line defines some parameters that control the display of the fitting program. The "initial values" line defines the starting values for the iterative search process, and "initial results" line is used to compute and display the fits of these initial parameters. The "final results" line calls the MATLAB program that is used to search for the best-fitting parameters. In this case, we are using an unconstrained, modified Newton-Raphson method. The input arguments to this program include the user-defined name of the program used to compute the fit of the model, the initial parameters, and the options for the display.

The function called "Fitr" is a user-supplied function that has only one input argument and one output argument. The input argument is a vector containing the parameters to be used to fit the data. The output argument is the value of the objective function. The "global" statement is used to access the data vector **P**, which was read into the main program. The next few lines redefine the names of the parameters using more convenient names, define the sample sizes, and define the time delays. The MATLAB notation (0:10) creates a vector of integers ranging from 0 to 10. The "prediction" line computes the 11 predictions from the model for the entire vector of 11 time delays (the dot that appears before each mathematical operation is used to instruct the program to perform operations elementwise, that is, separately on each element in the vector). The next pair of lines computes the log likelihoods for the cognitive retention model and for the saturated model, and the last line computes the G^2 lack-of-fit index.

Notes

1. There is an entire literature on time series analysis of the autocorrelations, and these autocorrelations may reveal important hidden cognitive processes (see Gilden, 2001).

2. The log likelihood for the binomial distribution also includes the log of the constant $[n_A!/(n_A! \cdot n_B!)]$, which is contributed by the number of sequences for obtaining n_A corrects out of n trials. However, this constant has no bearing on any subsequent analyses, and it can be ignored. In particular, it cancels out the expression for G^2 in Equation 3.7, which is introduced later.

3. For nonlinear models, it is possible for R^2 to be less than zero, that is, worse than the null model.

4. The sum of squared error criterion was used because there is no sampling error in these data sets, and the other two criteria are not defined in this ideal case.

5. For continuously distributed observations, such as response times, we would only need to change our definitions from probability masses to probability densities, and the rest would remain the same.

4

Application to Choice and Response Time Measures

Many studies in cognitive psychology include two primary measures of performance—choice probability and response time. This chapter presents methods for estimating parameters and comparing models using both these response measures. A study by Ratcliff, Thaper, and McKoon (2001) provides a very good example. They investigated the effects of aging on accuracy and response time in a signal detection task. As one might expect, they found that response times were longer for older participants. However, the important theoretical question is, why does this slowdown occur?

This chapter will describe a model for analyzing choice and response time measures using a fictitious data set generated to simulate the effects of aging on performance in a signal detection task. First, we describe a signal detection experiment that is similar to the actual study reported by Ratcliff et al. (2001) and we report the (fictitious) results of the experiment. Although the results are fictitious, they reflect some of the main findings reported by Ratcliff et al. (2001). Second, we present a cognitive theory that is designed to simultaneously model choice and response time measures for signal detection. Third, we describe methods for fitting the model to the choice and response time data, and estimating the parameters of this model. Finally, we present the results of model comparisons and tests of model parameters, and the implications of these analyses for understanding the aging process.

Many studies in cognitive psychology include two primary measures of performance—choice probability and response time. This chapter presents methods for fitting models, estimating parameters, and testing hypotheses using both these response measures simultaneously. Fitting a model to multiple response measures creates special difficulties, but it is well worth the effort because multiple response measures provide converging operations for discovering the underlying psychological constructs (Garner, Hake, & Erickson, 1956).

Great advances have been made in the development of models for choice probability and response time. The most successful class of models share the idea that information is sequentially sampled over time until a threshold criterion is reached for making a decision. Several versions of this basic idea have been developed (e.g., Ashby, 2000; Busemeyer & Townsend, 1993; Diederich, 1997; Laming, 1968; Link & Heath, 1975; Nosofsky & Palmeri, 1997; Pike, 1966; Ratcliff, 1978; Smith, 2000; Townsend & Ashby, 1983; Usher & McClelland, 2001; Vickers, 1979). See Ratcliff and Smith (2004) for comparisons of models. These models can be viewed as dynamic extensions of earlier static signal detection models (Green & Swets, 1966). This chapter will primarily rely on the Ratcliff (1978) version. The main purpose of this chapter is to describe how to fit a cognitive model to choice and response time measures simultaneously.

Signal Detection Task

Imagine that a researcher wished to study the effects of age on detection of targets in a military signal detection task.[1] To be more concrete, suppose the task is to detect the presence of an enemy target within a noisy background on a radar screen. On each trial, either a target is present (signal trial) within a noisy display or no target is present (noise trial), and the decision maker must choose to respond by pressing the signal or noise response buttons. There are four types of stimulus—response outcomes—for this task: A Hit occurs if it is a signal trial and the decision maker responds signal; a False Alarm (FA) occurs if it is a noise trial and the decision maker responds signal; a Miss occurs if it is a signal trial and the decision maker responds noise, and a Correct Rejection (CR) occurs if it is a noise trial and the decision maker responds noise. The decision maker's hypothetical payoff depends on which of these four outcomes occurs, according to the following payoff matrix:

Response	Signal Trial	Noise Trial
Respond Signal	Hit: Safe	FA: Lose another person's life
Respond Noise	Miss: Lose your own life	CR: Safe

If we assume that the idea of losing your own life is worse than losing another person's life, then this payoff matrix is slightly biased toward responding signal. Imagine that each participant made 600 decisions, half signal trials and half noise trials, randomly interspersed. Also suppose there are three age groups (young, middle, old) with 20 participants per age group. The (fictitious) results are described next. (The data were generated by computer simulation.)

Basic Findings

Table 4.1 presents the Hit rates (proportion of signal responses given that a signal was present) and FA rates (proportion of signal responses given that only noise was present), averaged across participants, for each of the three age groups. For the time being, focus only on the columns under the heading "Obs" for observed data; the columns under the heading "Pred" refer to predictions from a cognitive model discussed later.

As can be seen in this table, the Hit rates did not vary much across age groups and the FA rates decreased only slightly across age groups. Thus, age had little effect on the Hit and FA rates.

Age had a much larger effect on the response times. Tables 4.2a, 4.2b, 4.2c, and 4.2d show the three quartiles (25th, 50th, and 75th percentile) for the response times obtained from each of the four possible trial outcomes. The quartiles are always higher for the older as compared with the younger decision makers. These tables also show that errors were generally slower than correct decisions. For example, the second quartile (median) for Hits is generally faster than that for FA, and the same relation holds when we compare CR with Misses.

Table 4.1   Hit and False Alarm Rates Averaged Across Participants

	Obs Hit	Pred Hit	Obs FA	Pred FA
Young	.81	.80	.32	.30
Middle	.80	.81	.28	.29
Old	.81	.81	.26	.27

Table 4.2a   RT Quartiles for Hits Averaged Across Participants

	Q1 obs	Q1 pred	Q2 obs	Q2 pred	Q3 obs	Q3 pred
Young	0.58	0.6378	0.78	0.8748	1.17	1.3288
Middle	1.0217	1.0202	1.2868	1.2917	1.8209	1.8132
Old	1.4607	1.4100	1.7926	1.7180	2.4591	2.3085

Table 4.2b   RT Quartiles for CR Averaged Across Participants

	Q1 obs	Q1 pred	Q2 obs	Q2 pred	Q3 obs	Q3 pred
Young	0.7601	0.8113	1.0189	1.1058	1.4302	1.6013
Middle	1.2235	1.2122	1.5629	1.5477	2.1515	2.1177
Old	1.6725	1.6150	2.0879	1.9925	2.8310	2.6370

Table 4.2c   RT Quartiles for FA Averaged Across Participants

	Q1 obs	Q1 pred	Q2 obs	Q2 pred	Q3 obs	Q3 pred
Young	0.6209	0.6838	0.8739	0.9828	1.3184	1.5423
Middle	1.0941	1.0887	1.4698	1.4437	2.1339	2.1097
Old	1.5908	1.5055	2.0982	1.9280	2.9668	2.7180

Table 4.2d   RT Quartiles for Misses Averaged Across Participants

	Q1 obs	Q1 pred	Q2 obs	Q2 pred	Q3 obs	Q3 pred
Young	0.8254	0.9028	1.1225	1.2788	1.6335	1.8853
Middle	1.3661	1.3357	1.8325	1.7782	2.6140	2.5007
Old	1.9336	1.7810	2.5186	2.3015	3.5779	3.1560

The basic question that arises from this type of data is "Why are the older participants slower than the younger participants to make their decisions?" There are at least three major hypotheses: (a) The rate of information processing slows down with age; (b) the rate of information processing does not change with age, and instead the motor time to make a response slows down with age; (c) older people are more patient and so the threshold criterion increases with age. Of course, combinations of these are also possible. A cognitive model of performance on this task provides an analytical method for answering these questions.

A Dynamic Signal Detection Model

Dynamic models of signal detection have proven to be very effective for simultaneously analyzing choice probability and the response time distributions for signal detection tasks. The advantage of the dynamic models over the earlier static models is that whereas the static models only provide a model for the choice probabilities and do not provide a model for the response times, the dynamic models provide a common model and a common set of parameters for both measures. Although various types of dynamic signal detection models have been developed, we will present the one that was used in the aging research by Ratcliff, Thaper, and McKoon (2001). The basic idea of the dynamic signal detection model is presented next.

According to the theory, the stimulus presented on each trial generates evidence that the decision maker experiences, which may favor responding signal or noise. This evidence is accumulated over time until it is sufficiently strong to cross a threshold, and once this happens, the response favored by the evidence is chosen. The time it takes to reach the threshold determines the decision time.

Initial State

A state of evidence exists even before the stimulus is presented, which is called the initial state, labeled "$X(0)$." The initial state is determined by the prior probability that a signal is presented.[2] For example, if the signal appeared very infrequently across the previous trials, so that the prior probability of a signal is very low, then the decision maker starts each trial with a belief that a signal is unlikely to appear again. In the current task, there is an equal probability that a signal or noise trial is presented, and so this factor would lead the decision maker to start out in a neutral state, $X(0) = 0$, with no prior evidence for either hypothesis.

Evidence Accumulation

Once the stimulus is presented, the decision maker begins to process information in the display. At each moment in time, or time step of duration h, the decision maker samples some information from the display. The evidence, denoted V, may be positive, in which case it favors the signal response, or it may be negative, in which case it favors the noise response.[3] After the very first time step, h, the initial state of evidence $X(0)$ changes to a new state of evidence $X(h)$ by summing the initial state and the new evidence:

$$X(h) = X(0) + V(h).$$

This process continues over time and after n time steps, corresponding to time $t = n \cdot h$, the state of evidence changes as follows:

$$X(t) = X(t - h) + V(t) = X(0) + \sum_{j=1}^{n} V(j \cdot h) = X(0) + S(t),$$

where $X(0)$ is the initial state and $S(t)$ is the sum of all the evidence up to time t. This process continues until the cumulative evidence is strong enough to exceed a threshold bound, at which point in time a choice is made.

Stopping Rule

If the state of evidence first reaches the upper threshold bound, $+\theta_S$, then a signal response is made; but if the state of evidence first reaches the lower bound, $-\theta_N$, then a noise response is made.[4] The time required to make the decision is determined by the time required to reach one of the threshold bounds. Thus, the stopping rule is defined as

if $-\theta_N < X(t) < +\theta_S$, then continue sampling information,

if $X(t) \geq +\theta_S$, then stop and choose signal,

if $X(t) \leq -\theta_N$, then stop and choose noise.

This process is illustrated in Figure 4.1. The horizontal axis represents time ($h = 0.001$, say 1 millisecond, in this example), the vertical axis represents the state of evidence, and the sample trajectory indicates the state of evidence at each point in time for one simulated decision. The top line (intersecting the vertical axis at 0.8) represents the upper threshold for responding signal, and the bottom line (intersecting the vertical axis at −1.0) represents the lower threshold for responding noise. In this case, the state of evidence vacillates around zero for a while and then finally increases in strength to a sufficiently high level to reach the signal response threshold.

Model Parameters

In the current form, the model has two different threshold bounds—an upper bound for the signal response $+\theta_S$, and a lower bound for the noise response $-\theta_N$. However, it is useful to rearrange this form of the model by transforming the boundary parameters into two new parameters, a payoff-bias parameter and a speed-accuracy trade-off parameter. The payoff-bias parameter is defined as the difference $b = (\theta_N - \theta_S)/2$. If the response bias b is positive, then less evidence is required to respond signal as compared with noise, making it more likely to respond signal; if it is negative, then more evidence is required to respond signal as compared with noise, making it less likely to respond signal. This bias is assumed to be manipulated by the payoff matrix.

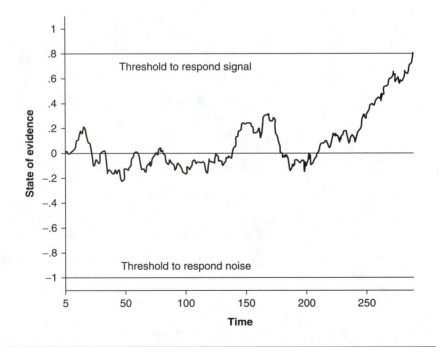

Figure 4.1   The Accumulation of Evidence Within a Single Trial Leading to a
Decision to Produce a Signal Response

For example, if the payoffs favor a signal response, so that there are bigger gains from correctly detecting a signal or smaller losses for incorrectly responding signal, then the decision maker will be more willing to choose the signal and require less evidence to make this response. In the example, the payoffs are biased to favor signal so that we would expect $b > 0$.

The speed-accuracy trade-off parameter is defined as the sum $\theta = (\theta_S + \theta_N)/2$. On the one hand, if speed is emphasized, so that θ is relatively small, then decisions are made quickly but less accurately; on the other hand, if accuracy is emphasized, so that θ is relatively large, then decisions take longer, but are more accurate. This factor is manipulated by the cost associated with waiting to make the decision relative to the payoffs for correct and incorrect decisions. For example, if waiting is almost as costly as the penalty for an error, then a low threshold is selected; but if the penalty for an error is much greater than the minor costs of waiting, then a high threshold is selected. Impulsive decision makers who can't wait tend to select a low threshold, while deliberative decision makers who wish to wait and be sure tend to select a high threshold.

Note that $+\theta - b = \theta_S$ and $-\theta - b = -\theta_N$ and so the decision process can be redescribed in terms of the payoff-bias and speed-accuracy parameters as follows:

if $-\theta - b < X(t) < +\theta - b$, then continue sampling information,

if $X(t) \geq +\theta - b$, then stop and choose signal,

if $X(t) \leq -\theta - b$, then stop and choose noise.

An equivalent way to describe this decision rule is as follows:

if $-\theta < X(t) + b < +\theta$, then continue sampling information,

if $X(t) + b \geq +\theta$, then stop and choose signal,

if $X(t) + b \leq -\theta$ then stop and choose noise.

Recalling that $X(t) = X(0) + S(t)$, we can rewrite the decision process as given below:

if $-\theta < [b + X(0)] + S(t) < +\theta$, then continue sampling information,

if $[b + X(0)] + S(t) \geq +\theta$, then stop and choose signal,

if $[b + X(0)] + S(t) \leq -\theta$, then stop and choose noise.

In this form, the bias from the payoffs can be combined with the bias from the prior probability to form a total response bias, denoted $\beta = [b + X(0)]$. From this point of view, the bias from the payoffs can be interpreted as an adjustment to the starting state. The response bias β from this dynamic model plays a role similar to the bias parameter in the static signal detection model.

The evidence that is sampled during each time step, $V(t)$, is assumed to be independently and identically distributed over time. The mean of the evidence per time step is given by the expectation $\mu = E[V(t)]$ and the variance of the evidence per time step is given by the expectation $\sigma^2 = E[(V(t) - \mu)^2]$. The ratio of the mean to the standard deviation is called the discriminability parameter, $d = (\mu/\sigma)$. This discriminability parameter d of the dynamic signal detection model is conceptually similar to the discriminability parameter used in the static signal detection model.[5] On signal trials, $d > 0$ will drive the state of evidence up toward the upper threshold boundary; on noise trials, $-d < 0$ will drive the state of evidence down to the lower threshold boundary. The magnitude of d represents the strength or intensity of the signal stimulus. Here, we assume that the magnitude of the discriminability parameter is the same for signal and noise trials, and only the sign changes across these two types of trials.

If the standard deviation of the evidence σ is constant across conditions, then it is not possible to estimate this parameter separately from the mean μ because only the ratio enters the prediction equations. Therefore, when the standard deviation is constant across conditions, it can be set to $\sigma = 1$ without loss in generality. Hereafter, we will assume this is the case.

The time required to make a decision is assumed to be determined by the time required to reach a threshold bound. This is a random variable that depends on the evidence that is sampled over time on a given trial (as shown, e.g., in Figure 4.1). This random decision time is denoted by DT. However, this decision time is not directly observable. Instead, the observed choice response time is also to be influenced by the motor response time. That is, once a decision is reached, it takes additional time to execute the motor response. The motor response time is another random variable denoted as MT. Thus, the total choice time is given by $CRT = DT + MT$.

The importance of the distribution for the motor time depends on the amount of variance produced by MT as compared with that produced by DT. On the one hand, if the motor response is complex, and the decision is simple, then the DT variance will be small relative to the MT variance, and the motor time distribution will be important. On the other hand, if the motor response is very simple (a button push), and the decision is very complex (decide whether an image on the radar screen is an enemy or a friendly aircraft), then most of the variance is contributed by DT, and the variance contributed by MT is trivial. In the latter case, we can approximate the effect of the motor time by assuming that it is simply an additive constant. The latter will be assumed in the analysis described below.

Finally, the time step h represents the small duration of time between samples of information. In this discrete time form, the model is called a random walk model. As the time step h approaches zero in the limit, the process converges to a continuous time model called a diffusion model. Ratcliff et al. (2001) use the continuous time version which assumes $h \to 0$. The analysis presented below is also based on the continuous time model.

In summary, the dynamic signal detection model has four critical parameters: (1) the response bias β, from the prior probabilities and payoffs; (2) the discriminability parameter d, representing the strength of evidence sampled at each time step; (3) the average distance between the bounds θ, controlling speed-accuracy trade-offs; and (4) the motor time constant for executing a response MT. This model is then used to predict both the choice probabilities and the distribution of decision times.

Ratcliff (1978) added an additional assumption to the model. He reasoned that the discriminability parameter does not remain constant across trials, and instead, it varies from one trial to the next. This variation in discriminability could result from several sources, but for aging research, one important potential source is variability in the participant's attention to the task from trial to trial. On some trials, the decision maker may be highly alert; but on other trials, the decision maker's attention may lapse or be distracted by uncontrollable events. The Ratcliff model assumes that the variability in discriminability across trials can be approximated by a normal distribution with a mean that we will now call the parameter d, and a standard deviation, symbolized η. Therefore, Ratcliff's model requires an additional parameter representing the variance in the discriminability parameter across trials.

Prediction Equations

The derivation of the choice probabilities and distribution of decision times from the dynamic signal detection model is fairly complex, and so this is given in the appendix to this chapter. For a fixed stimulus condition, the theoretical results are presented below. The probability of responding signal is given by

$$\Pr[R_s] = \frac{1 - e^{-2d(\theta + \beta)}}{1 - e^{-4d\theta}} \qquad (4.1)$$

$$= \frac{e^{4\theta d}}{e^{4\theta d}} \cdot \frac{1 - e^{-2d(\theta + \beta)}}{1 - e^{-4\theta d}} = \frac{e^{4\theta d} - e^{2d(\theta - \beta)}}{e^{4\theta d} - 1}.$$

The probability of choosing noise is one minus this value. The joint cumulative probability distribution for obtaining a choice response time less than T and responding signal is given by

$$\begin{aligned} \Pr[CRT < T \text{ and } R_S] &= \Pr[DT + MT < T \text{ and } R_S] \\ &= \Pr[DT < (T - MT) \text{ and } R_S] \\ &= \Pr[R_S] - 2\pi(2\theta)^{-2} e^{d(\theta - \beta)} \end{aligned} \tag{4.2}$$

$$\times \sum_{j=1}^{\infty} \frac{j \cdot e^{-\frac{1}{2}\left[\left(\frac{\pi j}{2\theta}\right)^2 + d^2\right] \cdot (T - MT)}}{\left(\frac{\pi j}{2\theta}\right)^2 + d^2} \cdot \sin\left(\frac{\pi(\theta - \beta) \cdot j}{2\theta}\right).$$

Equation 4.2 involves an infinite sum of terms, and each term is a product of two parts. The first part of each term (i.e., the exponential part) starts out positive and then monotonically decreases toward zero as j increases, while the second part (i.e., the sine part) remains less than one in magnitude. Thus, the magnitude of each term in the sum is bounded below the first part of each term. In practice, the summation can be terminated once the magnitude of the first part of each term becomes less than some very small tolerance level (e.g., 10^{-30}).

The conditional probability of obtaining a decision time less than T, given that a signal response is made, is obtained by dividing Equation 4.2 by Equation 4.1. The probabilities and distributions for responding noise are obtained by replacing d with $-d$ and replacing β with $-\beta$ (everywhere in the above equations). For signal trials, we have $d > 0$ and for noise trials, we have $d < 0$.

The Ratcliff model assumes that the variability in discriminability across trials can be approximated by a normal distribution with a mean that we call d, and a standard deviation symbolized by η. Therefore, Ratcliff's model requires an additional parameter representing the variance in the discriminability parameter across trials. So the prediction equations then have to be modified by multiplying Equations 4.1 and 4.2 by the normal probability density and then integrating over the theoretical range discriminability parameters:

$$\Pr[R_S] = \int \Pr[R_S | \text{discriminability} = x] \cdot f(x) \, dx \tag{4.3}$$

$$\begin{aligned} \Pr[DT < T - MT \text{ and } R_S] &= \int \Pr[DT < T - MT \\ \text{and } R_S | \text{discriminability} &= x] \cdot f(x) \, dx, \end{aligned} \tag{4.4}$$

where $f(x)$ is the normal density with mean d and standard deviation η. There are no explicit solutions for the above integrals, and so these must be computed by using numerical integration routines available in most mathematical programming languages such as MATLAB, Mathematica, GAUSS, or SAS.

Theoretical Questions

In the next sections, we use the cognitive model described above to address the following theoretical questions. First, is there a significant advantage gained by adding the assumption of variability in the discriminability across trials? This question will be answered by performing a model comparison between the model that assumes no variability in the discriminability parameter and the Ratcliff model that allows for trial-by-trial variability in this parameter. Second, what caused the slower response times for the older participants? This question will be answered by comparing the model parameters across age groups.

Data Representation

First, we need to be specific about the data to be analyzed. Table 4.1 shows the means of the quantiles, averaged across participants. However, the model analyses are based on estimates of the model parameters at the individual level of analysis.

The raw data that we obtain from each person consist of the 600 choices and response times made by each person. We could apply the maximum-likelihood method directly to these 600 responses. Alternatively, we could estimate the quantiles from each individual as we did for Table 4.1, and apply the maximum-likelihood method to the quantile statistics. The advantage of the former method is that it uses all the information available in the data (see Van Zandt, 2000). The disadvantage is that it may not be robust to outliers produced by violations of the model assumptions (see Heathcote & Brown, 2002; Ratcliff & Tuerlinckx, 2002). For example, we are assuming that the motor time variance can be ignored, but response execution errors (missing the button when trying to push it) could cause outliers that distort the estimation and fitting procedures. The advantage of the quantile method is that it is more robust to these outliers, however, at the cost of losing some information.

First, we compute the frequencies of each type of stimulus and response combination: the number of signal responses when a signal trial was present, N_{Ss}; the number of signal responses when a noise trial was present, N_{Sn}; the number of noise responses for signal trials, N_{Ns}; and the number of noise responses when noise was present, N_{Nn}. However, the frequencies must sum to the total number of trials (600) within each stimulus condition, leaving only one frequency that is free to vary within each stimulus condition.

The quantiles for each person can be computed using the following simple algorithm (also see Heathcote & Brown, 2002). Suppose we wish to divide the distribution into four categories each having an equal frequency, that is, $p = \frac{1}{4}$ in this case. In other words, we wish to calculate the first, second, and third quartiles, denoted as Q_1, Q_2, and Q_3, respectively. For a simple example, let $N_{Sn} = 22$ be the number of trials that a signal response was made to a noise stimulus. Consider the following ordered set of 22 such response times (in seconds): {0.501, 0.501, 0.507, 0.520, 0.523, 0.532, 0.567, 0.583, 0.590, 0.601, 0.616, 0.622, 0.652, 0.671, 0.688, 0.692, 0.724, 0.745, 0.747, 0.754, 0.792, 0.820}. The expected number of scores at or below the first quartile is defined as $n_1 = (p \cdot N_{Sn}) + 0.50 = (22/4) + 0.50 = 6$, and so the first quartile is located at the 6th ordinal position, that is, the response time score $Q_1 = 0.532$. The expected number of scores at or below the second quartile is defined as $n_2 = (2 \cdot p \cdot N_{Sn}) + 0.50 = (22/2) + 0.50 = 11.5$, and so the second quartile is located somewhere in between the 11th and 12th ordinal positions, that is, somewhere between $L_2 = 0.616$ and $U_2 = 0.622$. The exact position for the second quartile is defined as $L_2 + (U_2 - L_2) \cdot [n_2 - \text{truncate}(n_2)] = 0.616 + (0.622 - 0.616) \cdot (11.5 - 11) = 0.619$ (the notation, truncate(x), simply means to round x off to the next lowest integer). The expected number of scores at or below the third quartile is defined as $n_3 = (3 \cdot p \cdot N_{Sn}) + 0.50 = (3 \cdot 22/4) + 0.50 = 17$, and so the third quartile is located at the 17th ordinal position, that is, the response time $Q_3 = 0.724$. Thus, the three quartiles for this example are {$Q_1 = 0.532$, $Q_2 = 0.619$, $Q_3 = 0.724$}.

The above procedure was performed on the response times for the signal response to a noise stimulus, and this same procedure is repeated for the response times from the noise response to the noise stimulus, which produces another set of three quartiles. Finally, the procedure is repeated for the response times from the signal and noise responses to the signal stimulus. If we use quartiles, then the total number of free data points per individual is $4 \cdot 3 = 12$ quantiles + 2 response frequencies = 14 data points. The Ratcliff model has five parameters that must be estimated from the 14 data points for each individual. Therefore, the difference between the number of data points and number of parameters is $df = 14 - 5 = 9$ in this example.

Parameter Estimation

To estimate the five parameters of the Ratcliff model, a maximum-likelihood method for quantiles will be used, which was proposed by Heathcote and Brown (2002). Alternatively, a weighted least squares (i.e., Pearson chi-square) could be used to measure the fit, which would give similar results (see Ratcliff & Tuerlinckx, 2002). According to this method, the observed quantiles are used to divide the response time distribution into categories. Consider once again the earlier example involving $N_{Sn} = 22$ response times for a signal response to a noise stimulus. In this case, the range of response times is divided into four categories: Category 1 is defined by $CRT \leq Q_1 = 0.532$, Category 2 is defined by $Q_1 = 0.532 \leq CRT \leq Q_2 = 0.619$, Category 3 is defined by $Q_2 = 0.619 \leq CRT \leq Q_3 = 0.724$, and Category 4 is defined as $CRT > Q_3 = 0.724$. We then compute the observed frequencies within each of these categories, $n_{Sn,i}$ for category i (which, by construction, are expected to be equal). These observed category frequencies are then compared with the predicted probabilities computed from the model for these same category bounds. The predicted probabilities for each of the four categories are as follows:

$$p_1 = \Pr[DT < (Q_1 - MT) \text{ and } R_S]$$

$$p_2 = \Pr[DT < (Q_2 - MT) \text{ and } R_S] - \Pr[DT < (Q_1 - MT) \text{ and } R_S]$$

$$p_3 = \Pr[DT < (Q_3 - MT) \text{ and } R_S] - \Pr[DT < (Q_2 - MT) \text{ and } R_S]$$

$$p_4 = \Pr[DT > (Q_3 - MT)] = \Pr[R_S] - (p_1 + p_2 + p_3).$$

The joint probability of observing the frequencies within each of the four categories is determined by multinomial distribution (see Chapter 3):

$$L_{Sn} = K \cdot p_1^{n_{Sn1}} p_2^{n_{Sn2}} p_3^{n_{Sn3}} p_4^{n_{Sn4}}. \tag{4.5a}$$

The constant K equals the number of combinations that reproduce the observed frequencies. This constant is not a function of the model parameters, and consequently, it has no effect on the parameter estimation problem. Therefore, this constant can be dropped from the analysis without affecting any of the results. It is more convenient to use the log of the likelihood, which is

$$\begin{aligned}\ln(L_{Sn}) = \ln(K) &+ n_{Sn,1} \cdot \ln(p_1) + n_{Sn,2} \cdot \ln(p_2) \\ &+ n_{Sn,3} \cdot \ln(p_3) + n_{Sn,4} \cdot \ln(p_4).\end{aligned} \tag{4.5b}$$

This log likelihood is computed for each stimulus-response combination, and the four likelihoods are summed to produce the total log likelihood for all 600 trials for each individual:

$$\ln(L) = \ln(L_{Ss}) + \ln(L_{Sn}) + \ln(L_{Ns}) + \ln(L_{Nn}). \tag{4.6}$$

In sum, to fit the model to the data, we need to find the five parameters that maximize the total log likelihood $\ln(L)$ for the model (see Chapter 3).

The total log likelihood produced by the Ratcliff model can be compared with a total log likelihood of another model, called the saturated model. The saturated model simply sets the predicted probabilities for each category equal to the observed relative frequencies. Using the present example, we set p_j equal to the observed relative frequency for each category for the saturated model, and then we recompute the log likelihood given by Equations 4.5b and 4.6 using the observed relative frequencies as the predicted probabilities. If we denote the log likelihood for the Ratcliff model as $\ln(L_R)$ and the total log likelihood of the saturated model as $\ln(L_S)$, then we can compute the difference in the total log likelihoods: $[\ln(L_S) - \ln(L_R)]$. A lack of fit statistic, called G^2, is defined as two times this difference: $G^2 = 2[\ln(L_S) - \ln(L_R)]$. This lack-of-fit statistic must be positive because it is impossible to fit better than the saturated model. Note that maximizing the log likelihood of the Ratcliff model will minimize the lack-of-fit G^2 statistic, and so we can reframe the parameter estimation problem as one in which we find the model parameters that minimize this lack-of-fit statistic.

The parameter estimation problem for the Ratcliff model is nonlinear, and there are no known simple solutions for solving for the parameters that minimize the G^2 in this case. Thus, we must resort to using a nonlinear optimization program available in MATLAB, Mathematica, GAUSS, or some other mathematical programming language to find the optimal parameters for each participant (see Chapter 3). The results of this parameter search are summarized in Table 4.3, which presents the means and standard deviations of the model parameters, pooled across participants within each group. As can be seen in this table, only two parameters changed substantially across the age groups: One was the threshold bound, and the other was the motor response time. Thus, these parameters help us answer one of the main questions raised at the beginning of this chapter: Was the slowdown due to slower information processing rate or due to motor response time or change in threshold? The results suggest that the mean rate of information processing, measured by the mean of the discriminability parameter, did not change across ages. Instead, there was a large increase in the motor response times for the older participants. Additionally, the threshold increased with age, indicating that older subjects were more conservative.[6]

Table 4.3   Parameter Estimates and Chi-Square Fit Statistics Averaged Across
Subjects

	θ	d	η	β	MT	G^2
Young	1.10	.74	.71	.19	.33	9.12
	(.09)	(.13)	(.30)	(.05)	(.03)	(4.38)
Middle	1.21	.75	.75	.20	.66	8.79
	(.10)	(.14)	(.29)	(.05)	(.03)	(4.97)
Old	1.31	.76	.74	.20	1.0	7.88
	(.05)	(.08)	(.15)	(.05)	(.03)	(4.68)

NOTE: True parameters are $\theta = 1 + .2(\text{age} - 1)$, $d = .75$, $\eta = .75$, $\beta = .2$, $MT = \text{age}/3$.

Goodness of Fit

Once the parameters have been estimated for each participant, we can insert
these parameters back into the model and compute the predictions from the
model using Equations 4.1 through 4.4. Equation 4.1 directly provides the
choice probability. To find the predicted quartiles, we need to find the CRT
predicted by the model that produces a cumulative probability equal to the
corresponding quartile. The predictions from the individual participants are
averaged, and the average predictions for each group are shown alongside
the observed means in Tables 4.1 and 4.2a–d.

As can be seen from these tables, the predictions are fairly accurate. We
can quantitatively evaluate the accuracy of the predictions for each quartile
by computing a couple of auxiliary fit indices. For each group, there are a
total of 12 pairs of predicted and observed values for each quartile in Tables
4.2a–d. For convenience, we will label these as Q_i and Q'_i for the observed
and predicted values with i ranging from 1 to 12. One commonly used index
of fit is the proportion prediction defined as

$$R^2 = 1 - (SSE/TSS).$$

SSE symbolizes the sum of squared prediction errors,

$$SSE = \sum (Q_i - Q'_i)^2,$$

and *TSS* is the total sum of squares

$$TSS = \sum (Q_i - M)^2,$$

where $M = \sum Q_i/12$ is the mean of the 12 observed quartiles. For this example, $R^2 = .97$, $.95$, and $.92$ for the first, second, and third quartiles, respectively. Another commonly used measure of fit is the mean absolute deviation (MAE) defined as

$$MAE = \sum |Q_i - Q_i'|/12.$$

For this example, $MAE = .05$, $.09$, and $.17$ for the first, second, and third quartiles, respectively.

Lack-of-Fit Tests

For large samples sizes, the G^2 statistic can be used to perform a statistical test for lack of model fit, that is, if an important statistical assumption is true. The required assumption is that the observations on each trial be statistically independent, conditioned on the type of stimulus presented (see Chapter 3). This assumption is required for the use of the multinomial distribution (more simply, this is required whenever we express the joint probabilities as a product of the probabilities from each trial). If there are trial-to-trial dependencies so that the response probability on one trial depends on events from earlier trials (e.g., learning effects, drifting attention, or disturbances that carry over trials), then the statistical independence assumption will be violated. The statistical test also depends on using large sample sizes because the distribution of G^2 is not known for small sample sizes. What counts as a large sample is difficult to say a priori without performing Monte Carlo simulations to check on speed of convergence to a chi-square distribution for this model. In sum, we must assume that the sample size is sufficiently large to produce accurate results and that the observations are statistically independent. Then, we can test the null hypothesis, which states that the cognitive model is equivalent to the saturated model for this design. To do this, we compare the G^2 statistic to a table chi-square critical value using a stated significance level and using degrees of freedom equal to the difference between the number of parameters of the two models. The saturated model has the same number of parameters as the number of data points, which is equal to 14 in this example. The Ratcliff model has only 5 parameters, and so the degrees of freedom for the test is $df = (14 - 5) = 9$.

If we use a .05 significance level for rejecting the null hypothesis, then the critical chi-square equals 16.92. Thus, if the observed G^2 exceeds this critical value for a participant, then we can reject the null hypothesis: We conclude that there is a true difference between the saturated model and the cognitive model.

Referring to Table 4.3, we see that the average G^2 for each group is below the critical chi-square for rejecting the null hypothesis of no systematic discrepancy between the saturated model and the Ratcliff model. However, when we apply this test to each individual, we find that 3 out of 60 (5%) participants produced statistically significant discrepancies (0, 2, and 1 from the young, middle, and old groups, respectively), which is the rate expected by chance.

There is some controversy about the meaning of this statistical test. Most scientists would agree that the cognitive model is not perfectly correct, and thus the null hypothesis is known to be false from the beginning. Also, this statistical test is only accurate for large sample sizes, in which case there is usually sufficient power to detect even minor differences between the cognitive and the saturated model. Thus, a statistically significant lack of fit does not necessarily imply that the model is of no use.

Statistical Tests of Parameters

Suppose we wish to test a hypothesis regarding the variance of the discriminability parameter across trial, that is, the parameter denoted by η. According to the Ratcliff model, this parameter is substantially greater than zero. We can test this hypothesis by comparing the Ratcliff model with a simpler model that restricts this parameter to zero. To do this, we refit the data from each participant using only four parameters, and force $\eta = 0$, which generates a new chi-square fit statistic for each participant. Thus, the restricted model (zero variance) is a special case of the Ratcliff model, and the chi-square produced by the restricted model can only be larger (worse fit) than that produced by the Ratcliff model. The two models are nested, and so we can perform a chi-square difference test of the null hypothesis H_0: $\eta = 0$. This is done by computing the difference: G^2(restricted model) $- G^2$ (Ratcliff model). The obtained chi-square difference is then compared to a table chi-square with the degrees of freedom equal to the difference in the number of parameters used by each model. In this case, the Ratcliff model has five parameters and the restricted model has four, and so the test is based on 1 degree of freedom (alternatively, this is the number of restrictions placed on the Ratcliff model to reduce it to the simpler model). For the .05 level of significance, the critical value for rejecting the null hypothesis is a table chi-square value equal to 3.84. Table 4.4 displays the average chi-square difference for each group. As can be seen in this table, the observed average

Table 4.4   Chi-Square Differences Between Two Models

Age	Mean Chi-Square Difference
Young	8.73 (6.46)
Middle	9.31 (7.09)
Old	10.93 (5.10)
Average	9.66 (6.27)

NOTE: Standard deviations are shown in parentheses.

is greater than the critical value for rejecting the null hypothesis. However, if we perform this test separately for each individual, we find that 50 out of 60 (83%) of the participants produce statistically significant improvements by adding the extra parameter, allowing for variance in the discriminability parameter across trials. Based on the chi-square tests, there is strong evidence for parameter variability.

Qualitative Analysis

Another way to evaluate the restricted model is to evaluate whether or not its predictions capture all the main systematic qualitative patterns observed in the data. It turns out that one systematic pattern is not captured by the restricted model—it fails to predict the difference in the quartiles produced by error responses as compared with correct responses, when we hold the response that is made as a constant. More specifically, the restricted model predicts absolutely no difference between the quartiles for Hits and FAs; nor does it predict any difference between the quartiles for Misses and CRs. Note that the observed data in Table 4.1 do show a systematic difference between these quartiles for each age group. Also note that the Ratcliff model, which allows for variability in the discriminability across trials, accurately captures this pattern in the data. On this basis, one is led to reject the hypothesis of no variability in discriminability across trials.

Conclusion

This chapter began with an observation that the response time quartiles increased with age, and a question was raised as to whether this slow-down was caused by a slowing rate of information processing or a slower movement response time or a greater threshold criterion. It is difficult to separate out these important theoretical issues without the use of a cognitive model. Application of a dynamic model of the signal detection task allows one to estimate parameters from the data, and these parameters provide measurements of the theoretical component processes. In this (fictitious) example, the analysis indicated that the mean rate of information processing did not change with age, and the effect of age was primarily caused by the threshold and motor response time. This example was partly based on an experiment reported by Ratcliff et al. (2001) concerning the effects of age on signal detection performance. Ratcliff et al. (2001) found no differences among age groups on the discriminability parameter, and instead they found differences in both the motor response time and the criterion threshold: Both the latter parameters increased with age. The Ratcliff et al. (2001) article provides a very good example demonstrating the use of cognitive modeling for resolving important psychological issues.

Appendix

The purpose of this appendix is to derive the equations used with Ratcliff's diffusion model from elementary principles. The plan is to start with a simple discrete time random walk model and then build up to the more complex diffusion model. See Diederich and Busemeyer (2003) for more information about the matrix methods of analysis presented below, and see Smith (2000) for a review of the stochastic differential equation method of analysis.

Matrix Methods

First, consider the following simple "random walk" model for a signal detection task. In a signal detection task, the participant is asked to make a decision whether a signal or noise stimulus is present on a particular trial. Figure A4.1 provides a simplified representation of the decision process used to generate a response to the stimulus.

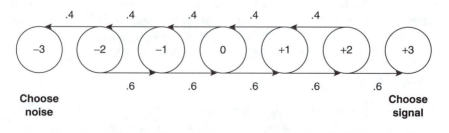

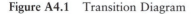

Figure A4.1   Transition Diagram

Suppose the decision maker starts out before the stimulus is presented in a neutral state, labeled "0" in the figure, which means the decision maker starts without any bias toward signal or response. This is called the initial state of evidence or starting state, and in general, it is denoted $X(0)$. Thus, $X(0) = 0$ indicates that the initial state starts out unbiased. However, the starting state does not have to be neutral, and the process could start out biased by starting in any one of the five possible initial states $\{-2, -1, 0, +1, +2\}$ in the figure. For example, the process could start out in the state $X(0) = +1$ indicating a slight bias favoring the signal response. The bias in the starting position is affected by the payoffs and prior probabilities of the task.

When the stimulus is presented, the decision maker obtains a sample of information from the stimulus, which provides evidence for a signal or noise response. The probability of sampling evidence in favor of the signal response equals .60 in the figure; the probability of sampling evidence favoring the noise response is .40. In general, the value of this probability is determined by the discriminability of a stimulus trial from a noise trial in the task.

If the first piece of evidence favors the signal, then the state changes from neutral, $X(0) = 0$ in the figure, to a state that moderately favors the signal, $X(1) = +1$ in the figure. But this evidence is not sufficiently strong to decide. The next piece of evidence may also favor signal, producing a step up to state $X(2) = +2$. But the third sample may provide evidence for the noise response so that the state of evidence moves back down a step to $X(3) = +1$. This process continues until one of the end states is reached, at which point the response is chosen. For example, if the evidence state reaches state +3 after, say, eight time steps, that is, $X(8) = +3$, then the cumulative evidence is sufficiently strong to make a decision in favor of the signal.

In this example, the two end states $\{-3 \text{ and } +3\}$ are called absorbing states, and the five intermediate states $\{-2, -1, 0, +1, +2\}$ are called transient states. Eventually, the state of evidence leaves the set of transient states and is captured by one of the absorbing states. The end states or absorbing states are also called the threshold bounds for making a decision. The threshold bound is used to control speed accuracy trade-offs. A high threshold bound produces slower but more accurate decisions, and a low threshold bound produces faster decisions but more errors. The threshold bound is affected by the time pressure or the cost of waiting to make a decision.

According to this simple model, the probability of choosing to respond signal is determined by the probability of eventually reaching the +3 absorbing state before reaching the −3 absorbing state. The time to make the decision is determined by the number of time steps required to reach an absorbing state. Below we will compute the joint probability of taking N transient steps and then taking a final step that reaches the boundary to choose signal, conditioned on each possible starting state.

The 7×7 matrix **T** shown below is a transition matrix corresponding to the transition diagram shown above. The row labeled "−3" represents the absorbing state for choosing noise, the row labeled "+3" represents the absorbing state for choosing signal, the row labeled "0" represents the neutral state, and the remaining rows represent the other transient states; the columns are organized in a corresponding manner. Each cell, q_{ij}, indicates the probability of transiting from a row state i to a column state j. For example, the probability of transiting from row state 0 to column state +1 is $q_{45} = .60$. Note that the process always leaves a transient state for one of the other states, but the process never leaves an absorbing state.

$$
\mathbf{T} =
\begin{array}{c}
\,\, -3 \;\, -2 \;\, -1 \quad\; 0 \;\, +1 \;\, +2 \;\, +3 \\
\begin{array}{c}
-3 \\ -2 \\ -1 \\ 0 \\ +1 \\ +2 \\ +3
\end{array}
\left[
\begin{array}{ccccccc}
1 & 0 & 0 & 0 & 0 & 0 & 0 \\
.4 & 0 & .6 & 0 & 0 & 0 & 0 \\
1 & .4 & 0 & .6 & 0 & 0 & 0 \\
0 & 0 & .4 & 0 & .6 & 0 & 0 \\
0 & 0 & 0 & .4 & 0 & .6 & 0 \\
0 & 0 & 0 & 0 & .4 & 0 & .6 \\
0 & 0 & 0 & 0 & 0 & 0 & 1
\end{array}
\right]
\end{array}
$$

First, we partition the transition matrix **T** into two submatrices. The first submatrix is formed by deleting the first row and column and the last row and column, and extracting the remaining probabilities between transient states {−2, −1, 0, +1, +2}. This is the 5×5 submatrix in the center of **T**, and it is called the transient state matrix (labeled **Q**):

$$
\mathbf{Q} =
\begin{bmatrix}
.0 & .6 & 0 & 0 & 0 \\
.4 & .0 & .6 & 0 & 0 \\
0 & .4 & .0 & .6 & 0 \\
0 & 0 & .4 & .0 & .6 \\
0 & 0 & 0 & .4 & .0
\end{bmatrix}.
$$

The second submatrix is taken from the middle five rows of the last column of **T**, and each element contains the probability of transiting to the +3 absorbing state from one of the transient states, which is called the transient to absorbing vector (denoted **R**):

$$
\mathbf{R} =
\begin{bmatrix}
0 \\
0 \\
0 \\
0 \\
.6
\end{bmatrix}.
$$

Next, we use Markov chain theory to do the calculations of the desired joint probabilities (see Bhattacharya & Waymire, 1990, chap. 3). The results of these calculations are symbolized by a 5×1 vector $\mathbf{P}(N)$, which contains the joint probability taking N transient steps followed by a last step to choose the signal response, conditioned starting from each one of the five transient states $\{-2, -1, 0, +1, +2\}$. The jth row of $\mathbf{P}(N)$, denoted $P_j(N)$, equals the probability of taking N transient steps and then a last step to choose the signal response, conditioned on starting at the state corresponding to row j.

Let us begin with the possibility that no transitions occur in the transient states ($N = 0$), in which case we simply use the probabilities of transiting directly from each transient state to the $+3$ absorbing state. These probabilities are given in the vector (shown above)

$$\mathbf{P}(N = 0) = \mathbf{R}$$

that has zero probability from each of the states $\{-2, -1, 0, +1\}$, and a .6 probability given that the process starts in state $+2$. For the next case, consider the possibility of taking one step within the transient states ($N = 1$), followed by a step that absorbs at state $+3$. In this case, we matrix multiply (see Strang, 1988) the probability of one transition by the probability of exiting and choosing signal:

$$\mathbf{P}(N=1) = \mathbf{Q} \cdot \mathbf{R} = \begin{bmatrix} 0 \\ 0 \\ 0 \\ .36 \\ 0 \end{bmatrix}.$$

Again, we have only one nonzero entry because there is only one way to take a transient step and then take a final step that absorbs at $+3$: The process must start at state $+1$ and take a positive step upward to $+2$ and then take a final positive step up to $+3$. If $N = 2$, transient steps occur followed by a step that absorbs at state $+3$, then we matrix multiply the probability of taking 2 transient steps times the probability of taking the last step that exits and chooses signal (see appendix of Chapter 2 for a review of matrix algebra):

$$P(N=2) = \mathbf{Q} \cdot \mathbf{Q} \cdot \mathbf{R} = \mathbf{Q}^2 \mathbf{R} = \begin{bmatrix} 0 \\ 0 \\ .216 \\ 0 \\ .1440 \end{bmatrix}.$$

Now there are two nonzero entries, indicating that the +3 absorbing state can be reached in two transient steps by starting either from the initial state 0 or the initial state +2. After taking $N = 8$ transient steps, the joint probabilities conditioned on each initial state are given by

$$P(N=8) = \mathbf{Q}^8 \mathbf{R} = \begin{bmatrix} .0582 \\ 0 \\ .0806 \\ 0 \\ .0279 \end{bmatrix}.$$

The first row indicates that the joint probability is .0582 given that the process starts out biased to say noise in state −2; middle row indicates that the joint probability is .0806 given that the process starts out in the neutral state, 0; and the last row indicates that the joint probability is .0279 given that the process starts biased to say signal in state +2. If the process starts out in state −1 or +1, then the process cannot exit after exactly $N = 8$ transient steps. More generally, the probability of taking N steps in the transient states and then taking a final step that exits and chooses the signal is

$$\mathbf{P}(N) = \mathbf{Q}^N \cdot \mathbf{R}. \tag{A4.1a}$$

If we assume that each transition requires a fixed amount of time, then Equation A4.1a provides the distribution of decision times for choosing the signal response.

The computation in Equation A4.1a can be greatly simplified by rewriting the transient state matrix $\mathbf{Q}$ in terms of its linearly independent matrix of eigenvectors $\mathbf{V}$ and its diagonal matrix of real-valued eigenvalues $\mathbf{\Lambda}$ (see appendix to Chapter 2 for a review of matrix algebra):

$$\mathbf{Q} = \mathbf{V} \cdot \mathbf{\Lambda} \cdot \mathbf{V}^{-1},$$

where $\mathbf{\Lambda} = \text{diag}[\lambda_1, \ldots, \lambda_j, \ldots, \lambda_m]$ and $0 < |\lambda_j| \leq 1$ is one of the eigenvalues. Note that

$$\mathbf{Q}^2 = \mathbf{Q} \cdot \mathbf{Q} = (\mathbf{V} \cdot \mathbf{\Lambda} \cdot \mathbf{V}^{-1})(\mathbf{V} \cdot \mathbf{\Lambda} \cdot \mathbf{V}^{-1}) = \mathbf{V} \cdot \mathbf{\Lambda}^2 \cdot \mathbf{V}^{-1},$$

and by induction we have $\mathbf{Q}^N = \mathbf{V} \cdot \mathbf{\Lambda}^N \cdot \mathbf{V}^{-1}$, where $\mathbf{\Lambda}^N = \text{diag}[\lambda_1^N, \ldots, \lambda_j^N, \ldots, \lambda_m^N]$. Thus, computing the Nth power of a matrix has been reduced to computing the Nth power of the eigenvalues:

$$\mathbf{P}(N) = (\mathbf{V} \cdot \mathbf{\Lambda}^N \cdot \mathbf{V}^{-1})\mathbf{R}. \tag{A4.1b}$$

To use Equation A4.1b, we need to determine three objects: the eigenvector matrix $\mathbf{V}$, the inverse eigenvector matrix $\mathbf{V}^{-1}$, and the eigenvalues $\mathbf{\Lambda}$. An easy way to do this in any application is to use a computer program such as MATLAB, Mathematica, GAUSS, or the R program, which has efficient numerical routines for computing these objects.

The cumulative probability of taking N transient steps or less and then a final step to choose the signal response, conditioned on each starting state, is simply obtained by summing all the joint probabilities of Equation A4.1 up to and including N:

$$\mathbf{C}(N) = \sum_{n=0}^{N} \mathbf{P}(N) = [\mathbf{Q}^0 + \mathbf{Q}^1 + \mathbf{Q}^2 + \cdots + \mathbf{Q}^N] \cdot \mathbf{R}.$$

This sum can be simplified as follows. Define

$$\mathbf{S} = [\mathbf{Q}^0 + \mathbf{Q}^1 + \mathbf{Q}^2 + \cdots + \mathbf{Q}^N]$$

then

$$\mathbf{Q} \cdot \mathbf{S} = [\mathbf{Q}^1 + \mathbf{Q}^2 + \mathbf{Q}^3 + \cdots + \mathbf{Q}^{N+1}]$$

and the difference is

$$\mathbf{S} - \mathbf{Q} \cdot \mathbf{S} = (\mathbf{I} - \mathbf{Q}) \cdot \mathbf{S} = (\mathbf{Q}^0 - \mathbf{Q}^{N+1}) = (\mathbf{I} - \mathbf{Q}^{N+1}).$$

Solving for $\mathbf{S}$ yields

$$\mathbf{S} = (\mathbf{I} - \mathbf{Q})^{-1} \cdot (\mathbf{I} - \mathbf{Q}^{N+1}),$$

where $\mathbf{Q}^0 = \mathbf{I}$ is the identity matrix. Replacing this solution for the sum in $\mathbf{C}(N)$ yields

$$\mathbf{C}(N) = (\mathbf{I} - \mathbf{Q})^{-1} \cdot (\mathbf{I} - \mathbf{Q}^{N+1})\mathbf{R}. \tag{A4.2}$$

Once again, if we assume that each transition requires a constant amount of time, then Equation A4.2 provides the cumulative distribution of decision times.

The marginal probability of choosing the signal, conditioned on each starting position, can be obtained from Equation A4.2 by allowing $N \rightarrow \infty$, in which case $\mathbf{Q}^{N+1} \rightarrow 0$ (zero matrix), and we obtain

$$\mathbf{C}(\infty) = (\mathbf{I} - \mathbf{Q})^{-1} \cdot \mathbf{R}. \tag{A4.3}$$

Each row of c_j of $C(\infty)$ contains the probability of choosing the signal response, conditioned on starting in the state corresponding to the jth row. Equation A4.3 entails finding a matrix inverse $(I - Q)^{-1}$. Programs such as MATLAB, Mathematica, GAUSS, or the R program have efficient routines for computing inverses of matrices.

The development of Equations A4.1a, b, A4.2, and A4.3 was based on a simple example that assumed a specific 7×7 transition matrix T. It is important to note, however, that none of the derivations for these equations depended on this example. All the formulas stated above in these equations continue to hold for an arbitrary number of states and arbitrary transition probabilities.

Elementary Formulas for the Random Walk

The purpose of this section is to derive more elementary formulas for Equations A4.1a, b, A4.2, and A4.3. Hereafter, we will refer to a process with an arbitrary number of transient states and an arbitrary pair of transition probabilities from each state. First, we let p represent the probability of taking a unit step up, and $q = 1 - p$ is the probability of taking a unit step down at each time step. In the previous example, $p = .6$ and $q = .4$. The upper absorbing state for responding signal is some arbitrary number of steps $+K$ above zero; and the lower absorbing state is $-K$ steps below zero. In the previous example, $+K = +3$ and $-K = -3$. Hereafter, we will let $m = 2K - 1$ denote the number of transient states, $\{-K + 1, \ldots, -1, 0, +1, \ldots, + K - 1\}$. In the previous example, $m = 2 \cdot 3 - 1 = 5$. The initial starting position, $X(0)$, is located in row $i = [K + X(0)]$ of Q. In the previous example, the neutral starting position, $X(0) = 0$, corresponded to row $(3 + 0) = 3$ of Q. The transient state matrix Q is an $m \times m$ matrix containing all the transient state transition probabilities.

$$q_{ij} = q \text{ if } j = i - 1, \; q_{ij} = p \text{ if } j = i + 1, \text{ and } 0 \text{ otherwise.}$$

The vector R is an $m \times 1$ vector with all zeros except p in the last row.

Marginal Choice Probability

First, we derive an elementary formula for the marginal probability of choosing a signal response, conditioned on each initial state. Note that Equation A4.3 can be rewritten as

$$(I - Q) \cdot C = R \text{ or } C = R + Q \cdot C.$$

This matrix equation implies that the marginal probabilities contained in C can be obtained by solving a set of m simultaneous linear equations of the form

$$c_1 = p \cdot c_2$$

$$c_i = q \cdot c_{i-1} + p \cdot c_{i+1}, \, i = 2, \ldots, m - 1$$

$$c_m = q \cdot c_{m-1} + p,$$

where c_i = Pr[Choose signal | initial state in row i]. We can also include the two absorbing states to this definition: c_0 = Pr[Choose signal | start at lower bound] and c_{m+1} = Pr[Choose signal | start at upper bound], and by definition we know that $c_0 = 0$ and $c_{m+1} = 1$. Then, all the above equations satisfy the common equation:

$$c_j = q \cdot c_{i-1} + p \cdot c_{i+1}, \, j = 1, \ldots, m.$$

The above equation is a second-order linear difference equation, which is known to have a solution of the form (see Luenberger, 1979; chap. 2)

$$c_i = x^i.$$

Inserting this into the linear difference equation produces

$$x^i = q \cdot x^{i-1} + p \cdot x^{i+1} \rightarrow x = q \cdot x^0 + p \cdot x^2 \rightarrow p \cdot x^2 - x + q = 0.$$

Thus, x^i satisfies the difference equation by setting x equal to either of two unique solutions or roots of this quadratic form:

$$x_1 = \frac{1 - \sqrt{1 - 4 \cdot pq}}{2p}$$

and

$$x_2 = \frac{1 + \sqrt{1 - 4 \cdot pq}}{2p}.$$

Note that

$$\sqrt{1 - 4pq} = \sqrt{1 - 4p(1 - p)} = \sqrt{1 - 4p + 4p^2}$$
$$= \sqrt{(1 - 2p)^2} = (1 - 2p)$$

and so $x_1 = 1$ and $x_2 = (q/p)$. The general solution is a linear combination of these two particular solutions:

$$c_i = ax_1^i + bx_2^i = a(1) + b(q/p)^i.$$

To satisfy $c_0 = 0$, we must have $a + b(q/p)^0 = 0$ or $b = -a$; and to satisfy $c_{m+1} = 1$ we have $a(1) + (-a) \cdot (q/p)^{m+1} \rightarrow a - a \cdot (q/p)^{m+1} = 1 \rightarrow a = [1 - (q/p)^{m+1}]^{-1}$. Thus, the final solution for the marginal probability of choosing the signal, conditioned on starting in the state corresponding to row i is (recall that $m + 1 = 2 \cdot K$)

$$c_i = ax_1^i + bx_2^i = \frac{1 - (q/p)^i}{1 - (q/p)^{m+1}} = \frac{1 - (q/p)^i}{1 - (q/p)^{2K}}. \tag{A4.4}$$

Distribution of Decision Time

Next, we determine an elementary formula for the joint probability of taking N transient steps and then taking a final step to respond signal. This is more difficult, and it requires solving for three objects, the eigenvectors in $\mathbf{V}$, the inverse eigenvectors in $\mathbf{V}^{-1}$, and the eigenvalues in $\mathbf{\Lambda}$. To determine the "right-side" eigenvectors in the columns of the matrix $\mathbf{V}$, recall (see Strang, 1988) that the jth column vector in $\mathbf{V}$, denoted as

$$\mathbf{V}_j = \begin{bmatrix} v_{1j} \\ v_{2j} \\ . \\ . \\ v_{mj} \end{bmatrix}$$

satisfies the following "right-side" property:

$$\mathbf{Q} \cdot \mathbf{V}_j = \lambda_j \cdot \mathbf{V}_j.$$

For the transient state matrix $\mathbf{Q}$, this implies the following linear equalities:

$$p \cdot v_{2j} = \lambda_j \cdot v_{1j} \tag{A4.5a}$$

$$q \cdot v_{i-1, j} + p \cdot v_{i+1, j} = \lambda_j \cdot v_{ij} \tag{A4.5b}$$

$$q \cdot v_{m-1, j} = \lambda_j \cdot v_{m, j}. \tag{A4.5c}$$

Equation A4.5b is a second-order linear difference equation with respect to the row index i, and as before, it has a solution of the form

$$v_{ij} = x^{i-1}.$$

Inserting this solution into Equation A4.5b yields

$$qx^{i-2} + px^i = \lambda_j \cdot x^{i-1} \rightarrow qx^0 + px^2 = \lambda_j \cdot x^1 \rightarrow px^2 - \lambda_j x^1 + q = 0.$$

This quadratic form has two complex roots or solutions:

$$x_1 = \frac{\lambda_j - \sqrt{\lambda_j^2 - 4pq}}{2p} = \frac{\lambda_j - i\sqrt{4pq - \lambda_j^2}}{2p},$$

$$x_2 = \frac{\lambda_j + \sqrt{\lambda_j^2 - 4pq}}{2p} = \frac{\lambda_j + i\sqrt{4pq - \lambda_j^2}}{2p}.$$

The squared magnitude of each root reduces to the following simple expression:

$$x_1^2 = x_2^2 = \left(\frac{\lambda_j}{2p}\right)^2 + \left(\frac{\sqrt{4pq - \lambda_j^2}}{2p}\right)^2 = \frac{4pq}{4p^2} = \frac{q}{p},$$

and so the magnitude of each root is $|x_1| = |x_2| = \sqrt{q/p}$.

The general solution is a linear combination of these two special cases:

$$v_{ij} = a \cdot x_1^{i-1} + b \cdot x_2^{i-1}.$$

The eigenvectors are only unique up to a multiplicative constant (see Strang, 1988), so without loss in generality, for $i = 1$, we can set the first coordinate v_{1j} equal to $v_{1j} = ax_1^0 + bx_2^0 = 1$ (later we adjust the inverse eigenvectors to compensate for setting $v_{1j} = 1$), which then implies that $b = (1 - a)$. To find the constant a, we use the top boundary Equation 4.5a:

$$p \cdot v_{2j} = \lambda_j \cdot v_{1j} \rightarrow p[ax_1 + (1 - a)x_2] = \lambda_j$$

$$\rightarrow a = \frac{(\lambda_j/p) - x_2}{x_1 - x_2}.$$

Note that

$$\frac{\lambda_j}{p} - x_2 = \frac{2 \cdot \lambda_j}{2p} - \left[\frac{\lambda_j + \sqrt{\lambda_j^2 - 4pq}}{2p}\right] = \frac{\lambda_j - \sqrt{\lambda_j^2 - 4pq}}{2p} = x_1,$$

so that $a = x_1/(x_1 - x_2)$ and $b = -x_2/(x_1 - x_2)$ and the solution for the "right" eigenvalues is

$$v_{ij} = \frac{x_1 x_1^{i-1} - x_2 x_2^{i-1}}{x_1 - x_2} = \frac{x_1^i - x_2^i}{x_1 - x_2}.$$

To simplify this solution, it is useful to express the complex roots in polar form (see Strang, 1988, p. 218):

$$x_1 = r[\cos(\phi) - i\,\sin(\phi)] \text{ and } x_2 = r[\cos(\phi) + i\,\sin(\phi)],$$

where $r = |r_1| = |r_2| = \sqrt{p/q}$ and $i = \sqrt{-1}$. These definitions require that the phase ϕ, is defined in such a way that it satisfies the pair of equations:

$$\sin(\phi_j) = \sqrt{p/q}\frac{\sqrt{4pq - \lambda_j^2}}{2p}, \quad \cos(\phi_j) = \sqrt{p/q}(\lambda_j/2p).$$

This pair of equations implies a simple relation between each eigenvalue and the corresponding phase:

$$\lambda_j = 2\sqrt{pq}\cos(\phi_j).$$

Inserting these definitions for the roots yields a simple solution for v_{ij}:

$$v_{ij} = \frac{\sqrt{q/p}^i[\cos(\phi \cdot i) - i\,\sin(\phi \cdot i)] - \sqrt{q/p}^i[\cos(\phi \cdot i) + i\,\sin(\phi \cdot i)]}{\sqrt{q/p}[\cos(\phi) - i\,\sin(\phi)] - \sqrt{q/p}[\cos(\phi) + i\,\sin(\phi)]}$$

$$= \sqrt{q/p}^{i-1}\frac{\sin(\phi \cdot i)}{\sin(\phi)}. \tag{A4.6}$$

Here we used de Moivre's law that

$$[\cos(\phi) + i \cdot \sin(\phi)]^i = \cos(\phi \cdot i) + i \cdot \sin(\phi \cdot i).$$

We still need to determine the phase, ϕ_j, corresponding to each eigenvalue λ_j. The phase must satisfy the constraint imposed by Equation A4.5c:

$$q \cdot v_{m-1,j} = \lambda_j \cdot v_{mj}$$

$$\rightarrow q\sqrt{q/p}^{\,m-2} \frac{\sin(\phi_j \cdot (m-1))}{\sin(\phi_j)} = 2 \cdot \sqrt{pq}\cos(\phi_j)\sqrt{q/p}^{\,m-1} \frac{\sin(\phi_j \cdot m)}{\sin(\phi_j)}$$

$$\rightarrow \sin(\phi_j \cdot (m-1)) = 2 \cdot \cos(\phi_j)\sin(\phi_j \cdot m)$$

$$= \sin(\phi_j \cdot (m+1)) + \sin(\phi_j \cdot (m-1))$$

$$\rightarrow \sin(\phi_j \cdot (m+1)) = 0,$$

which is satisfied for $\phi_j = [\pi \cdot j/(m+1)] = (\pi \cdot j/2K)$ where $2K = m + 1$. Substituting this final solution for the phase ϕ_j generates the final solution for the "right-sided" eigenvectors:

$$v_{ij} = \sqrt{q/p}^{\,i-1} \frac{\sin\left(\frac{\pi \cdot j \cdot i}{2K}\right)}{\sin\left(\frac{\pi \cdot j}{2K}\right)}, \tag{A4.7}$$

with corresponding eigenvalues

$$\lambda_j = 2\sqrt{pq} \, \cos\left(\frac{\pi \cdot j}{2K}\right). \tag{A4.8}$$

We still need to determine the inverse eigenvector matrix $\mathbf{V}^{-1}$. The "left-side" eigenvector

$$\mathbf{W}_j = [w_{j1}, w_{j2}, \ldots, w_{jm}]$$

in the jth row of the matrix $\mathbf{W}$ satisfies the "left-side" property

$$\mathbf{W}_j\mathbf{Q} = \lambda_j \cdot \mathbf{W}_j.$$

For the transient state matrix $\mathbf{Q}$, this implies the following linear equalities:

$$q \cdot w_{j2} = \lambda_j \cdot w_{j1} \tag{A4.9a}$$

$$p \cdot w_{j, k-1} + q \cdot v_{j, k+1} = \lambda_j \cdot w_{jk} \tag{A4.9b}$$

$$p \cdot w_{j, m-1} = \lambda_j \cdot w_{j, m}. \tag{A4.9c}$$

Once again this is a linear difference equation, and following the same line of reasoning as before, we obtain the solution:

$$w_{jk} = \sqrt{p/q}^{\,-k-1} \frac{\sin\left(\frac{\pi \cdot j \cdot k}{2K}\right)}{\sin\left(\frac{\pi \cdot j}{2K}\right)}. \qquad \text{(A4.10a)}$$

Note that the inverse property demands that $\mathbf{W} \cdot \mathbf{V} = \mathbf{V}^{-1} \cdot \mathbf{V} = \mathbf{I}$. Equations A4.7 and A4.10 satisfy the orthogonality relation $\mathbf{W}_k \cdot \mathbf{V}_i = 0$ for $i \neq k$. However, the lengths of the "left-side" eigenvectors are not normalized properly (recall that we arbitrarily set $v_{1j} = 1$) and

$$\mathbf{W}_j \cdot \mathbf{V}_j = \frac{2K}{2\sin^2(\pi \cdot j/2K)},$$

which does not satisfy the requirement $\mathbf{W}_j \cdot \mathbf{V}_j = 1.0$. But this can be achieved by modifying Equation A4.10a by dividing out this factor

$$\begin{aligned}
w_{jk} &= \sqrt{p/q}^{\,-k-1} \frac{\sin(\pi \cdot j \cdot k/2K)}{\sin(\pi \cdot j/2K)} \cdot \frac{2}{2K} \cdot \sin^2\left(\frac{\pi \cdot j}{2K}\right) \\
&= \frac{2}{2K} \sqrt{p/q}^{\,-k-1} \cdot \sin\left(\frac{\pi \cdot j \cdot k}{2K}\right) \cdot \sin\left(\frac{\pi \cdot j}{2K}\right).
\end{aligned} \qquad \text{(A4.10b)}$$

Now we have determined all three ingredients: the entries for the eigenvector matrix $\mathbf{V}$ are given by Equation A4.7, the entries for the inverse eigenvector matrix $\mathbf{V}^{-1}$ are given by Equation A4.10b, and the eigenvalues are given by Equation A4.8. When we substitute these equations into Equation A4.1b, and evaluate the ith row of P in Equation A4.1b, then the following result is obtained:

$$P_i(N) = \sum_{j=1,m} (\lambda_j^N \cdot v_{ij} \cdot w_{jm}) \cdot p$$

$$= p2^N \left(\frac{2}{2K}\right) \sqrt{pq}^{\,N} \sqrt{q/p}^{\,i-1} \sqrt{p/q}^{\,m-1}$$

$$\times \sum_j \cos^N\left(\frac{\pi \cdot j}{2K}\right) \frac{\sin(\pi \cdot i \cdot j/2K)}{\sin(\pi \cdot j/2K)} \sin\left(\frac{\pi \cdot j \cdot m}{2K}\right) \sin\left(\frac{\pi \cdot j}{2K}\right)$$

$$= p \frac{2^{N+1}}{2K} \sqrt{pq}^{\,N} \sqrt{p/q}^{\,2K-i-1} \sum_j \cos^N\left(\frac{\pi \cdot j}{2K}\right) \sin\left(\frac{\pi \cdot j \cdot i}{2K}\right) \sin\left(\frac{\pi \cdot j \cdot m}{2K}\right)$$

$$= \frac{2^{N+1}}{2K} \sqrt{pq}^{N+1} \sqrt{p/q}^{2K-i}$$
$$\times \sum_j \cos^N\left(\frac{\pi \cdot j}{2K}\right) \sin\left(\frac{\pi \cdot j \cdot (2K-i)}{2K}\right) \sin\left(\frac{\pi \cdot j}{2K}\right). \tag{A4.11}$$

The above formula goes back to Lagrange and it has been derived by many authors using various methods. Here we used what is called the "spectral" method presented in Bhattacharya and Waymire (1990, p. 241). Feller (1968, p. 353) earlier derived the same formula using the "generating function" method.

Wiener Diffusion Model

The model developed so far assumes discrete steps of unit size during discrete time intervals of unit size, which is called a random walk model. If the time interval between steps become arbitrarily small, and the step sizes also become arbitrarily small, and consequently the number of steps to reach the bound become arbitrarily large, then the discrete time random walk model converges in distribution to a continuous time Wiener diffusion model (Bhattacharya & Waymire, 1990, p. 386; Feller, 1968, p. 359).

To formalize this convergence process, define h as a small time unit, and then $t = h \cdot N$ is the amount of time required to make a decision. Also define $\Delta(t)$ as a small step up or down at time t. The time unit and step size are linked by the relation $|\Delta(t)| = \Delta = \sqrt{h}$. The absorbing states for the model are now denoted as $+\theta = +k \cdot \Delta$ and $-\theta = -k \cdot \Delta$. The initial starting position is now denoted as $z = X(0) = (i - k) \cdot \Delta$. As before, we let p denote the probability of taking a positive step up, and $q = 1 - p$ is the probability of taking a negative step down. Thus, at each time step h the new cumulative state of evidence is related to the old state of evidence by

$$X(t + h) = X(t) + \Delta(t + h).$$

The transition probability p can be determined from another parameter of the random walk process, namely, the mean change of evidence during the time period h, denoted $d \cdot h$, which is defined by the following expectation:

$$d \cdot h = E[X(t + h) - X(t)] = E[\Delta(t)]$$
$$= (p\Delta - q\Delta) = (p - q)\Delta. \tag{A4.12}$$

This equation allows us to solve for the transition probability p of the random walk process in terms of the mean of the random walk process as follows:

$$d \cdot h = (p - q)\Delta = [p - (1 - p)] \cdot \Delta = (2p - 1)\sqrt{h},$$

and solving for p then produces

$$p = \tfrac{1}{2}(1 + d \cdot \sqrt{h}).$$

The predictions for the continuous time Wiener diffusion model are obtained from the discrete time random walk model by inserting the above definition for p into Equation A4.4, and then taking the limit as $h \to 0$. In the limit (using the Sterling formula),

$$\left(\frac{q}{p}\right)^{i} \to \left(\frac{1 - d\sqrt{h}}{1 + d\sqrt{h}}\right)^{\frac{(\theta + z)}{\Delta}} \to e^{-2d(\theta + z)}$$

and

$$\left(\frac{q}{p}\right)^{2K} \to \left(\frac{1 - d\sqrt{h}}{1 + d\sqrt{h}}\right)^{\frac{2\theta}{\Delta}} \to e^{-4d\theta}$$

and so the marginal probability of choosing signal, conditioned on starting at position $X(0)$, converges to

$$c_z = \frac{1 - e^{-2 \cdot d \cdot (\theta + z)}}{1 - e^{-4 \cdot d \cdot \theta}}. \tag{A4.13}$$

The eigenvalues converge to

$$\lambda_j^t = e^{-\frac{1}{2}\left[\left(\frac{\pi \cdot j}{2 \cdot \theta}\right)^2 + d^2\right] \cdot t},$$

and the product of the eigenvectors converges to

$$v_{ij} \cdot w_{jm} \cdot p \to (2\theta)^{-1} e^{d \cdot (\theta - z)} \left(\frac{j \cdot \pi}{2 \cdot \theta}\right) \cdot \sin\left(\frac{\pi \cdot (\theta - z) \cdot j}{2 \cdot \theta}\right),$$

and Equation A4.11 converges to the probability distribution for the continuous time Wiener diffusion process (see Feller, 1968, p. 359):

$$P_z(t) = (2\theta)^{-1} e^{d \cdot (\theta - z)} \sum_{j=1, \infty} \lambda_j^t \cdot \left(\frac{\pi \cdot j}{2 \cdot \theta}\right) \cdot \sin\left(\frac{\pi \cdot (\theta - z) \cdot j}{2 \cdot \theta}\right)$$

$$P_z(t) = \pi \cdot (2\theta)^{-2} e^{d \cdot (\theta - z)}$$

$$\times \sum_{j=1, \infty} j \cdot e^{-\frac{1}{2}\left[\left(\frac{\pi \cdot j}{2 \cdot \theta}\right)^2 + d^2\right] \cdot t} \cdot \sin\left(\frac{\pi \cdot (\theta - z) \cdot j}{2 \cdot \theta}\right), \quad (A4.14)$$

where z is the initial starting position of the process. Integration with respect to time t of Equation A4.13 then gives the cumulative joint distribution

$$C_z(T) = \int_0^T P_z(t) \, dt$$

$$= \pi \cdot (2\theta)^{-2} e^{d \cdot (\theta - z)} \sum_{j=1}^{\infty} \frac{2 \cdot j}{\left(\frac{\pi \cdot j}{2 \cdot \theta}\right)^2 + d^2}$$

$$\times \left(1 - e^{-\frac{1}{2}\left[\left(\frac{\pi \cdot j}{2\theta}\right)^2 + d\right]^2 \cdot T} \cdot \sin\left(\frac{\pi \cdot (\theta - z) \cdot j}{2 \cdot \theta}\right)\right)$$

Note that as $t \to \infty$, $e^{-\frac{1}{2}\left[\left(\frac{\pi \cdot j}{2\theta}\right)^2 + d^2\right] \cdot t} \to 0$ and $C_z(\infty) = c_z$ as shown in Equation A4.13. Consequently, the above equation can be simplified as follows:

$$C_z(T) = c_z - 2\pi \cdot (2\theta)^{-2} e^{d \cdot (\theta - z)}$$

$$\times \sum_{j=1}^{\infty} \frac{j}{\left(\frac{\pi \cdot j}{2\theta}\right)^2 + d^2} e^{-\frac{1}{2}\left[\left(\frac{\pi \cdot j}{2\theta}\right)^2 + d^2\right] \cdot T} \cdot \sin\left(\frac{\pi \cdot (\theta - z) \cdot j}{2 \cdot \theta}\right) \quad (A4.15)$$

which is equivalent to that given in Ratcliff (1978). To obtain the formula for the noise response, simply replace the parameters $\{d, z\}$ in Equation A4.15 with $\{-d, -z\}$, respectively.[7]

Notes

1. The design and analysis of the fictitious study described here was inspired by research reported by Ratcliff, Thaper, and McKoon (2001). However, the design and results presented here were generated to meet the pedagogical needs of this chapter.

2. For an optimal Bayesian inference model, $X(0)$ = log prior probability of signal − log prior probability of noise.

3. For an optimal Bayesian inference model, V = log likelihood of the sample information given signal − log likelihood of the sample information given noise.

4. Ratcliff (1978) defines $-\theta_N = 0$ and $+\theta_S = a$.

5. Ratcliff (1978) uses ξ to symbolize what we define as μ and he sets $\sigma = .10$ instead of $\sigma = 1$.

6. Recall that these are just simulated results. Real data are reported by Ratcliff et al. (2002). They found no difference in the discriminability parameter across age groups, but they reported a larger threshold criterion for older as compared with younger participants as well as a longer motor time.

7. Ratcliff gives the formula for the noise response, whereas we give the formula for the signal response. Also the correspondence between Ratcliff's parameters and the present parameters is as follows (Ratcliff's on the left-hand side, ours on the right-hand side): $a/s = 2\theta$, $\zeta/s = z + \theta$, $\xi/s = d$.

5

Quantitative Model Comparisons

The purpose of this chapter is to provide a detailed example of a quantitative comparison of three different cognitive models. For the purpose of introducing students to the basic methods and techniques of cognitive modeling, it is best to start with a fairly simple example. Although the example is simple, it entails all the steps of cognitive modeling. Moreover, the procedures learned with this simple example can also be applied to the more complex models.

The example presented in this chapter was chosen for reasons beyond just simplicity. One is that this is an application of cognitive modeling to issues of interest in several fields of psychology, including decision making, clinical psychology, and cognitive neuroscience. Another reason is that it illustrates a model involving interactions among several cognitive processes, including evaluation, learning, and decision making. A third reason is because the experiment and data reviewed in this chapter are based on actual research by Bechara and Damasio (2005) and the models are based on previous published ones on this topic by Busemeyer and Stout (2002).

This chapter is organized as follows. First, we describe a simulated gambling task that has become popular in cognitive neuroscience. We present the (fictitious) basic findings from this experiment. Although the findings are fictitious, they reflect the actual results reported by Bechara and Damasio (2005) using individuals with damage to orbital-frontal cortex. Second, we present three different cognitive models for this task, which have been examined earlier by Busemeyer and Stout (2002). Third, we present the problem of estimating the parameters for the models. Fourth, we present model comparisons using various new methods for quantitatively comparing models. Finally, we examine the parameters of the models, and we use these parameters to help understand the nature of the decision-making deficit in brain-damaged individuals.

Cognitive models are often built up from simple units that conform to a small number of elementary principles of cognition. However, once a large number of these units are connected together into an interrelated and dynamic system, the behavior of the system becomes fairly complex, and computer analysis is usually required to derive the predictions from the system. Under these circumstances, it becomes very difficult to derive qualitative tests of the competing models, and consequently, the researcher must resort to quantitative model comparisons. Quantitative model comparisons are performed by first finding the best-fitting model parameters and then comparing the quantitative accuracy of the predictions based on the optimal parameters. However, these comparisons are difficult because the models differ in complexity, which needs to be taken into consideration. Model complexity is based on the type and number of fundamental assumptions, the functional forms used to mathematically represent the assumptions, and the number of model parameters. In other words, the selection of the best model must satisfy a balance of both accuracy and parsimony.

The purpose of this chapter is to provide a detailed example of a quantitative comparison of three different cognitive models. The example presented below was chosen for three reasons. One is that this is an application of cognitive modeling to issues of interest that span across several fields, including decision making, clinical psychology, and cognitive neuroscience. A second reason is that this example illustrates a model involving interactions among several cognitive processes, including motivation, learning, and decision making. Third, the models that we compare are qualitatively different in their assumptions and number of parameters. This last feature is very common in cognitive modeling, but it makes the process of comparison much more difficult.[1]

Bechara's Simulated Gambling Task

The cognitive neuroscience, psychopathology, and drug abuse literatures have become interested in the use of a laboratory-based simulated gambling paradigm developed by Bechara, Damasio, Tranel, and Damasio (1997). This task has been used to experimentally study the neuropsychological basis of deficits in decision making exhibited by brain-damaged, psychopathic, antisocial, and drug-abusing populations. The Bechara task was designed to examine the complex interplay between cognitive and motivational processes, and it has been very successful for revealing striking individual differences in decision-making performance. However, performance on this task is confounded by complex interdependencies between cognitive, motivational, and response processes, making it difficult to sort out and identify the specific processes responsible for the observed behavioral deficits. Cognitive models provide a theoretical basis for decomposing complex tasks into separate processes, thus providing a theoretically based means for assessment of the hidden components. This chapter compares three competing cognitive decision models of the Bechara task in terms of their ability to explain the performance deficits observed in patients with orbital-frontal cortex damage as compared with healthy controls. The parameters of the best-fitting model are used to decompose the observed performance deficits of the patients with orbital-frontal cortex damage into cognitive, motivational, and response sources.

Procedure

The gambling task involves the use of four decks of cards (labeled here as D_1, D_2, D_3, and D_4). On each of several hundred trials of the game, the player is asked to choose a card from any one of the four decks. Once a card is chosen, it is turned over, the amount of money won or lost for choosing that card is revealed, and any wins and losses are included in the player's holdings. The player is never told the distribution of wins and losses associated with each deck, and instead the distributions are learned from experience.

The four decks are designed in such a way that two of the decks (labeled here as decks D_1 and D_2) are advantageous, while the other two decks (labeled here as decks D_3 and D_4) are disadvantageous in the following sense. Each advantageous deck produces an average gain of $2.50, averaged across every 10 cards within a deck, whereas each disadvantageous deck produces an average loss of $2.50, averaged across every 10 cards within a deck. However, the payoffs are arranged and sequenced in a manner that makes it difficult for the player to learn this fact. The advantageous decks always produce a small immediate win of $.50, while the disadvantageous decks always produce a large immediate win of $1.00. Thus, the disadvantageous decks appear at first sight to be superior, at least with respect to the amount to win. But this is misleading because the disadvantageous decks also produce larger losses than the advantageous decks. The advantageous deck D_1 yields a loss of $2.50 once every block of 10 cards within its deck, whereas the disadvantageous deck D_3 yields a loss of $12.50 once every block of 10 cards within its deck. The other advantageous deck D_2 yields five losses of $.50 within each block of 10 cards in that deck for a total loss of $2.50 within each block, whereas the other disadvantageous deck D_4 yields losses of $1.50, $2.00, $2.50, $3.00, and $3.50 within each block of 10 cards in that deck for a total loss of $12.50 within each block.

Basic Results

Bechara et al. (1997) compared the decision-making performance of patients with orbital-frontal cortex damage with healthy controls on the gambling task. The main dependent measure is the proportion of choices taken from the advantageous decks as a function of training trials. A typical finding reported with this task is that healthy control participants gradually learn to favor the advantageous decks, but people with orbital-frontal cortex damage persist in favoring the disadvantageous decks (see Bechara et al., 1997). The typical pattern of results is shown in Figure 5.1.[2] This figure shows the proportion of advantageous choices as a function of training for a group of 50 (fictitious) healthy controls and a second group of 10 (fictitious) brain-damaged individuals.

Poor performance by the patients with orbital-frontal cortex damage on these tasks has been attributed to the inability of these patients to anticipate the long-term negative consequences of disadvantageous choices. A problem arises, however, when attempting to theorize the exact causes of these decision-making deficits. Because decision making is produced by complex cognitive-motivational interactions, it is difficult to sort out and identify the specific cognitive processes responsible for the observed behavioral deficits. Performance on the task depends on multiple processes, including remembering

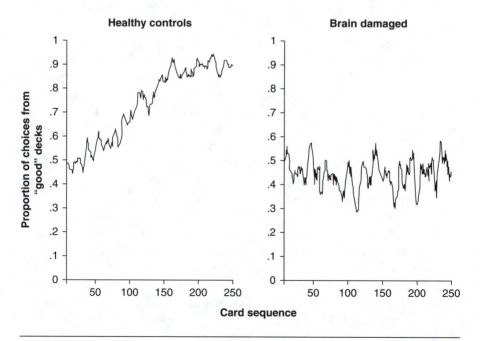

Figure 5.1   Fictitious Results for the Bechara Task

past outcomes, learning long-term contingencies, evaluating immediate wins relative to the longer-term losses, and finally choice mechanisms controlling the decision maker's impulsiveness and recklessness. Thus, the decision-making deficits exhibited by brain-damaged patients may result from individual differences on any combination of the above processes. Cognitive modeling is helpful for sorting this out and identifying which of these processes are mainly responsible for the observed deficits.

Three Cognitive Models

The first step in any type of cognitive modeling application is to compare and test competing models for the task. The best-fitting model from this competition is then selected and used to provide the basis for parameter estimation and interpretation of the results. Busemeyer and Stout (2002) proposed three different cognitive models for the Becahara task: One is called the strategy-switching model, the second is called the Bayesian utility model, and the third is called the expectancy valence model. These three models were selected for consideration according to several criteria. First, each of the models had received some general support from previous research in the decision-making literature. Second, all the models are simple and entail only a small number of free parameters, which are needed for the efficient statistical estimation of parameters. Third, the models differ fundamentally in terms of their basic processing assumptions. The purpose of the last criterion is to avoid simply testing small variations on a single idea and failing to contrast completely different ideas. The models use different assumptions and principles to describe how decision makers learn to choose from the decks across trials. The basic ideas are briefly described next.

One major approach to human decision making is based on the idea that decision makers employ simple heuristic strategies, and they learn to adapt or switch strategies depending on the decision environment and task demands (see Payne, Bettman, & Johnson, 1993). The strategy-switching model is an application of these ideas to the Bechara task. According to this model, the decision maker initially hypothesizes that the high immediate payoff decks are best, and thus starts with a tendency to choose from the disadvantageous decks. But after experiencing a series of large losses produced by the disadvantageous decks, he or she switches hypotheses and changes toward a tendency to choose more from the advantageous decks. According to this model, the brain-damaged patients fail to learn to deviate from the disadvantageous strategy.

Another major approach to human decision making is based on the idea that people use bounded rational decision strategies. That is, they attempt to optimize their decisions under constraints imposed by human information processing limitations. The Bayesian utility model is an application of these ideas to the Bechara task. According to this model, Bayes's rule is used to update prior estimates of the payoff probabilities into posterior probabilities. This updating is based on experience with the outcome observed by the choice made on each trial. Using these probability estimates, the expected utility of each deck is computed on each trial. Finally, the deck that maximizes expected utility is chosen on each trial. According to this model, brain-damaged patients choose from the disadvantageous decks because the utility of the gains are emphasized relative to the losses.

The third model has conceptual roots that date back to a classic learning and choice theory proposed by Tolman (1948), but these ideas have reemerged in more recent neural-network-type models of learning called reinforcement learning models (see Sutton & Barto, 1998). According to the expectancy valence model, the decision maker integrates the gains and losses experienced on each trial into a single affective reaction called a valence. Expectancies about the valence of a deck are learned from the trial-by-trial feedback by a simple adaptive learning mechanism. Finally, these expectancies serve as the inputs into a probabilistic choice mechanism that selects the choice on each trial. According to this model, poor performance by brain-damaged patients may be caused by failure to learn expectancies for each deck.

Definitions and Notation

Before describing these models in more detail, we need to introduce some notations. The two advantageous decks are labeled D_1 and D_2, and the two disadvantageous decks are labeled D_3 and D_4. The time index t is used to denote the trial number, that is, the total number of cards selected by a particular decision maker at some point during training. The deck chosen on trial t is denoted as $D(t)$, so that, for example, $D(t) = D_2$ if the second "advantageous" deck is chosen on trial t. The reward or gain received by choosing deck D is denoted $R(D)$, that is, $R(D) = \$50$ for "advantageous" choices, and $R(D) = \$100$ for disadvantageous choices. The loss received from choosing deck D on trial t is denoted $L(D(t))$. For example, if a "disadvantageous" deck is chosen on trial $t = 10$ and a loss of $\$1,250$ occurs, then $L(D(10)) = -\$1,250$.

Strategy-Switching Model

There are many ways to formulate a strategy-switching model, and the following is just one specific version. Figure 5.2 illustrates a version that is our formalization of Bechara and Damasio's suggestions about the learning process.

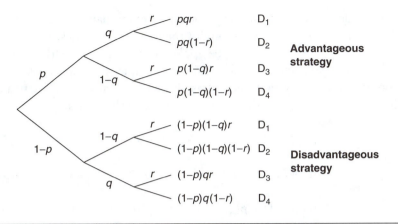

Figure 5.2   Probability Tree for the Strategy-Switching Model

On each trial, the decision maker first selects either the advantageous strategy with probability p or the disadvantageous strategy with probability $(1 - p)$. If the advantageous strategy is selected (move up on the first branch in Figure 5.2), then there is a high probability q of choosing one of the advantageous decks, and a low probability $(1 - q)$ of choosing one of the disadvantageous decks. If the disadvantageous strategy is selected (move down on the first branch in Figure 5.2), then there is a high probability q of choosing one of the disadvantageous decks, and a low probability $(1 - q)$ of choosing one of the advantageous decks. Finally, if one of the advantageous decks is chosen (move up on the second branch in Figure 5.2), the probability of choosing the low-frequency loss deck (deck D_1) is r, and the probability of choosing the high-frequency loss deck (deck D_2) is $(1 - r)$. Similarly, if one of the disadvantageous decks is chosen (move down on the second branch in Figure 5.2), the probability of choosing the low-frequency loss deck (deck D_3) is r, and the probability of choosing the high-frequency loss (deck D_4) is $(1 - r)$.

Consider the possibility of choosing deck D_1 on any particular trial. This particular choice can happen in two ways. On the one hand, the decision maker may select the advantageous strategy (with probability p) *and* choose one of the advantageous decks (with probability q) *and* choose the low-frequency deck (with probability r). The joint probability of these three independent events is pqr. On the other hand, the decision maker may select the disadvantageous strategy (with probability $1 - p$), but still choose one of the advantageous decks (with probability $1 - q$), and choose the low-frequency deck (with probability r). The joint probability of these three events is $(1 - p)(1 - q)r$.

Choosing deck D_1 is the union of these two mutually exclusive events, and the union probability is the sum of the joint probabilities: $pqr + (1 - p)$ $(1 - q)r$. This same principle can be applied to the other three decks to produce the other three choice probabilities. In sum, let the symbol $Pr[D_i|t + 1]$ denote the probability that deck D_i is chosen on trial $t + 1$. The strategy-switching model produces the following choice probabilities:

$$Pr[D_1|t + 1] = pqr + (1 - p)(1 - q)r \qquad (5.1a)$$

$$Pr[D_2|t + 1] = pq(1 - r) + (1 - p)(1 - q)(1 - r) \qquad (5.1b)$$

$$Pr[D_3|t + 1] = p(1 - q)r + (1 - p)qr \qquad (5.1c)$$

$$Pr[D_4|t + 1] = p(1 - q)(1 - r) + (1 - p)q(1 - r). \qquad (5.1d)$$

Bechara and Damasio (2005) suggested that the probability p of switching from a disadvantageous strategy to an advantageous strategy (the first branch of Figure 5.2) depends on the experience of the big losses from the disadvantageous decks. To formalize this idea, we will let the symbol $S(t)$ represent the sum of all the losses produced by the choosing from the disadvantageous decks up to and including t. The probability of switching to the advantageous strategy on trial $t + 1$ is assumed to be determined from this sum as follows:

$$p = \frac{e^{aS(t)}}{e^{aS(t)} + e^b}. \qquad (5.1e)$$

Equation (5.1e) is called the logistic distribution function, and it was selected because it provides a smooth S-shaped curve that is an increasing function of the loss sum $S(t)$. At the beginning of training, $S(0) = 0$, and the probability of choosing the disadvantageous strategy is at its maximum level. As training progresses and losses accumulate from the disadvantageous decks, the probability of switching to the advantageous strategy gradually increases. The logistic function has only two parameters: The parameter a determines how rapidly the function rises from its minimum to maximum level and the parameter b determines the initial probability of choosing the advantageous deck when the loss sum is zero.

In summary, the strategy-switching model requires the estimation of four free parameters from the data: the parameters a and b, which determine the probability for the first branch in Figure 5.2; the parameter q, which determines probability for the second branch of Figure 5.2; and the parameter r,

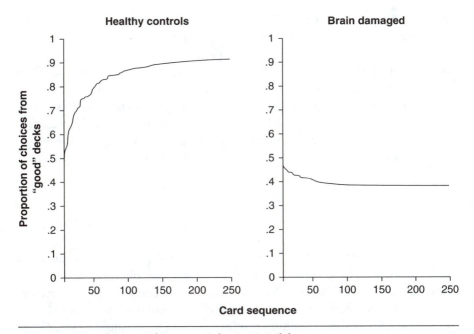

Figure 5.3   Predictions of Strategy Selection Model

which determines the probability in the third branch in Figure 5.2. Figure 5.3 illustrates the predictions generated by a computer simulation of this model when the parameters are set to $a = .1$, $b = .5$, $q = .92$, and $r = .5$ for the healthy controls and $a = -.05$, $b = .5$, $q = .62$, and $r = .5$ for the brain-damaged group.

It is important to note how the predictions change depending on the selection of parameter values. Both curves were generated from exactly the same model, and only the parameters were changed across the two groups. Nevertheless, the predicted patterns are dramatically different. If we used the same parameters for both groups, then of course we could not predict the group differences. Thus, the selection of parameter values is a crucial step for evaluating the models. This figure was generated using typical, but not necessarily the best, parameter values for each group.

Bayesian Utility Model

Once again, there are many ways to formulate the Bayesian utility model, but here we chose one of the simplest forms. This model assumes that the decision maker learns the probabilities of losing from each deck from experience. The decision maker also has to learn the winning value for each deck, but this is trivial for the Bechara task, because the same win value occurs on every trial for a given deck. Therefore, we will assume that the win values are learned almost immediately and focus on learning the losses.

The symbol $p_i(t)$ denotes the decision maker's estimate of the probability of a loss given that deck D_i is chosen on trial t. Bayesian learning is based on the idea that the decision maker integrates prior beliefs with experience. Before any experience, the decision maker is assumed to have a prior expectation about the probability of losing from each deck, which we represented by the ratio $1/n(0)$. After experience, Bayes's rule is used to update the expectations for the probability of losing, which implies[3] the following updating rule:

$$p_i(t) = \frac{f_i(t) + 1}{n_i(t) + n(0)} \, . \tag{5.2a}$$

In the above equation, $f_i(t)$ symbolizes the number of cards producing a loss experienced by choosing deck D_i up to and including trial t; $n_i(t)$ symbolizes the total number of trials that deck D_i was chosen up to and including trial t. The parameter $n(0)$ determines the initial estimate before any experience: Small values produce fast learning and large values produce slow learning. Note that this updating rule provides a computationally simple and intuitively reasonable model for learning the probabilities of each deck.

On each trial, the decision maker receives a gain and possibly a loss, denoted as $R(D(t))$ and $L(D(t))$ for trial t, where $L(D(t))$ may be zero on some trials and negative on other trials. The net payoff, denoted as $x(t)$, for trial t is the sum of the gains and losses, $x(t) = R(D(t)) + L(D(t))$. The decision maker's subjective evaluation of this net payoff, denoted as $u[x(t)]$, is called the utility of the net payoff. In general, the utility function is a possibly nonlinear but monotonically increasing function of the net payoff. A standard assumption made by decision theorists (see Luce, 2000) is to represent the utility function by a pair of power functions. Power functions are used because they are monotonic but flexible in shape, and they provide a simple way to represent different risk attitudes. This assumption will be used here as well, in which case the utilities of the gains and losses are computed as follows:

$$u[x] = x^a \text{ if } x > 0 \text{ and } u[x] = -|x|^b \text{ if } x < 0. \tag{5.2b}$$

The exponents of the power functions, $a > 0$ and $b > 0$, are parameters to be estimated from the choice data. Different exponents are allowed for the gains and the losses, which are used to represent individual differences in risk attitudes. Exponents between 0 and 1 produce risk aversion, and exponents greater than 1 produce risk seeking. For example, a person who is risk averse for gains and risk seeking for losses is represented by setting $a < 1$ and $b > 1$; another person who is risk averse for both gains and losses is represented by setting $a < 1$ and $b < 1$; a third person who is risk neutral for both gains and losses is represented by $a = 1$ and $b = 1$.

The choice on each trial is made on the basis of a comparison of the expected utilities estimated for each deck, and the deck producing the maximum expected utility is chosen. The expected utility of choosing deck D_i on trial t, denoted as $Eu[D_i|t]$, is computed as follows:

$$Eu[D_i|t] = [1 - p_i(t)] \cdot u[R(D_i)] + p_i(t) \cdot u[R(D_i)+L(D_i)]. \qquad (5.2c)$$

Finally, deck D_i is chosen on trial $t + 1$ if

$$Eu[D_i|t] = \max\{Eu[D_1|t], Eu[D_2|t], Eu[D_3|t], Eu[D_4|t]\}.$$

To allow for occasional random guessing, it is assumed that the decision maker chooses the maximum expected utility option on a trial with probability q and otherwise guesses randomly among the four decks with equal probability.

In sum, the Bayesian expected utility model requires the estimation of five parameters from the data: The first two parameters $f(0)$ and $n(0)$ determine the prior expectations for each deck, another two parameters a and b determine the shape of the utility function for gains and losses, and the last parameter q allows for some proportion of random guessing. Figure 5.4 illustrates the predictions generated by a computer simulation of this model when the parameters are set to $n(0) = 1$ for both groups, $a = 1$, $b = 1$, and $q = .15$ for the healthy control group, and $a = 1$, $b = .5$, and $q = .73$ for the brain-damaged group. Once again, the predictions change dramatically depending on the selection of parameter values.

At this point, one might be tempted to compare the predictions generated by the Bayesian utility model shown in Figure 5.4 with the data shown in Figure 5.1; and also compare the predictions generated by the strategy-switching model shown in Figure 5.3 with the data shown in Figure 5.1. The Bayesian model seems to learn too fast, and the strategy-switching model seems to approximate the rate of learning better for the healthy control group. But this comparison is unfair for the following reason. The parameters that we chose to illustrate these predictions were chosen arbitrarily and do not represent the best selections for fitting the data. For example, increasing $n(0)$ for the prior probability can slow down the learning rate for the Bayesian utility model. This is why it is crucial to find the best-fitting parameters for each model before conducting a model comparison.

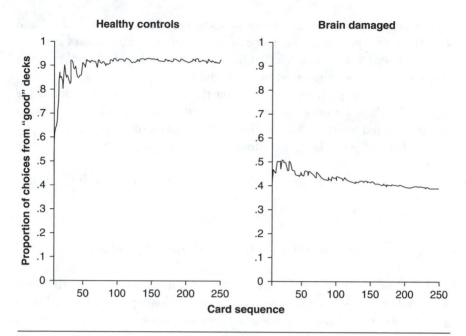

Figure 5.4   Predictions of the Bayesian Utility Model

Expectancy Valence Learning Model

According to this model, the gains and losses experienced after making a choice produce an affective reaction in the decision maker called a valence. The valence experienced after choosing deck D on trial t, denoted as $v(t)$, is represented as a weighted average of the gains and losses:

$$v(t) = [(1 - w) \cdot R(D(t)) + w \cdot L(D(t))]. \tag{5.3a}$$

The weight parameter, $0 < w < 1$, allows for the possibility that different amounts of attention or importance are given to the losses as compared with the gains.

The decision maker learns expectancies between the cues for each deck and the valences produced by choosing each deck. Define $x_i(t)$ as the cue that is used to indicate that deck D_i has been selected on trial t, where $x_i(t) = 1$ if $D(t) = D_i$ and 0 otherwise. Define $Ev[D_i|t]$ as the expected valence associated with deck D_i on trial t, and these expectancies start at 0 before training begins. The expectancies are updated after each choice, according to a delta learning rule (see Chapter 2):

$$Ev[D_i|t + 1] = Ev[D_i|t] + a \cdot \{v(t) - Ev[D_i|t]\} \cdot x_i(t),$$

where $0 < a < 1$ is the learning rate. This equation can be simplified in this case as follows. If deck D_i is chosen on trial t, then the expectancy for this deck is a weighted average of the previous expectancy and the most recently experienced valence:

$$Ev[D_i|t + 1] = (1 - a) \cdot Ev[D_i|t] + a \cdot v(t). \qquad (5.3b)$$

This learning model produces expectancies that are a weighted average of the past valences, and the weights decrease as a function of the lag (number of choices back in time) of the experience. Recently experienced valences receive more weight than more remotely experienced valences. In Equation 5.3b, the parameter a represents the updating rate ($0 < a < 1$). Large rates produce fast changes, strong recency effects, short associative memories, and rapid forgetting. Small rates produce slow changes, weak recency effects, long associative memories, and slow forgetting.

The choice made on each trial is a probabilistic function of the expectancies associated with each deck. The probability of choosing deck D_i is an increasing function of the expectancy for that deck, and a decreasing function of the expectancies for the other decks. This principle is captured by the following ratio of strengths rule for choice probabilities (see Chapter 2):

$$\Pr[D_i|t + 1] = \frac{e^{cEv[D_i|t]}}{\sum\limits_{j=1}^{4} e^{cEv[D_j|t]}}. \qquad (5.3c)$$

The parameter c in Equation 5.3c is called the sensitivity parameter. It determines the sensitivity of the choice probabilities to the expectancies. If the sensitivity parameter is set to zero, then choices are completely random and independent of the expectancies. As the sensitivity parameter increases in magnitude, the choices become more strongly dependent on the expectancies. For very large values of the sensitivity parameter, choice becomes deterministic and the deck producing the largest expectancy is chosen with certainty.

In sum, the expectancy valence model has three parameters. One is the weight w given to losses as opposed to gains; the second is the learning or updating rate parameter a, and the third is the parameter c that controls the sensitivity of choice to expectancies. Figure 5.5 illustrates the predictions generated by a computer simulation of this model when the parameters are set to $a = .05$, $w = .5$, and $c = .08$ for the healthy control group, and $a = .05$, $w = .25$, and $c = .01$ for the brain-damaged group. Of course, the predictions change depending on the selection of parameter values, and the methods for doing this are described in the next chapter.

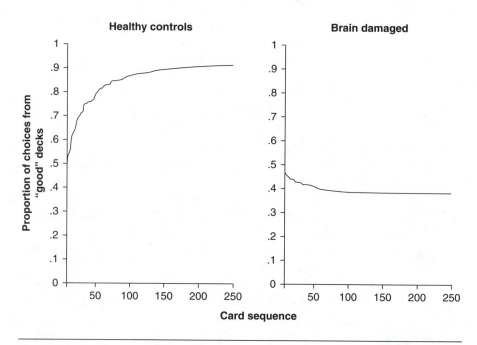

Figure 5.5   Predictions of the Expectancy Valence Model

Baseline Model

In addition to the above three cognitive models, a baseline model was used as a standard for comparison with each model. The baseline model is a statistical rather than a cognitive model, and it assumes that a multinomial process generates choices with constant probabilities across trials. The probability of choosing from deck D_1 is denoted p_1, the probability of choosing from deck D_2 is denoted p_2, the probability of choosing from deck D_3 is denoted p_3, and finally the probability of choosing from deck D_4 is $p_4 = 1 - (p_1 + p_2 + p_3)$. The baseline model has three parameters that must be estimated from the data, p_1, p_2, and p_3. Unlike the cognitive models, this model simply assumes that the choices are independently and identically distributed across trials. Thus, the baseline model simply predicts flat lines across training. Nevertheless, the baseline model is a strong competitor because it can perfectly reproduce the marginal choice probabilities, pooled across trials. Thus, a cognitive model can only perform better than this model if it succeeds in explaining how the choices depend on the sequence of trial-by-trial feedback.

Ad Hoc Assumptions

So far, we have presented four competing models (including the baseline model) for the Bechara task. In each case, we started with a general framework and constructed a specific model to correspond with each general framework. However, each framework was insufficient for specifying the general idea, and we had to add specific assumptions to complete the model. Considering the strategy-switching model, we assumed that the probability of selecting the lower-frequency loss deck r was the same regardless of whether the advantageous or disadvantageous decks were chosen. Considering the Bayesian utility model, we assumed that the utility function was a simple power function. Considering the expectancy valence model, we assumed that the initial expectancies were zero at the beginning of training. We could relax some of these assumptions by adding extra parameters, but then we run into the problem of trying to estimate too many parameters from the limited data that we have. Thus, the ad hoc assumptions help keep the models simple in terms of reducing the number of free parameters. The drawback is that we introduce arbitrary constraints on the model that do not directly follow from the general framework. If we reject one of these models, the failure may be due to the simplifying or ad hoc assumptions rather than a principle derived from the general framework.

Estimating the Parameters for Each Model

For this example application, all three decision models are able to reproduce the basic qualitative pattern of results shown in Figure 5.1, provided that we allow the model parameters to change across groups. At this point, the models need to be compared with respect to the accuracy of their quantitative predictions. However, the predictions depend on the specific values of the parameters, and we would not want to reject a model simply because we arbitrarily chose a poor set of parameters. Therefore, we first need to estimate the optimal parameters from each model.

Data Representation

The first step is to determine what data to use for estimating the parameters. In this example, we have data from a total of 60 participants and choices from 250 trials for each participant. Once again, we will use the individual data-fitting approach. Using this approach, we fit the trial-by-trial data from each individual separately. Table 5.1 is an example of a (fictitious) data set from one of the individuals in the control group. The first column indicates the trial number (or number of cards selected), the second column indicates the deck that was chosen by this individual on each trial, and the last two columns show the gains and losses incurred by the choice on each trial. Using this approach, we would estimate the parameters for this one individual using the data shown in the table. This procedure would be repeated independently for each participant, producing 60 different parameter estimates, one for each of the 60 participants.

Generating Predictions

Consider the problem of fitting the expectancy valence model to the data in Table 5.1. Recall that this model has three parameters: the weight w, the updating rate a, and the sensitivity θ. Let us make an arbitrary selection of

Table 5.1   Data Set From One (Fictitious) Participant on the Bechara Gambling Task

Trial	Deck	Gain	Loss	Prediction
1	4	100	0	.25
2	4	100	0	.29
3	2	50	0	.22
4	1	50	0	.22
5	2	50	0	.24
6	2	50	0	.25
7	1	50	50	.23
8	1	50	0	.22
9	4	100	1,250	.29
10	3	100	350	.27
...				
249	1	50	50	.56
250	1	50	50	.54

parameter values to illustrate how to calculate predictions from the model. In particular, let us begin by simply setting $a = .05$, $w = .5$, and $c = .08$. This may not be the best choice of parameters, but we will wait until later to see how to find the best parameters.

We insert the three parameter values $a = .05$, $w = .5$, and $c = .08$ into Equations 5.3a, 5.3b, and 5.3c above to generate the predictions for each trial for the expectancy valence model. This produces the column of predictions shown in the last column of Table 5.1. Consider the first row in Table 5.1, and note that Deck 4 was chosen on the first trial. Consequently, we need to compute the probability of obtaining this observation from the model. Reviewing Equation 5.3c, the probability that Deck 4 is chosen at the beginning of the first trial is denoted $Pr[D_4|t = 1]$, and we see from the right-hand side of the equation that this requires determining the expectancies before any feedback on the first trial, that is, $Ev[D_i|t = 0]$ for all four decks. But it is assumed that the expectancy for each deck equals zero before any training so that $Ev[D_i|t = 0] = 0$ for all four decks. Inserting these values into the right-hand side of Equation 5.3c produces $e^0/4e^0 = ¼ = .25$ for each deck (recall that $e^0 = 1$), which is the prediction shown on the first trial in Table 5.1.

Now consider the second row in Table 5.1, and note that Deck 4 was chosen again on the second trial. Consequently, we need to compute the probability of this observation from the model, that is, $Pr[D_4|t = 2]$. To do this computation, we first need to compute the expectancies $Ev[D_i|t = 1]$ for each deck after the first trial. Deck 4 was chosen on the first trial, and so the expectancies for Decks 1, 2, and 3 remain unchanged, and stay at the previous values, $Ev[D_i|t = 1] = Ev[D_i|t = 0] = 0$, for $i = 1, 2,$ and 3. The expectancy for Deck 4 was changed by the valence, $v(1)$, experienced on the first trial. According to Equation 5.3a, the valence for the first trial, $v(1)$, is a weighted average of the gain of 100 and loss of zero, and with the weight set equal to $w = .50$, this produces $v(1) = (.5)100 + (.5)0 = 50$. Inserting this valence into Equation 5.3b, and using the learning rate $a = .05$, produces the new expectancy for Deck 4 after Trial 1, $Ev[D_4|t = 1] = (.95)Ev[D_4|t = 0] + (.05)v(1) = (.95)(0) + (.05)(50) = 2.5$. Finally, inserting the four expectancies $(0, 0, 0, 2.5)$ back into Equation 5.3c, and setting the sensitivity to $c = .08$, produces a choice probability for Deck 4 on Trial 2 equal to

$$e^{(.08)(2.5)}/[e^{(.08)(2.5)} + 3e^0] = 2.7183^{(.20)}/[2.7183^{(.20)} + 3] = .289,$$

which was rounded off to .29 in Table 5.1.

Let us do one more trial in detail. Now consider the third row in Table 5.1, and note that Deck 2 was chosen on the third trial. Consequently, we need to compute the probability of this observation from the model, that is, $Pr[D_2|t = 3]$.

To do this computation, we first need to compute the expectancies $Ev[D_i|t = 2]$ for each deck after the second trial. Deck 4 was chosen on the second trial, and so the expectancies for Decks 1, 2, and 3 remain unchanged, and stay at the previous values, $Ev[D_i|t = 2] = Ev[D_i|t = 1] = 0$, for $i = 1$, 2, and 3. The expectancy for Deck 4 was changed by the valence $v(2)$ experienced on the second trial. Inserting the payoffs for Deck 4 on Trial 2 into Equation 5.3a produces the valence for the second trial $v(2)$; this equals $v(2) = (.5)100 + (.5)0 = 50$. Inserting this valence into Equation 5.3b and using the learning rate $a = .05$ produces the new expectancy for Deck 4 after Trial 1, $Ev[D_4|t = 2] = (.95)Ev[D_4|t = 1] + (.05)v(2) = (.95)(2.5) + (.05)(50) = 2.375 + 2.5 = 4.875$. Finally, inserting the four values (0, 0, 0, 4.875) for the four expectancies after Trial 1 back into Equation 5.3c, and setting the sensitivity to $c = .08$, produces a choice probability for Deck 2 on Trial 3 equal to

$$e^{(0)}/[e^{(.08)(4.875)} + 3e^0] = 1/[2.7183^{(.39)} + 3] = .2233,$$

which was rounded off to .22 in Table 5.1.

The remaining predictions in Table 5.1 were computed in a similar manner for each time step. Actually, this was done by a computer program that uses a loop to compute the predictions for each trial, similar to the program shown in Figure 5.6. In this program, the dummy variable x1(t) is set to one if Deck 1 was chosen on trial t, otherwise zero; the dummy variable x2 was set to one if Deck 2 was chosen on trial t, and otherwise zero; similarly for dummy variables x3 and x4. The variables Win(t) and Loss(t) store the wins and losses from each trial. Programs such as this make it very easy to compute the model predictions.

```
Ev1=0; Ev2=0; Ev3=0; Ev4=0;
P1(1)=.25; P2(1)=.25; P3(1)=.25; P4(1)=.25;
For t = 1 to 250
    v  = (1-w)*Win(t)-w*Loss(t);
    Ev1 = (1-x1(t))*Ev1 + x1(t)*((1-a)*Ev1 + a*v );
    Ev2 = (1-x2(t))*Ev2 + x2(t)*((1-a)*Ev2 + a*v);
    Ev3 = (1-x3(t))*Ev3 + x3(t)*((1-a)*Ev3 + a*v);
    Ev4 = (1-x4(t))*Ev4 + x4(t)*((1-a)*Ev4 + a*v);
    S1 = exp(Ev1*c);  S2 = exp(Ev2*c);
    S3 = exp(Ev3*c);  S4 = exp(Ev4*c);
    Sum = S1+S2+S3+S4;
    P1(t+1) = S1/Sum; P2(t+1) = S2/Sum;
    P3(t+1) = S3/Sum; P4(t+1) = S4/Sum;
End
```

Figure 5.6   Program for Computing Expectancy Valence Model Predictions

The Likelihood Function

The predictions shown in Table 5.1 were generated by using the parameter values $a = .05$, $w = .5$, and $c = .08$. Now we need to evaluate how accurately the model fits the data using these parameter values. The next step is to formulate a measure of the fit between the model predictions and the data for a given set of parameter values.

There are several different objectives that we could use to measure the fit to the data, but here we will focus on what is called the likelihood objective (see Chapter 3). Intuitively, we compute the likelihood that the model would generate the observed data, for a given model and a fixed set of parameter values. Referring to Table 5.1, the likelihood, denoted as L, is computed by multiplying all the conditional probabilities under the predicted column:

$$L = (.25)(.29)(.22)(.22)(.24)(.25)(.23)(.22)(.29)(.27) \ldots (.56)(.54).$$

As you might expect, the product of all these probabilities turns out to be a very small number, and so it is more convenient to work on the log scale by taking the logarithm of the product, which is called the log likelihood. (Recall that the natural log of a product equals the sum of the logs.) In this case, we obtain

$$\ln(L) = \ln(.25) + \ln(.29) + \ln(.22) + \ln(.22) +$$
$$\ln(.24) + \ln(.25) + \ln(.23) + \ln(.22) + \ln(.29) +$$
$$\ln(.27) + \ldots + \ln(.56) + \ln(.54) = -262.86.$$

The log likelihood is negative because the log of a proportion is negative. It is usually converted into a badness-of-fit statistic, called G^2, by multiplying the log likelihood with (-2), which yields in this case $G^2 = 525.72$ (the reason for multiplying by 2 will become evident later when we perform model comparisons). Note that both the likelihood and the log likelihood are measures of goodness of fit, or in other words, greater likelihoods or log likelihoods imply better fits. However, the sign is reversed for G^2, and so G^2 is a measure of badness of fit—larger G^2 statistics imply worse fits.

Parameter Optimization

Recall that the predictions shown in Table 5.1 were generated from the expectancy valence model using the parameter values $a = .05$, $w = .5$, and $c = .08$. These parameters yielded $G^2 = 525.72$. If we change to a slightly different set of parameter values, say $a = .04$, $w = .5$, and $c = .08$, then the

G^2 statistic decreases slightly to a better value, $G^2 = 514.91$; alternatively, if we change the parameters slightly again to even another set, say $a = .06$, $w = .5$, and $c = .08$, then G^2 increases to a slightly worse value, $G^2 = 538.71$. In short, our lack-of-fit measure G^2 changes as a function of the three parameters. What we need to do at this point is search for the parameters that produce the smallest lack-of-fit measure for G^2. This is a fairly complex search problem, and there is no general solution. Highly technical optimization programs available in many mathematical programming languages such as GAUSS, Mathematica, MATLAB, R program, or SAS are available for conducting the search for the optimal parameters (see Chapter 3). A steepest-descent type of algorithm (a modified Newton-Raphson algorithm) was used to estimate the parameters that maximized the likelihood (minimized G^2) for each model separately for each individual.

Quantitative Comparison of the Models

One of the most important goals of science is to construct theories that are predictive—those that explain previous results and predict new findings. Another important goal of science is to construct theories that are parsimonious—those that entail few ad hoc assumptions and few parameters. On the one hand, if two theories are equally accurate for prediction, but one theory requires fewer parameters, then the simpler and more parsimonious theory is preferred. On the other hand, if two theories are equally complex, but one makes more accurate predictions, then the more accurate model is preferred. Unfortunately, accuracy and parsimony usually trade off, so that increasing one decreases the other. So we are often confronted with a situation where one model is both more complex and more accurate, making it difficult to decide whether the gain in accuracy offsets the loss in parsimony. This makes it difficult to compare models that differ in the number of free parameters.

Chi-Square Tests

If two major conditions are satisfied, then we can perform a classic statistical significance test between two cognitive models. The first condition is that one of the models must be nested within the other model, that is, one of the models is a restricted case of the other more general model. The more general model can reproduce any set of predictions that can be generated by the restricted model. In this case, the more general model must produce a lack of fit that is equal or better than the restricted model. For example, we could compare a three-parameter expectancy valence model (with parameters a, w, and c all free) with a two-parameter expectancy valence model, which is restricted by constraining the weight parameter to assign equal attention to gains and losses (a and c are free but $w = .50$). The second condition is that we measure lack of fit by using the likelihood objective: $G_m^2 = -2\ln(L_m)$, where L_m represents the likelihood of the data given that Model m generated the data, and we use the maximum-likelihood parameter estimates to compute the likelihood (m is just an index used to label each model).

Given that these two conditions are satisfied (as well as some other technical assumptions, see Rao, 1965, pp. 350–351), then a chi-square test can be performed by computing the difference ($G_{\text{restircted}}^2 - G_{\text{general}}^2$). The null hypothesis states that the population or true parameters of the general model do satisfy the constraints of the restricted model (e.g., the extra parameters are truly zero). If the null hypothesis is correct, then difference in G^2 will be approximately chi-square distributed with degrees of freedom equal to the number of restrictions (i.e., the difference in the number of free parameters between the two models). This is a large sample test and so the approximation to a chi-square distribution improves as the sample size increases. Thus, we evaluate the p value, $p = \Pr[\chi^2 > \text{observed difference}|H_0]$, which is the probability of observing a chi-square value as large as the observed difference given that the null hypothesis is correct. If p is less than some significance level, say $\alpha = .05$, then we reject the null hypothesis, that is, we reject the restricted model in favor of the general model. Another way to do this test is to compare the observed difference in G^2 with a cutoff read from a chi-square table using the degrees of freedom equal to the difference in number of free parameters, and using the specified significance level (e.g., $\alpha = .05$). If the difference in G^2 exceeds the chi-square table cutoff, then we reject the null hypothesis, that is, we reject the restricted model and select the more general model. Alternatively, if the difference in G^2 fails to exceed the cutoff, then we retain the null hypothesis, that is, we select the restricted model. This is essentially the same principle for model selection that is used to test coefficients in a multiple regression model or used to test treatment effects in an analysis of variance model.

As an example, consider once again the data from subject, shown in Table 3.1 of Chapter 3. We compare the three-parameter expectancy valence model to the two-parameter version in which the weight has been fixed at $w = .50$. The G^2 produced by the three-parameter model is 508.74, and the G^2 produced by the two-parameter model is 509.47, so the difference is (509.47 − 508.74) = 0.73. These two models differ by only one parameter, so we refer to the chi-square table using $df = 1$ and $\alpha = .05$, to find the cutoff equal to 1.8. Finally, we note that the difference in G^2, 0.73, is less than the cutoff, and so we retain the null hypothesis, that is, we retain the simple two-parameter model. In other words, we conclude that this individual placed equal attention weight on the gains and losses.

There are several problems in this method of model comparison (Myung, 2000). First of all, the most interesting comparisons are between models that are not nested. For example, none of the three cognitive models described in this chapter are nested. Second, even if the models are nested, the power of the test increases as the sample size increases, and so we may reject the null hypothesis even though there may be no practical or scientifically meaningful difference between the two models. In short, the significance test simply tells us whether or not we have a sufficiently large sample size to reject the simpler model in favor of the more complex model.

Bayesian Model Comparison

A Bayesian approach to model comparison is based on the principle of choosing the model that is most likely to be the correct model given the sample data evidence. To compare any pair of models, we can determine the ratio of the two probabilities

$$\frac{\Pr[\text{Model A}|\text{data}]}{\Pr[\text{Model B}|\text{data}]} = \frac{\Pr[\text{Model A}]}{\Pr[\text{Model B}]} \cdot \frac{\Pr[\text{data}|\text{Model A}]}{\Pr[\text{data}|\text{Model B}]}$$
$$= \text{priors} \cdot \text{Bayes factor}$$

If we wish to ignore the prior odds for each model, we can set them equal, and just concentrate on what is called the Bayes factor, which is the ratio of the evidence for each model. For large sample sizes, the natural log of the Bayes factor can be approximated by a statistic called the Bayesian information criterion or BIC for short (also known as the Schwarz criterion; see the appendix to this chapter for more details). The BIC index for comparing two models is defined as follows (the difference is arranged so that positive values indicate that A is more likely than B):

$$2 \cdot \text{BIC}_{AB} = (G_B^2 - G_A^2) - (k_A - k_B) \cdot \ln(N), \tag{5.4a}$$

where k_A is the number of free parameters for Model A, and k_B is the number of free parameters in Model B, and N is the number of observations used to compute the likelihood. BIC provides a measure of the evidence for Model A as compared with Model B. If BIC_{AB} is positive, then we choose A over B, and if it is negative, we choose B over A. When there are more than two models to consider, it is more convenient to compute the index BIC_m separately for each model as follows:

$$2 \cdot BIC_m = G_m^2 + k_m \cdot \ln(N). \qquad (5.4b)$$

Here, we choose the model producing the smaller BIC_m. Note that $BIC_{AB} = (BIC_B - BIC_A)$ and so either way we get the same answer.[4]

The first term in Equation 5.4a represents the improvement in predictive accuracy obtained by using Model A as compared with Model B. The second term represents a penalty for the number of free parameters required by Model A as compared with Model B. Thus, the BIC criterion provides a simple formula for balancing accuracy and parsimony.

The BIC index can be converted back into the Bayes factor by the following simple calculation:

$$\text{Bayes factor} = e^{BIC_{AB}} = \frac{\Pr[\text{data}|\text{Model A}]}{\Pr[\text{data}|\text{Model B}]}. \qquad (5.4c)$$

The Jeffrey rating scale of evidence can be used to interpret this ratio (see Wasserman, 2000). Assume that we arrange the ratio so that the most likely model is in the numerator, and the ratio is greater than or equal to 1. Then, Bayes factors ranging from 1 to 3 provide weak evidence, those ranging from 3 to 10 provide moderate evidence, and those greater than 10 provide strong evidence for the numerator model over the denominator model.

Consider the example discussed earlier, where we compared the three-parameter expectancy valence model with the two-parameter model with the weight fixed at .50, using the data shown in Table 5.1. Recall that earlier we found that in this case $(G_B^2 - G_A^2) = 0.73$. The difference in parameters is one, and so the penalty for the three-parameter model is one times the natural log of $N = 250$, which is $\ln(250) = 5.215$. Using this penalty, we obtain $2 \cdot BIC_{32} = .73 - 5.215 = -4.4825$, or $BIC_{32} = -2.2413$, and because this is negative, we choose the simpler two-parameter model. Finally, let us compute the Bayes factor, that is, the odds favoring the three-parameter model over the two-parameter model. To do this, we take the exponential of BIC_{32}, which gives us $e^{-2.2413} = .1063$. To interpret this evidence, it may be easier to reconsider the Bayes factor in terms of evidence favoring the two-parameter model over the three-parameter model, that is, the reciprocal of the previous factor, and this equals $1/(.1063) = 9.4051$. This means that the odds are nine times greater for the two-parameter model, which is considered moderate evidence against the three-parameter model (according to the Jeffrey rating scale of evidence).

There are several advantages for using the BIC method as compared with the chi-square test method. First, the BIC index can be used to compare non-nested models that differ with respect to the number of parameters. Second, the BIC index is derived from a rational set of assumptions (Bayesian probability theory). Third, the BIC index provides a simple way to evaluate models with respect to the two main criteria for model selection: accuracy and parsimony.

Another approach to model selection is the Akaike information criterion or AIC (see Bozdogan, 2000, for a review). The AIC method was designed to select the model that generates a distribution that is closest to the true distribution (see the appendix to this chapter for more details). Although it is based on different principles, under large sample sizes, it leads to a formula that is closely related to the BIC:

$$\mathrm{AIC}_m = G_m^2 + 2 \cdot k_m. \tag{5.5}$$

The AIC index is interpreted as an estimate of the discrepancy between a model and the true generating process, and so we choose the model that has the minimum AIC. Note that the only difference between the AIC and the BIC (besides the signs of the indices) is the penalty term for the number of parameters: For $N > 7$, the penalty is larger for the Bayesian index. A third approach to model selection comes from computer science. It is based on the principle of choosing the model that describes the data with the minimum description length (see Grunwald, 2000). Interestingly, this principle leads to a formula that is linearly related to the BIC under large sample sizes, and so we will just refer to the BIC index here.

Cross-Validation and Generalization Methods

The BIC and AIC indices are based on evaluating models using all the available data. An alternative way is to employ a two-stage approach: The first stage, called the calibration stage, uses only part of the data to estimate parameters; the second stage, called the test stage, uses another part of the data for model testing. In this case, during the test stage, the models must make new predictions for data points that were not used to estimate parameters. The predictive accuracies of the model are evaluated only in the second stage, where all models are making new predictions for new data. This approach can be used to evaluate models that are non-nested and differ according to the number of parameters. There are two ways to partition the data between calibration and test sets: One is called the cross-validation method (see Brown, 2000) and the other is called the generalization method (see Busemeyer & Wang, 2000).

According to the cross-validation method, the complete data set containing N data points is *randomly* divided into two samples (they do not have to be of the same size). For example, considering the data shown in Table 5.1, we could randomly sample 150 of the 250 trials for the calibration sample (e.g., we could pick trials 71, 163, 13, 245, . . . , etc.), and the remaining 100 trials are held back for the test stage. The first calibration sample is used to estimate the parameters of each model. For example, we could find the parameters that compute the maximum likelihood of the observations on the 150 trials in the calibration data set. Then these same parameters are used to make predictions for the second sample. For example, G^2 can be computed for each model on the remaining 100 trials of data from the test data set. But note that no parameters are estimated during the testing stage. We simply determine how well the model performs using the parameters obtained from the calibration stage. Finally, we choose the model that produces the most accurate predictions (e.g., the lowest G^2) during the test stage. The whole process can be repeated many times by new random divisions of calibration and test data sets, producing distribution of G^2 for each model.

The generalization test differs from cross-validation in the way that the data set is divided into calibration and test data sets. Rather than randomly dividing the data set into two parts, the data are systematically divided into two parts. The sampling for the calibration data set is restricted to sampling only from specified experimental conditions, and the sampling for the test data set is restricted to exclusively new experimental conditions. For example, in an experiment that manipulates stimulus intensity, we could restrict the calibration stage to the intermediate stimulus intensities, and restrict the test to the extrapolation regions of extreme lower and extreme upper stimulus intensities. Note that a cross-validation test would not be restricted from any regions of intensity and would allow observations to be included from any stimulus intensity conditions. As another example, consider once again the data shown in Table 5.1. We could use early training conditions (e.g., the first 150 trials) to estimate the model parameters, and then see how well the models extrapolate to the later training conditions (the last 100 trials). The generalization test will be illustrated below when we present a comparison of models using all the 60 participants.

Multiple Methods

Of course, there is nothing that prevents one from using any combination of the above model comparison methods.[5] By using the BIC method on all the data, one obtains more accurate parameter estimates, and one can see how well each model can fit the entire data set. By using the cross-validation or generalization test, the parameters are not estimated as well, but we can examine how well the models predict brand new data points that were not fit to the model. The two approaches complement each other. In fact, for large sample sizes, some of the methods tend toward the same conclusions. In particular, for large sample sizes, the G^2 statistics from the test stage of cross-validation will produce the same result as the AIC index (see Brown, 2000). However, this is not true for the generalization test.

BIC Application

Recall that we wish to compare the three cognitive models: the strategy-switching model with four free parameters, the Bayesian utility model with four free parameters, and the expectancy valence model with three free parameters. We also wish to compare each of these cognitive models with a baseline model, which has three free parameters. Note that these models are not nested and they differ in terms of number of parameters.

The BIC method was used to compare the models using all 60 (fictitious) participants and all 250 trials, which generated Figure 5.1. The first step was to estimate the parameters using maximum likelihood for each of the 60 participants and for each model. Then, we computed differences in G^2 between each cognitive model and the baseline model, separately for each of the 60 participants. Finally, we computed the BIC_m index for each of the 60 participants (Equation 5.4b). For example, $BIC_{strategy-switch}$ for the strategy-switching model was computed as follows: the median G^2 difference between the strategy-switching model and the baseline model equals 34.62; the difference in number of parameters between these two models equals $4 - 3 = 1$; the sample size for each person equals 250; and so the $2 \times BIC_{strategy-switch} = 34.62 - 1 \cdot \ln(250) = 34.62 - 5.52 = 29.10$, which is the value shown in the first row and column of the table.

The summary results are shown in Table 5.2. The first column indicates the model, the second column indicates the number of free parameters, the third column shows the median G^2 improvement of each cognitive model over the baseline model, the fourth column shows the mean for these same-fit statistics, the fifth column shows the number of participants for which the cognitive model fit better than the baseline model, and the last column shows the median BIC. As can be seen in this table, the Bayesian utility model clearly performed far below the other two cognitive models. The expectancy valence model performed better than the strategy-switching model on all aspects except the percent positive improvement, for which there is no real difference. We also computed the percentage of participants for which the BIC for the expectancy valence model exceeded the BIC for the

Table 5.2   Model Comparisons Based on All Data

Model	Number of Parameters	Median G^2 Improvement Over Baseline	Mean G^2 Improvement Over Baseline	Percent Positive Improvement	Median $2 \cdot BIC$ Comparison
Strategy-switching	4	34.62	38.77	.93	29.10
Bayesian utility	4	−15.20	−20.28	.18	−20.20
Expectancy valence	3	41.84	39.29	.92	41.84

NOTE: According to the BIC index, the expectancy valence model produced a better fit than the strategy-switching model for 68% of the participants. According to a z test, this proportion is significantly greater than .50 ($z = 2.84$, $p < .01$).

strategy-switching model. The result was 68%, which is significantly different from .50, according to a sign test. Thus, if we were to choose one model, then we would conclude that the expectancy valence model is the best choice from this set.

Generalization Criterion Application

Although the fits for the expectancy valence model were better than for the strategy-switching model according to the BIC criterion, the difference was not so convincing. Therefore, these two models were compared again using the generalization criterion. We divided each participant's data set into two parts: The first 150 trials were used for the calibration data set and the last 100 trials were used for the generalization test. The parameters were estimated from the calibration stage using maximum likelihood. Then these same parameters were used to make new predictions for the test stage. Only the controls were used for this test, because these data, being less noisy, provided a stronger discrimination between the two models.

The summary results for the G^2 improvement of each model over the baseline model results are shown in Table 5.3. For the calibration stage, the strategy-switching model (with four parameters) fits slightly better in terms of G^2 than the expectancy valence model (with three parameters); however, there is almost no difference with respect to the BIC for the calibration stage. Considering the crucial generalization test stage, the expectancy valence model clearly predicted better than the strategy-switching model, and this was true for each of the 50 controls.

Table 5.3   Generalization Test Results

Model	Number of Parameters	Mean Calibration G^2 Improvement	Mean Calibration BIC	Mean Generalization G^2 Improvement	Percent Better Generalization
Strategy-switching	4	21.30	16.29	7.62	0
Expectancy valence	3	16.44	16.44	38.10	100

Figure 5.7 illustrates the predictions of the two models, averaged across the 50 control participants. The predictions generated by the expectancy valence model are shown on the left, and the predictions for the strategy-switching model are shown on the right. The predictions for the first 150 trials represent the fit to the calibration stage, and the predictions for the last 100 trials represent the extrapolation of each model to these new training conditions. As can be seen in this figure, the expectancy valence model does much better extrapolating to the last 100 trials of training.

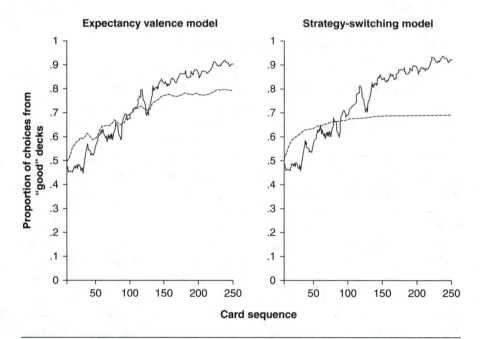

Figure 5.7   Predictions From Each Model for the Generalization Test

To complete our analysis, Figure 5.8 shows the predictions of the expectancy valence model when the parameters were fit to all 250 trials. As can be seen by comparing this to Figure 5.7, the model provides a much better fit to the last 100 trials when it is fit to all the data rather than attempting to predict this from the past.

In summary, two different approaches were used to compare the models. One was based on fitting each model to all the data and comparing the models with respect to a Bayesian information criterion. The second was based on a generalization test that compared each model in terms of its ability to predict brand new data points that were not fit by the parameters. Both methods led to the same conclusion in this example, but this is not always the case (see, e.g., Busemeyer & Wang, 2000). In case the two methods disagree, one can always design new experiments that seek for stronger evidence.

Interpreting Parameters

Now we will examine the parameter estimates produced by the best of the three cognitive models—the expectancy valence model. A constrained

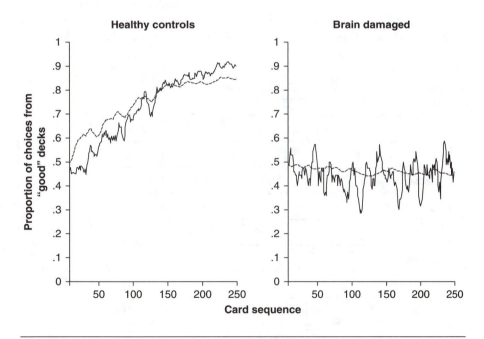

Figure 5.8   Predictions of the Expectancy Valence Model When Fit to All 250 Trials

Newton-Raphson optimization program was used to find the maximum-likelihood estimates for each of the 60 participants. The results are shown in Table 5.4. (Recall, however, that this is simulated data and not real.) The first block of rows in the table shows the summary results for the 50 control participants, and the second block of rows shows the results for the 10 brain-damaged participants. The three rows within a block show the median, mean, and standard deviations of the statistics separately for each group. The first column shows the results for the G^2 statistic (here we did not subtract out the baseline), the second column shows the results for the update parameter a, the third column shows the results for the weight parameter w, the fourth column shows the results for the sensitivity parameter c, and the last column indicates the sample size.

The first thing to note is that the model fits the control participants better than the brain-damaged participants. But the more important question concerns the differences between the groups with respect to the parameters. Any one of the three parameters may be responsible for the differences in performance observed in Figure 5.1.

First, consider the update rate parameter. There are 50 participants in the control group, and for this group, the mean and median are about the same, and the standard deviation is relatively small. There are only 10 brain-damaged participants, and for the group, the mean greatly exceeds the median, indicating a large positive skew in the distribution. Also, the variance is much larger for the brain-damaged group. If we focus on the median, which is less

Table 5.4   Expectancy-Valence Model Results

	G^2	Update	Weight	Sensitivity	N
Group 1					
Median	578	.028	.487	.096	50
Mean	576	.035	.488	.082	50
SD	42	.020	.098	.028	50
Group 2					
Median	687	.078	.257	.011	10
Mean	686	.300	.264	.013	10
SD	7	.406	.294	.009	10

sensitive to outliers, then we see that the update rate was slightly larger for the brain-damaged group, indicating that they were more sensitive to recent outcomes and tended to forget past events more rapidly than the controls.

Now we turn to the attention weight parameter. The median and means closely agree, suggesting that the distributions are not very skewed for this parameter. The standard deviation is relatively small for the control group, but it is much larger for the brain-damaged group. If we focus on the medians, we see that the attention weight to losses was much larger for the control group as compared with the brain-damaged group.

Finally, consider the sensitivity parameter. The means and medians closely agree and the standard deviations are relatively small for both groups. The median value for the control group was larger than the median for the brain-damaged group, indicating that the brain-damaged group responded more randomly in their choices as compared with the controls.

At this point, we could conduct statistical tests, such as t tests, or nonparametric tests, to determine which of the parameters produce statistically significant group differences. We could also correlate these parameter estimates with other individual difference measures such as IQ scores, memory test scores, or personality test scores.

Conclusion

One of the important contributions of cognitive modeling is that the parameter estimates provide theoretically based individual difference measures of the component cognitive processes. The performance that we observe in any cognitive task is the result of complex and dynamic interactions among many underlying cognitive processes. For example, the performance deficit observed in brain-damaged patients on the Bechara task may have resulted from motivational, learning, or decision processes, and it is impossible to isolate or specify these contributions without a cognitive modeling analysis. Signal detection theory (Green & Swets, 1966) was perhaps the first and most important application of this idea: It provided a theoretical basis for estimating discriminability and bias parameters from Hit and False Alarm choice probabilities. More recently, however, several new applications of cognitive modeling to individual difference assessment have appeared in the literature in aging and clinical psychology (see, e.g., Batchelder, 1998; Busemeyer & Stout, 2002; Maddox & Filoteo, 2001; Ratcliff, Thaper, & McKoon, 2001). All these applications differ from intelligence or personality assessment methods because the latter are founded on psychometric rather than cognitive theory.

Appendix

This appendix covers several topics concerning model selection criteria in more detail. First, we present an example to illustrate the importance of considering a balance between accuracy and parsimony when selecting a model. Then, we discuss principles underlying the several model selection criteria that are designed to achieve this balance.

Parsimony and Generalization

To illustrate the potential advantages of using simple rather than complex models, consider the hypothetical example shown in Figure A5.1 (see Myung, 2000). The circles shown in the figure represent the brightness judgments on a 0 to 100 rating scale as a function of stimulus intensity. The data were generated by the model labeled *true*, where the variable t in the equation represents the stimulus intensity (t ranges from 0 to 10), J represents the judged brightness, and ε is a normally distributed error with mean zero and standard deviation 2.

$$J = 10 + 70/[1 + e^{-(1.5) \cdot (t-5)}] + \varepsilon, \qquad \text{(True model)}$$

$$J = 100/[1 + e^{-c \cdot (t-b)}] + \varepsilon. \qquad \text{(Model A: Logistic)}$$

$$J = b_0 t^0 + b_1 t^1 + b_2 t^2 + \ldots + b_{10} t^{10} + \varepsilon. \quad \text{(Model B: Polynomial)}$$

A total of $n = 1,000$ samples were generated from the true model for each of the 10 stimulus intensities, and so the grand total sample size is $N = 11 \cdot 1,000 = 11,000$. The logistic model is almost the same form as the true model, except that the minimum and maximum of the function differs. The minimum and maximum is restricted to rating scales within 20 to 80 for the true model, as if participants did not want to use the extreme values of the scales. The range for the logistic model is 0 to 100, which represents the physical lower and upper limits of the rating scale. The predictions of the logistic model are restricted to an increasing S-shaped function. The polynomial model is a very flexible model that can fit a wide variety of functional relations.

Consider comparing a logistic with a polynomial model for explaining the observed results. The logistic model has only two parameters c and b, but the polynomial model has eight parameters. Suppose we fit both models to the intermediate stimulus intensity values 1 through 9, and leave the two extreme intensities for a generalization test. First, we estimate the parameters that minimize the sum of squared prediction errors for the nine intermediate

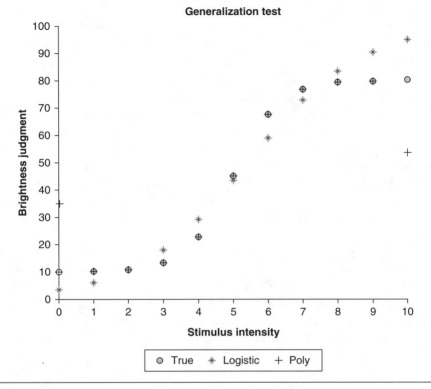

Figure A5.1   Comparison of Simple and Complex Models

intensities. From these estimates, we find that the polynomial fits 9.27 times better than the logistic model on the nine intermediate intensities ($SSE_P/N =$ 3.992 for polynomial, $SSE_L/N = 37.00$ for logistic). As seen in Figure A5.1, the polynomial model almost perfectly reproduces the observed data for the intermediate stimulus values, but the logistic model misses in several locations.

Using these same parameters, now we see which model makes the best prediction for the extreme stimulus intensities. As can be seen in Figure A5.1, the polynomial is way far off the mark, producing outrageous predictions of a large increase at the low extreme and a large decrease at the upper extreme. The logistic model still makes errors at the extremes, but the predictions remain in the correct direction, and the sizes of the errors are much smaller than those produced by the polynomial. To obtain a quantitative comparison for the generalization test stimuli, we computed the average of the squared deviations between the prediction and the observed mean for the two extreme stimulus intensities. The results now show that the logistic model predicts 5.14 times better than the polynomial model ($SSE_p/2 = 659.82$ for the polynomial model, and $SSE_L/2 = 128.49$ for the logistic model).

How can this happen? There are a couple of reasons. One is that the polynomial model has an abundance of parameters, and so it has many opportunities to fit noise in the data as well as the systematic relationships. The second reason is that the polynomial model is too flexible, and it is not constrained to satisfy any basic principles for cognition. For example, one basic principle for this case is monotonicity—judgments generally increase toward an asymptote. The polynomial model is not constrained to satisfy this basic principle, but the logistic model must obey this property. In sum, by using too many parameters, a more complex model may fit better, but it may also fail to generalize to new conditions.

Bayesian Model Selection

The BIC index is a Bayesian criterion that provides a balance between accuracy and parsimony. To understand how the BIC is related to the Bayes criterion, let us examine the Bayesian principle for model selection in more detail. Recall that the Bayesian method for comparing any pair models is based on the ratio

$$\frac{\Pr[\text{Model A}|\text{data}]}{\Pr[\text{Model B}|\text{data}]} = \frac{\Pr[\text{Model A}]}{\Pr[\text{Model B}]} \cdot \frac{\Pr[\text{data}|\text{Model A}]}{\Pr[\text{data}|\text{Model B}]}.$$

If we assume equal priors for the two models, then the Bayesian criterion only depends on the Bayes factor, which can be written in the following form:

$$B_{AB} = \frac{\Pr[\text{data}|\text{Model A}]}{\Pr[\text{data}|\text{Model B}]} = \frac{\int f_A(\theta) L_A(\theta)\, d\theta}{\int f_B(\theta) L_B(\theta)\, d\theta} = \frac{E[L_A(\theta)]}{E[L_B(\theta)]}. \quad \text{(A5.1)}$$

$L_m(\theta)$ is the likelihood of the data when θ is used with Model m, $f_m(\theta)$ represents the prior density for θ under Model m, and $E[L_m(\theta)]$ is the mean likelihood averaged over all the parameters for Model m. In general, the prior density is based on the researcher's beliefs about the parameters. In practice, a noninformative prior is used, such as the Jeffrey's prior (see Wasserman, 2000).

Equation A5.1 makes it clear that the Bayesian criterion selects the model that has the largest average likelihood. In other words, the model that robustly produces accurate predictions across a wide range of parameter values tends to be selected. Suppose Model A and Model B have the same maximum likelihood, but Model A produces large likelihoods across a wide range of parameters, whereas Model B produces very small likelihoods everywhere except at the maximum point. In this case, the average likelihood for Model A will exceed that for Model B, and so the Bayesian criterion will select Model A over Model B. If we add extra parameters to a model, then we have to average across a larger domain; if the points in the extended domain produce low likelihoods, then they will dilute the average and lower the average likelihood. In this way, models that add useless parameters are rejected.

A difficulty implementing the Bayesian criterion is computing the mean likelihood for each model, $E[L_m(\theta)]$, which requires integrating over the entire parameter space. In practice, this can be achieved by a technique called the Markov Chain Monte Carlo methods (see Andrieu, 2003). A computer program called BUGS is available for implementing this method, which can be downloaded free from the Web. Alternatively, when the Jeffrey's noninformative prior is assumed, and the sample size is large, then one can approximate $\ln\{E[L_m(\theta)]\}$ by $\ln(L_m) - (k_m/2) \cdot \ln(N)$, where L_m is the maximum likelihood for Model m and k_m is the number of parameters in Model m and N is the number of observations entering into the likelihood (see Wasserman, 2000, for more details). Substituting this approximation for the mean likelihood then reduces the Bayes factor to the BIC index:

$$
\begin{aligned}
\ln(B_{AB}) &= \ln\{E[L_A(\theta)]\} - \ln\{E[L_B(\theta)]\} \\
&= [\ln(L_A) - (k_A/2) \cdot \ln(N)] - [\ln(L_B) - (k_B/2) \cdot \ln(N)] \\
&= [\ln(L_A) - \ln(L_B)] - [(k_A/2) - (k_B/2)] \cdot \ln(N) \\
&= (1/2) \cdot \{(G_B^2 - G_A^2) - (k_A - k_B) \cdot \ln(N)\} = \text{BIC}_{AB}.
\end{aligned}
$$

Alternatively,

$$
\text{BIC}_m = (1/2) \cdot [G_m^2 + k_m \cdot \ln(N)], \qquad \text{(this is the traditional form)}
$$

and then $\text{BIC}_{AB} = \text{BIC}_B - \text{BIC}_A$. If the difference BIC_{AB} is positive, then we select Model A; and if it is negative, then we choose Model B.

The penalty of the BIC index is proportional to $\ln(N)$, and so it seems to increase as the sample size increases. However, this is a bit misleading because G^2 also tends to increase as the sample size increases. For example, normal and binomial distributions both produce log likelihoods that are proportional to N. If we divide G^2 by N, we obtain the average discrepancy, for example, the error variance for the normal distribution. If we examine the average BIC

$$(\text{BIC}_m /N) = (1/2) \cdot [G_m^2 /N + k_m \cdot \ln(N)/N],$$

we see that the average penalty, $k_m \cdot \ln(N)/N$, decreases with N. Therefore, as $N \to \infty$, $\text{BIC}_m/N \to 1/2 \; G_m^2 / N$, and so the model with the smallest lack of fit, G_m^2 / N, is chosen.

There are a couple of philosophical issues that arise with the use of the Bayesian criterion. One concerns the use of prior probabilities to compute the Bayes factor. However, this issue is usually resolved by using noninformative priors. Another issue arises from the notion that we do not strongly believe that the true model is even in the small set of cognitive models we are considering. In this case, how can we compute a posterior probability for each model given the data? In other words, if we wish to compute Pr[Model m|data] for each model in the set, then these probabilities must sum to one across all the models in the set that we are considering. One way to deal with this issue is the following. Do not compute posterior probabilities; simply compare evidence for models. If we assume that each model that we compare has the same (perhaps infinitely small) prior probability, so that the priors are equal, then we are justified in using the Bayes factor to compare the relative amount of evidence supporting each model.

Akaike Information Criterion

This criterion does not assume that any of the models within the set under consideration are true. Instead, the Akaike criterion is based on the concept of selecting the model that produces a probability distribution that is closest to the (unknown) true distribution. Note that the observed sample data provide only an estimate of the true distribution, and so the Akaike criterion does not necessarily select the best fit to the sample data. More formally, if we define $T(y)$ as the true density of observing the data y and we define $P(y)$ as the predicted density from our model, then the discrepancy between the predicted and true is defined by the Kullback-Leibler information measure $K(T, P) = \int T(y) \cdot \{\ln[T(y)] - \ln[P(y)]\} \; dy$. Given a set of models, we choose the model that produces the smallest discrepancy K. For large sample sizes, this discrepancy is approximated by the Akaike index (see Bozdogan, 2000):

$$\text{AIC}_m = (G_m^2 + 2k_m). \tag{A5.2}$$

The AIC measures the discrepancy of a model from the true model, so we wish to choose the model with the smallest AIC.

When comparing two models, say Model A with Model B, we can compute the difference in discrepancies as follows:

$$\text{AIC}_{AB} = \text{AIC}_B - \text{AIC}_A = \{(G_B^2 - G_A^2) - (k_A - k_B) \cdot 2\}.$$

If the difference AIC_{AB} is positive, then we select Model A, and if it is negative we choose Model B.

The penalty for parameters used in the Akaike index is smaller than that for the BIC whenever the sample size is greater than 7, which is almost always the case. Recall that G^2 generally increases proportional to the sample size, and if we divide by the sample size, then $(\text{AIC}/N) = (G_m^2/N) + (2k_m/N)$, which disappears as $N \rightarrow \infty$. In other words, for very large N, the penalty for parsimony has little or no effect.

Cross-Validation

Although the Akaike criterion was mathematically derived from the principle of selecting the model closest to the truth based on the Kullback-Leibler distance, it can also be derived from the principle of cross-validation. As discussed in this chapter, cross-validation divides the total sample of N observations randomly into two subsets, the calibration set with N_1, and the validation set with N_2 observations. Parameters are estimated from the first set, and these same parameters are used to make predictions for the second set. Surprisingly, it can be proved (see Brown, 2000) that the cross-validation index asymptotically converges to an affine transformation of the AIC index as sample sizes within each set approach infinity, $N_i \rightarrow \infty$. In other words, for large sample sizes, the AIC can be used to approximate the cross-validation index. It is interesting that two completely different concepts for model selection lead to the same result, at least for large sample sizes.

Minimum Description Length

The minimum description length (MDL) principle for model selection recommends picking the model that reproduces the data with the lowest stochastic complexity. For a model that satisfies certain regularity conditions, the stochastic complexity is derived from complexity theory to be (see Grunwald, 2000)

$$\text{MDL}_m = (1/2)\{G_m^2 + k_m[\ln(N) - \ln(2\pi)]\} + C_m(\theta), \qquad (A5.3)$$

where $C_m(\theta) = \ln\int |I(\theta)|^{.5} \, d\theta$, and $I(\theta)$ is the Fisher information matrix, which is defined as E[**H**], and **H** is the Hessian matrix with elements $h_{ij}(\theta) = \dfrac{\partial^2 \ln[L_m(\theta)]}{\partial\theta_i\partial\theta_j}$. The first term in this equation is a measure of lack of fit, the second term is a penalty for the number of parameters, and the last term is a penalty for variation in model fit depending on the parameters (model complexity).

A difficulty with this method is to find the integral for the model complexity $C(\theta)$. In practice, this could be done using Markov Chain Monte Carlo methods. However, a simpler solution is obtained for large sample sizes. Note that the last term in Equation A5.3 does not increase with the sample size N, and so its contribution diminishes as the sample size increases. Thus, for large sample sizes, the MDL criterion is linearly related to the BIC criterion. Once again, it is interesting to note that the same criterion is derived from two very different principles.

Generalization Criterion

One of the goals of science is to be able to make a priori predictions to brand new conditions without estimating any parameters. Consider, for example, the Newtonian theory of planetary motion. Isaac Newton built his theory of planetary motion on parameters fit by Johannes Kepler to astronomical data by collected by Tycho Brae. At that early time, many scientists remained unconvinced of its validity, and this skepticism lingered until Edmond Halley used Newton's theory to make a brand new startling prediction—he predicted the precise time of arrival of the comet that is now given his name. The precision of this a priori prediction overwhelmed scientists, and Newton's theory was considered validated. A similar story can be told of Einstein's theory, which was validated by the predicted bending of light near the sun. This startling prediction led Einstein's theory to be accepted as an advancement of Newtonian theory. Thus, making a priori predictions for new conditions is a hallmark of good science, and all theories strive to achieve this goal.

Generalization differs from cross-validation in a fundamental property (see Busemeyer & Wang, 2000). Consider the example shown in Figure A5.1 once again. To apply cross-validation, we form the calibration set by randomly sampling a subset of observations from *all* the stimulus intensities. The sampling is not restricted with respect to the experimental conditions. Thus, during the calibration stage, the model is fit to all conditions, but only part of the data from all the conditions is used to fit the model. To perform a generalization test, we form the calibration set by restricting the stimulus intensities to which the model is fit, and we use all the observations within these restricted conditions. Then, we use the parameters estimated from the calibration stage to predict the remaining stimulus intensities in the generalization test phase. In this example, we restricted the calibration phase to the intermediate stimulus intensities, and we held out the extreme conditions for the generalization test phase.

The model indices reviewed above purport to select models that achieve the standard of generalizability. However, this is an assumption rather than a proven fact. Let us see how these indices perform in practice on the example shown in Figure A5.1. First, we note that with $n = 1,000$ observations per condition and 11 conditions, the sample size for the complete design, $N = 11,000$, is very large, and so it is reasonably safe to use the asymptotic results for each index, although the penalty for parsimony is relatively small in this case. We reproduced all the results with smaller sample sizes using only $n = 100$ observations per condition and $n = 10$ observations per condition. Also recall that in the large sample case, the BIC and the MDL agree, also the AIC and cross-validation criteria agree. Thus, we only need to examine the BIC and AIC.

The top half of Table A5.1 shows the ratio of SSE/N for the two models, the difference in BIC, and the difference in AIC indices. These indices were computed in two ways: In the top row, all 11 stimulus intensity values were included to fit the models; in the second row, only the intermediate 9 stimulus values were used to fit the model (excluding the extreme generalization test stimuli). In both cases, the indices all choose the polynomial model, even though the logistic model was shown to produce better generalization in this example.

Table A5.1 Model Fit Indices Applied to Data Used in Figure A5.1

$n = 1,000$	SSE_L/SSE_P	$2 \cdot BIC_{LP}$	$2 \cdot AIC_{LP}$
All 11 intensities	12.78	−27,957	−28,001
Intermediate 9 intensities	9.27	−19,985	−20,028
$n = 100$	SSE_L/SSE_P	$2 \cdot BIC_{LP}$	$2 \cdot AIC_{LP}$
All 11 intensities	12.36	−2,724	−2,754
Intermediate 9 intensities	9.13	−1,950	−1,979
$n = 10$	SSE_L/SSE_P	$2 \cdot BIC_{LP}$	$2 \cdot AIC_{LP}$
All 11 intensities	18.10	−230	−307
Intermediate 9 intensities	9.13	−207	−222

The middle and bottom halves of Table A5.1 show the results fitted to the data for the smaller sample size. Essentially, these results reproduce the same conclusion: The polynomial model is selected. However, if we again examine the generalization test conditions and compute the mean of the squared deviations for the two extreme stimulus intensities, we find that the logistic model does an order of magnitude better than the polynomial model ($SSE_p/SSE_L = 130$ for $n = 100$, and $SSE_p/SSE_L = 367$ for $n = 10$).

In this example, the model selection indices failed to pick the model that produced the most accurate predictions for generalization. However, this conclusion is just based on one example (for others see Busemeyer & Wang, 2000; Forster, 2000), and in many cases the indices may work well for this goal. The main point is that it is worthwhile to use multiple methods for evaluating models rather than relying on a single method. If they all agree, then one gains greater confidence; if they disagree, then this provides information about different performance aspects of the models.

Notes

1. The fictitious research described here is based on empirical research by Bechara et al. (1997) and theoretical analyses by Busemeyer and Stout (2001).

2. These data are fictitious but similar to Bechara et al. (1997).

3. Technically, we are using what is called the Beta prior distribution (see Berger, 1985).

4. For nested models, one can interpret the parsimony penalty term in the BIC index as the criterion that needs to be exceeded in order to reject the simpler model in favor of the more complex model, much like the criterion used to perform a chi-square significance test.

5. See the special issue on Model Comparison and Model Validation that appeared in *Cognitive Science* in 2008.

6

Hierarchical Modeling

This chapter describes how to estimate parameters and evaluate a model to an ensemble of observations pooled across individuals, but at the same time, allowing parameter variability across individuals in the analysis. This is a new yet very important methodology. In the past, researchers have either assumed that participants are all the same (homogeneity of parameters across people) and estimated parameters from the mean of all participants or they have assumed that each individual is completely different and estimated the parameters separately from the data for each person. The first method has the advantage of making use of all the data across people to estimate parameters, but it can produce misleading results because the average result may not be like any individual. The second method has the advantage of allowing full differences among people, but it is problematic to estimate parameters when there is only a small amount of data from each person. The hierarchical Bayesian method provides an ideal compromise by modeling the individual differences using what are called hyperparameters, and thus it allows the analysis of data from all the participants while allowing for differences among people. The first section reviews Bayes's rule, and then provides an elementary introduction to hierarchical Bayesian modeling, and it finishes with several detailed applications of this method that have appeared in the cognitive literature.

Individual differences are pervasive in cognitive tasks. So far, we have treated this issue by fitting models separately to each individual. This is a reasonable method when there are a small number of participants with many data points per individual. However, in many studies, a large number of participants provide a small number of observations. In this case, it would be better to use what is called a hierarchical modeling approach. This involves fitting a model simultaneously to the data from all participants, but at the same time allowing for individual differences in the model parameters.

Hierarchical modeling has become increasingly attractive to many scientific fields over the past decades. In the social sciences, hierarchical linear models have a longer tradition and have been extensively applied to educational research questions for many years now, especially for students' achievement scores; but also in sociology and political sciences, in particular for survey data; for biometric applications, for example, for growth rates and dose-response curves; and in the econometric literature (e.g., Allenby & Rossi, 2006; Collins, 2006; Cudeck & Harring, 2007; Goldstein, 2003; Hox, 2002; Raudenbush & Bryk, 2002; Snijders & Bosker, 1999). Hoffman and Rovine (2007) provide a comprehensive overview of hierarchical models for experimental psychologists who usually apply analysis of variance (ANOVA) or analysis of covariance (ANCOVA) to their data. Hierarchical linear modeling is a generalization of linear and generalized linear modeling in which regression coefficients are themselves given a model whose parameters are also estimated from the data (see Gelman, 2006). "Hierarchical" refers to the dependence among the parameters and not necessarily to the hierarchical structure of the data, although the two often go together (Raudenbush, 2001). A typical example for a hierarchical data structure is students nested within schools nested within regions, states, or countries, including longitudinal aspects.

More recently, hierarchical modeling became attractive for cognitive scientists, in particular for analyzing reaction time distributions when very few participants but many data points per participant were collected (e.g., Peruggia, Van Zandt, & Chen, 2002) or when many participants with very few data points were available (e.g., Rouder, Sun, Speckman, Lu, & Zhou, 2003). Here, the more general hierarchical modeling approach for nonlinear models, usually called hierarchical Bayesian modeling, is applied.

Most recently, hierarchical Bayesian modeling is used with psychological models. For instance, Rouder and Lu (2005) and Rouder, Lu, et al. (2007) apply hierarchical Bayesian modeling to signal detection theory; Lee (2006) applies it to human decision making on an optimal stopping problem; Lee (2008) to three cognitive models: multidimensional scaling models for stimulus representation, the generalized context model of categorical learning, and a signal detection theory model for decision making; Rouder, Morey, Speckman, and Pratte (2007) to subliminal priming; Rouder, Lu, Morey, Sun, and Speckman (2008) to the Jacoby process-dissociation model; and Lee, Fuss, & Navarro (2007) and Vandekerckhove, Tuerlinckx, and Lee (2008) to diffusion process models of decision making.

Hierarchical Bayesian modeling should not be confused with Bayesian models on cognition in general whose framework for probabilistic interference seeks to provide a general approach for understanding how problems of induction can be solved and how they might be solved in the human mind (see Griffiths, Kemp, & Tenenbaum, 2008, for an overview).

Bayesian Analysis

Before we discuss hierarchical Bayesian modeling, let us first briefly introduce some basic concepts on Bayesian analysis. For a detailed presentation, we refer to the books by Gelman, Carlin, Stern, and Rubin (2004) and Berger (1985), which we highly recommend. See also Griffiths et al. (2008) for a short introduction and a numerical example and Sivia & Skilling (2006) for a Bayesian tutorial on data analysis.

From probability theory, we know that the condition probability of A given B, $Pr(A|B)$, is

$$Pr(A|B) = \frac{Pr(A, B)}{Pr(B)} \qquad (6.1)$$

and likewise, the conditional probability of B given A is

$$Pr(B|A) = \frac{Pr(A, B)}{Pr(A)}.$$

Rearranging these equations yields $Pr(A|B)\,Pr(B) = Pr(A,B) = Pr(B|A)Pr(A)$, and substituting the right-hand side in Equation 6.1 yields

$$Pr(A|B) = \frac{Pr(B|A)\,Pr(A)}{Pr(B)}. \qquad (6.2)$$

which is called *Bayes's theorem* or sometimes *Bayes's rule*. In the Bayesian framework, the event A usually represents a specific hypothesis H and $Pr(H)$ is the *prior probability* of H, before any (new) evidence is considered. H may be the hypothesis about the fairness of a coin, the chance of winning a car (rather than a goat) in the famous Monty Hall problem, the probability of cancer, and so on. The event B is considered as data D consistent or inconsistent with the hypothesis. Note that the event D may be available data such as tossing a coin several times or prior beliefs about all possible hypotheses.

Pr(D) is called the *marginal probability* or *a priori probability* of D. It expresses the probability of observing the data under all possible hypotheses. Therefore, the marginal probability may be written as $\Pr(D) = \sum_i \Pr(D|H_i)\,\Pr(H_i)$, where $\Pr(H_i)$ is the prior probability of the hypothesis H_i and $\Pr(D|H_i)$ is called the *conditional probability* or *likelihood* of observing data D given that hypothesis H_i is true. Finally, $\Pr(H|D)$, or more general, $\Pr(H_i|D)$ is the *posterior probability* of hypothesis H_i given the data D. It is *posterior* to the revelation of the data. In a more general form, Bayes's theorem in Equation 6.2 may be written as

$$\Pr(H_j|D) = \frac{\Pr(D|H_j)\,\Pr(H_j)}{\sum_i \Pr(D|H_i)\,\Pr(H_i)} \tag{6.3}$$

The denominator of the right-hand side of Equation 6.3, the marginal probability, is a normalization constant since it does not explicitly depend on the hypothesis. For convenience, we will abbreviate the marginal as $m(\cdot)$. Omitting the marginal is fine for many data analysis problems, for instance, for those involving parameter estimation. But the term becomes crucial for other problems such as model selection (Sivia & Skilling, 2006). When omitted, it is written as

$$\Pr(H_j|D) \propto \Pr(D|H_j)\,\Pr(H_j), \tag{6.4}$$

that is,

$$\text{posterior} \propto \text{likelihood} \times \text{prior}, \tag{6.5}$$

where $\propto$ means proportional.

For two hypotheses H_i and H_j, Bayes's theorem in the form of

$$\frac{\Pr(H_i|D)}{\Pr(H_j|D)} = \frac{\Pr(D|H_i)}{\Pr(D|H_j)} \cdot \frac{\Pr(H_i)}{\Pr(H_j)} \tag{6.6}$$

is called *posterior odds*. The terms of the right-hand side of the equation are called *likelihood ratio* and *prior odds*, respectively. Taking the logarithm of Equation 6.6 yields

$$\log\frac{\Pr(H_i|D)}{\Pr(H_j|D)} = \log\frac{\Pr(D|H_i)}{\Pr(D|H_j)} + \log\frac{\Pr(H_i)}{\Pr(H_j)} \qquad (6.7)$$

and is called log-posterior odds, log-likelihood ratio, and log-prior odds, respectively.

For infinitely many hypotheses, H is a continuous random variable. In that case, we have probability densities, and the sum over hypotheses becomes an integral. That is, for probability densities, Bayes's theorem can be written accordingly, and the parts in Equation 6.3 are labeled posterior distribution or posterior density or *posterior*, for short; prior distribution or *prior*, for short; likelihood distribution and marginal distribution or marginal density or *marginal*, for short.

Example

Imagine the sensitivity of a medical test for Disease A, that is, the probability of a positive test result ($T+$) given the patient has the disease ($A+$) is $\Pr(T+|A+) = .97$ and the specificity of this test, that is, the probability of a negative test result ($T-$) given the patient does not have the disease ($A-$) is $\Pr(T-|A-) = .94$. A large sensitivity value indicates that the test is good in detecting the disease if the patient has it, and a large specificity value indicates that the test is good in detecting the absence of the disease in case the patient does not have it. Assuming that the prevalence of the disease is $\Pr(A+) = .08$, then the probability that the patient actually has the disease when the test result was positive or not is

$$\begin{aligned}\Pr(A+|T+) &= \frac{\Pr(T+|A+)\cdot\Pr(A+)}{\Pr(T+|A+)\cdot\Pr(A+) + \Pr(T+|A-)\cdot\Pr(A-)}\\[2mm] &= \frac{.97\cdot.08}{.97\cdot.08 + .06\cdot.92} = .5843\end{aligned}$$

and

$$\begin{aligned}\Pr(A+|T-) &= \frac{\Pr(T-|A+)\cdot\Pr(A+)}{\Pr(T-|A+)\cdot\Pr(A+) + \Pr(T-|A-)\cdot\Pr(A-)}\\[2mm] &= \frac{.03\cdot.08}{.03\cdot.08 + .94\cdot.92} = .0028.\end{aligned}$$

Note that there is only a 58.43% chance that the disease is present when the test result is positive.

Notation

Before we develop the full Bayesian model, a few remarks on the notion taken here are appropriate. Throughout this chapter, we use the notion proposed by Gelman et al. (2004) with few exceptions. The book is now a standard text and we refer to it quite often.

For convenience, we will now label our hypotheses in terms of parameters θ and observed data as y. Greek letters stand for parameters (vectors), lowercase Roman letters for observed or observable scalars and vectors, and uppercase Roman letters for observed or observable matrices. No distinction is made between continuous density functions and discrete probability distributions (mass functions); in both cases, they are denoted by $p(\cdot|\cdot)$ for conditional probability distributions (densities) and by $p(\cdot)$ for marginal distributions. Different distributions in the same equation will each be denoted by $p(\cdot)$. Distributions are denoted by the name, for example, $\theta \sim N(\mu, \sigma^2)$ or more explicit, $\theta|\mu, \sigma^2 \sim N(\mu, \sigma^2)$, means that θ is a normally distributed random variable with mean μ and variance σ^2; and $p(\theta) = N(\theta|\mu, \sigma^2)$ or more explicit, $p(\theta|\mu, \sigma^2) = N(\theta|\mu, \sigma^2)$, is used for density functions.

Example

Assume a binomial experiment such as tossing a coin with y observed successes in n trials; observing y infected animals in a total of n; or diagnosing y children with attention-deficit hyperactivity disorder (ADHD) in a class with n students.

The parameter of interest, θ, follows a binomial distribution, that is, $\theta \sim Bin(n, p)$, where n is the sample size and $p \in [0, 1]$ is the probability of a specified outcome (e.g., success). Thus, the likelihood is

$$p(y|\theta) = Bin(y|n, \theta) = \binom{n}{y}\theta^y(1-\theta)^{n-y} \qquad (6.8)$$

and the posterior is

$$p(\theta|y) = \frac{p(y|\theta)p(\theta)}{\int_0^1 p(y|\theta)p(\theta)\,d\theta} = \frac{\binom{n}{y}\theta^y(1-\theta)^{n-y}p(\theta)}{\int_0^1 \binom{n}{y}\theta^y(1-\theta)^{n-y}p(\theta)\,d\theta}. \qquad (6.9)$$

Here, it becomes obvious that Bayesian inference about a parameter θ is made in terms of probability statements. To make a probability statement about θ for a given set of data y, the joint probability distribution for θ and y is determined as the product of two distributions. The prior distribution $p(\theta)$ expresses prior information about the parameter, and the other is the sampling distribution or likelihood $p(y|\theta)$. Conditioning on the known values of the data y yields the posterior distribution $p(\theta|y)$. Omitting constant factors in the distributions (e.g., the marginal distribution and for fixed n and y the binomial factor $\binom{n}{y}$ does not depend on the unknown parameter θ) yields the unnormalized posterior probability distribution, that is,

$$p(\theta|y) \propto \theta^y (1 - \theta)^{n-y} p(\theta) \cdot \qquad (6.10)$$

The question is what the prior distribution is for θ.

Prior Distributions

In Bayesian analysis, special attention is paid to the prior distribution. It represents the information about the uncertain parameter (vector) θ that is combined with the data distribution to yield the posterior distribution. Gelman et al. (2004) consider two basic interpretations of the prior distribution: the *population* interpretation, where the prior distribution represents a population of possible parameter values from which the parameter θ has been drawn; second, the *state of knowledge* interpretation, where knowledge and uncertainty about θ is expressed in terms of a random realization from the prior distribution. The prior distribution reflects the decision maker's belief and prior knowledge about the inference problem at hand. Bayesian statisticians consider this a virtue rather than a drawback, different from the classical statistics perspective using maximum-likelihood estimation and other methods that do not involve prior knowledge. In determining the prior distributions, it is crucial what information goes into it and what the properties of the resulting posterior distribution are. Prior distributions are classified as informative and noninformative prior distributions. Within the class of informative prior distributions, it is often distinguished between conjugate and nonconjugate prior distributions, and within the noninformative between proper and improper priors.

Noninformative Prior Distributions

When no specific assumptions about the form and/or parameters of a prior distribution seem appropriate, a *noninformative* (also called *flat* or *diffuse*) prior distribution is used. It contains no information about θ, that is, equal weight is given to all possible values of θ. For example, when the parameter set of θ is finite with *n* elements, then a noninformative prior gives each θ probability $1/n$. When the parameter set is infinite, each element of the parameter set gets equal density, which is a uniform noninformative prior $p(\theta) \equiv c$. A prior distribution is called *proper* when the function used integrates to 1. It is called *improper* when the function used has an infinite integral and is therefore not a probability function in a strict sense. For example, suppose the mean of the normal distribution is the parameter of interest and the parameter space is $(-\infty, \infty)$. When choosing a noninformative prior distribution, all possible values of θ get the same weight. In particular, for $p(\theta) = c > 0$ (since the choice of *c* is unimportant, it is usually set to 1), the prior distribution has infinite mass, that is, the integral is infinite and not a proper density. However, when combining with the data distribution, the resulting posterior distribution may well be a proper distribution. For example, for $y \sim N(\theta, \sigma^2)$ with known variance σ^2 and noninformative prior $p(\theta) = 1$, the posterior distribution is

$$p(\theta|y) = \frac{p(y|\theta)p(\theta)}{m(y)} = p(y|\theta) = \frac{1}{\sqrt{2\pi}\sigma} \exp\left(\frac{-(\theta - y)^2}{2\sigma^2}\right),$$

since

$$m(y) = \int_{-\infty}^{\infty} p(y|\theta)\, d\theta = \frac{1}{\sqrt{2\pi}\sigma} \int_{-\infty}^{\infty} \exp\left(\frac{-(y - \theta)^2}{2\sigma^2}\right) d\theta = 1.$$

That is, the posterior distribution of θ given *y* is $N(y, \sigma^2)$.

Informative Prior Distributions

Sometimes the decision maker has specific beliefs or prior knowledge about the prior distribution, for instance, when scientific information is available on the parameters in the model. Prior distributions with known distribution and known parameters are called *informative* priors. One family of prior distributions is particularly convenient since it leads to a simple posterior distribution. Take again the example of the binomial data distribution in Equation 6.8. For a Bayesian inference, a prior distribution for θ needs to be specified. The data distribution in Equation 6.8 can be written in an unnormalized form as

$$p(y|\theta) \propto \theta^a (1 - \theta)^b. \tag{6.11}$$

If the prior distribution $p(\theta)$ is of the same form with different exponents, then the posterior distribution $p(\theta|y)$ will be of the same form. Let

$$p(\theta) \propto \theta^{\alpha-1}(1-\theta)^{\beta-1}, \tag{6.12}$$

which is a beta distribution with parameters α and β: $\theta \sim \text{Beta}(\alpha, \beta)$. Both parameters determine the shape of the distribution as we will discuss in more detail in the context of hierarchical Bayesian modeling. The parameters of the prior distribution are often called *hyperparameters*. Assuming the parameter values for α and β are given, the posterior distribution for θ can be determined as

$$
\begin{aligned}
p(\theta|y) &\propto \theta^y(1-\theta)^{n-y}\theta^{\alpha-1}(1-\theta)^{\beta-1} \\
&= \theta^{y+\alpha-1}(1-\theta)^{n-y+\beta-1} \\
&= \text{Beta}(\theta|\alpha+y, \beta+n-y).
\end{aligned} \tag{6.13}
$$

The property that the posterior distribution follows the same parametric form as the prior distribution is called *conjugacy*. Obviously, conjugate prior distributions are computational convenient because the parametric form of the posterior distribution is known. As Berger (1985) points out, when dealing with conjugate priors, there is generally no need to explicitly calculate the marginal distribution. Since $p(\theta|y) = p(y, \theta)/m(y)$, the factors involving θ in $p(\theta|y)$ must be the same as θ in $p(y, \theta)$. Only factors involving θ in $p(y, \theta)$ need to be considered. If these can be recognized as belonging to a particular distribution, then $p(\theta|y)$ is that distribution. For example, assume that $y \sim \text{Poisson}(\theta)$. With n observations, the likelihood function is

$$p(y|\theta) = \prod_{i=1}^{n}\left[\frac{\theta^{y_i}e^{-\theta}}{y_i!}\right] = \frac{\theta^{n\bar{y}}e^{-n\theta}}{\prod_{i=1}^{n}(y_i!)}, \tag{6.14}$$

where $\bar{y}$ is the mean of the ys.

Realizing that this resembles a gamma distribution, the ideal candidate for a conjugate prior distribution belongs to that family, that is, $\theta \sim \text{Gamma}(\alpha, \beta)$ with density function

$$p(\theta) = \frac{\theta^{\alpha-1}e^{-(\theta/\beta)}}{\Gamma(\alpha)\beta^{\alpha}}, \quad \theta > 0. \tag{6.15}$$

Putting both equations together yields

$$p(y|\theta)p(\theta) = \frac{\theta^{n\bar{y}+\alpha-1}e^{-\theta(n+1/\beta)}}{\Gamma(\alpha)\beta^{\alpha}\prod\limits_{i=1}^{n}(y_i!)}, \quad \theta > 0. \tag{6.16}$$

This belongs to a gamma distribution $\text{Gamma}(n\bar{y}+\alpha, [n+1/\beta]^{-1})$ and must be the posterior $p(\theta|y)$. The marginal $m(y) = p(y, \theta)$ does not include θ and is omitted.

Obviously, conjugate prior distributions have very attractive properties. However, they should not be used if available information contradicts the assumption. For complex models, it might be even impossible to employ a conjugate prior distribution and a nonconjugate prior distribution (i.e., prior and posterior distributions do not follow the same parametric form) is the appropriate choice.

A list of data distributions with their conjugate prior is found in Appendix A of Gelman et al. (2004).

Assuming that the form of the prior is known, there is still the question as to what parameters should be selected. Belief and prior knowledge of the decision maker are important sources, but there are other several possible ways to select a prior distribution. We mention two approaches briefly, empirical Bayes and hierarchical Bayes. For various other methods, see Berger (1985, chap. 3).

Empirical Bayes

Empirical Bayes methods use empirical data to estimate or approximate conditional probability distributions in a Bayesian analysis. The approach combines Bayesian and frequentists' perspectives on estimating parameters. For example, it uses estimates (e.g., maximum-likelihood estimation) to approximate the marginal and expresses the hyperparameters of the prior in terms of empirical mean and variance, which in turn is used for a prior distribution for future experiments.

Empirical Bayes uses past data, and the so-called compound decision problem uses current data. However, often both approaches go under the name empirical Bayes. Two classes of empirical Bayes methods are usually distinguished—the *parametric empirical Bayes* (PEB) and the *nonparametric empirical Bayes* (NPEB). PEB assumes that the prior distribution of θ is in some parametric class with unknown hyperparameters, while NPEB assumes only that the θ_i are independently and identically distributed (iid). We only provide an example for the first one. (For more details, NPEB, and examples, see, e.g., Berger 1985, chap. 4.5; Casella, 1985; Efron, 2003).

Suppose 3 children in a class of 20 fourth graders are diagnosed with ADHD and the goal is to estimate the parameter θ for that population. We assume a binomial model for the number of cases y and assume the conjugate prior $\theta \sim \text{Beta}(\alpha, \beta)$. The parameter values, however, are not known.

Suppose past data are available, that is, reports from J schools, and for the jth school y_j children are diagnosed with ADHD in a class of n_j students. Let each y_j be a random sample with conditional density $p(y_j/\theta_j)$ and let $(\theta_1, \ldots, \theta_J)$ iid from the density $p(\theta)$, which is a Beta distribution. Assuming that this Beta distribution is a good description of the population distribution of the θs of the data observed in the past, the structure of the model is $(\alpha, \beta) \rightarrow \theta_j \rightarrow y_j$ for all j.

The observed sample mean and standard deviation from the J values y_j/n_j can then be used to determine the prior distribution for the new experiment. Assuming that the mean and standard deviation are 0.2 and 0.1, respectively, and setting the mean and standard deviation of the population distribution to these values yields $\alpha = 3$ and $\beta = 12$.[1] The prior is then Beta(3, 12), and we observed 3 cases out of 20 in the new study; therefore, the new posterior distribution for the current experiment is Beta $(3 + 3, 12 + 17) = \text{Beta}(6, 29)$.

Hierarchical Prior Distributions

The predictions of the Bayesian model may critically depend on the chosen prior distribution as well as on the parameters. Take, for instance, the prior distribution from the example above with $\theta \sim \text{Beta}(\alpha, \beta)$. Depending on the parameters α and β, the distribution can take on all kinds of shapes as illustrated in Figure 6.1. With $\alpha = \beta$, the distribution is symmetric around 0.5 but very different in shape, ranging from a U-shape ($\alpha = \beta = 0.5$) to a flat line ($\alpha = \beta = 1$, uniform distribution) or unimodal ($\alpha = \beta = 2$ and $\alpha = \beta = 5$). For $\alpha \neq \beta$, the shape depends on the relation between α and β. It can be strictly decreasing (reversing the parameters results in a strictly increasing function) or unimodal skewed.

Reconsider the example above with $y = 3$ children out of $n = 20$ students diagnosed with ADHS. The posterior distribution of θ is, therefore, Beta $(\alpha + 3, \beta + 17)$. The posterior means for parameters α and β used in Figure 6.1 are given in Table 6.1.

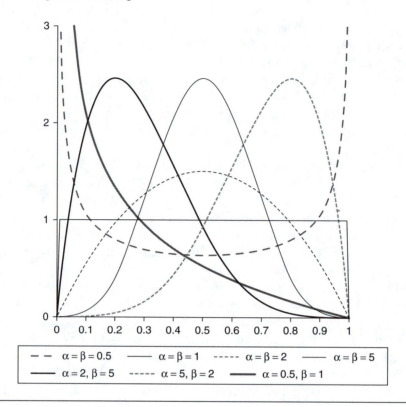

Figure 6.1   Beta Distribution

Table 6.1   Posterior Means for Parameters α and β Used in Figure 6.1

Beta Parameters	Posterior Means
$\alpha = \beta = 0.5$	0.1667
$\alpha = \beta = 1$	0.2083
$\alpha = \beta = 2$	0.2667
$\alpha = \beta = 5$	0.2083
$\alpha = 2, \beta = 5$	0.2667
$\alpha = 5, \beta = 2$	0.1818
$\alpha = 0.5, \beta = 1$	0.1667

Obviously, the estimates for θ may be quite different depending on the assumed parameters. Prior knowledge of decision maker, of course, may rule out some parameters. But what if there is a lack of this knowledge or prior belief and no historical data are available?

One important type of prior distribution is a hierarchical prior distribution. Structural and subjective information about the prior distribution are available and incorporated into the model simultaneously. This is often done in stages. For instance, the empirical Bayes used the structural assumption of independence of the θ_j parameters to determine the predictive distribution. Similar ideas are applied here. The prior distribution is

$$p(\theta) = \prod_{j=1}^{J} p(\theta_j). \tag{6.17}$$

This is called a first-stage prior distribution. The prior distribution for each group j may be considered as a sample from a common population distribution. The hierarchical approach is to put in a second-stage prior distribution, $p(\phi)$, on the first-stage prior distribution. The second-stage prior distribution is sometimes called a *hyperprior distribution*.

The joint prior distribution is

$$p(\phi, \theta) = p(\phi)p(\theta|\phi) \tag{6.18}$$

and the joint posterior distribution is

$$\begin{aligned} p(\phi, \theta|y) &\propto p(\phi, \theta)p(y|\phi, \theta) \\ &= p(\phi, \theta)p(y|\theta). \end{aligned} \tag{6.19}$$

The simplification holds because the data distribution, $p(y|\phi, \theta)$, depends only on θ and ϕ, and affects y only through θ (see Gelman et al., 2004, p. 124). As Berger (1985) points out, the hierarchical structure is a *convenient* presentation for a prior distribution and not an entirely new entity. Any hierarchical prior can be expressed as a standard prior distribution, that is, $p(\theta)$ can be written as

$$p(\theta) = \int \left[\prod_{j=1}^{J} p(\theta_j|\phi) \right] p(\phi) \, d\phi. \tag{6.20}$$

Furthermore, there is no theoretical reason to limit the hierarchical prior distribution to two stages. As before, a prior distribution for the second stage needs to be determined; common use for it is the noninformative prior distribution. However, if an improper hyperprior distribution is applied, it must be checked that the posterior distribution is proper.

Gelman et al. (2004) propose the following steps to conduct a hierarchical Bayesian analysis (p. 126).

1. Write the likelihood part of the model, $p(y \mid \theta)$, ignoring any factors that do not involve θ.

2. Write the joint posterior density, $p(\theta, \phi \mid y)$, in unnormalized form as a product of the likelihood $p(y \mid \theta)$, the population distribution[2] $p(\theta, \mid \phi)$, and the hyperprior distribution $p(\phi)$, that is,

$$p(\theta, \phi|y) \propto p(y|\theta)p(\theta|\phi)p(\phi). \tag{6.21}$$

3. Determine analytically the conditional posterior density of θ given the hyperparameters ϕ; for fixed observed y, this is a function of ϕ, $p(\theta \mid \phi, y)$. This is relatively easy for conjugate prior distributions. Conditional on ϕ, the population distribution for θ is $p(\theta|\phi) = \prod_{j=1}^{J} p(\theta_j|\phi)$, so that the conditional posterior distribution is a product of conjugate posterior distributions for the parameters θ_j.

4. Estimate ϕ by determining the marginal posterior distribution, $p(\phi \mid y)$, that is,

$$p(\phi|y) = \int p(\theta, \phi|y) \, d\theta, \tag{6.22}$$

or for many standard models algebraically by using the conditional probability formula

$$p(\phi|y) = \frac{p(\theta, \phi|y)}{p(\theta|\phi, y)}. \tag{6.23}$$

For illustration, we take the example from above. The data from the experiment $j = 1, \ldots, J$ follow independent binomial distributions:

$$y_j \sim \text{Bin}(n_j, \theta_j),$$

where the number of students in each class, n_j, is assumed to be known. The parameters θ_j are assumed to be independent samples from a beta distribution (a conjugate prior distribution, see above):

$$\theta_j \sim \text{Beta}(\alpha, \beta),$$

and since the decision maker has no prior knowledge of the hyperparameters, a noninformative hyperprior distribution is assigned to the hyperparameters.

Second, the joint posterior density in unnormalized form as the product of the likelihood, the population distribution, and the hyperprior distribution is

$$p(\theta, \alpha, \beta|y) \propto p(y|\theta, \alpha, \beta)p(\theta|\alpha, \beta)p(\alpha, \beta) \tag{6.24a}$$

and

$$\propto \prod_{j=1}^{J} \theta_j^{y_j}(1-\theta_j)^{n_j-y_j} \prod_{j=1}^{J} \frac{\Gamma(\alpha+\beta)}{\Gamma(\alpha)\Gamma(\beta)}\theta_j^{\alpha-1}(1-\theta_j)^{\beta-1}p(\alpha, \beta). \tag{6.24b}$$

Third, the conditional posterior density for θ, given the hyperparameters α and β, for fixed observed y is

$$p(\theta|\alpha, \beta, y) = \prod_{j=1}^{J} \frac{\Gamma(\alpha+\beta+n_j)}{\Gamma(\alpha+y_j)\Gamma(\beta+n_j-y_j)} \theta_j^{\alpha+y_j-1}(1-\theta_j)^{\beta+n_j-y_j-1}. \tag{6.25}$$

Fourth, the marginal posterior distribution of α and β is obtained by substituting Equations 6.24b and 6.25 in Equation 6.23,

$$p(\alpha, \beta|y) = \frac{p(\theta, \alpha, \beta|y)}{p(\theta|\alpha, \beta, y)} \propto \prod_{j=1}^{J} \frac{\Gamma(\alpha+\beta)}{\Gamma(\alpha)\Gamma(\beta)} \frac{\Gamma(\alpha+y_j)\Gamma(\beta+n_j-y_j)}{\Gamma(\alpha+\beta+n_j)} p(\alpha, \beta). \tag{6.26}$$

Finally, the noninformative hyperprior distribution has to be set up. Care has to be taken to assign one that results in a proper *posterior* distribution (see above). Gelman et al. (2004) provide the following solution. First, they reparameterize the Beta parameters: for α the logit[3] of the mean $\alpha/(\alpha+\beta)$, which is $\log(\alpha/\beta)$, is taken and for β the logarithm of the "sample size"[4] of the Beta distribution, $\log(\alpha+\beta)$, is taken. After some transformation, the hyperprior distribution yields (Gelman et al. 2004, p. 128)

$$p\left(\log\left(\frac{\alpha}{\beta}\right), \log(\alpha+\beta)\right) \propto \alpha\beta(\alpha+\beta)^{-5/2}.$$

To summarize the hierarchical model so far:

$$y_j \sim \text{Bin}(n_j, \theta_j), \text{ where } n_j \text{ is known } \theta_j \sim \text{Beta}(\alpha, \beta)$$

$$\alpha \sim \text{flat}$$

$$\beta \sim \text{flat}.$$

Furthermore, a directed acyclic graph (DAG) showing the dependencies of each variable on others is another representation of Equation 6.24a, and it becomes very convenient, in particular, when more complex models are constructed (see Figure 6.2).

Before we come to estimation procedures (Markov Chain Monte Carlo, MCMC), we report on several applications of hierarchical modeling in cognitive psychology.

Applications in Cognitive Psychology

We start with two studies in which hierarchical models are used for analyzing reaction time distributions. In one study, data from several participants are available, but only with a small number of observations per participant (Rouder et al., 2003; Rouder, Lu, Speckman, Sun, & Jiang, 2005); in the other very few participants took part but many data points per participant were collected (Peruggia, Van Zandt, & Chen, 2002). Rouder et al. (2005) distinguish between statistical modeling and substantive modeling. Statistical models, such as general linear models (e.g., ANOVA, regression), are used for estimation and inference. Substantive models, such as decision field theory, are tested as authentic models of phenomena (see Chapter 1 for more discussion on these).

A Hierarchical Weibull Model
for Reaction Time Distributions

Rouder et al. (2003, 2005) use the hierarchical Bayesian approach to provide a statistical framework for estimating higher-order characteristics of

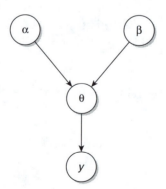

Figure 6.2   Directed Acyclic Graph

response time distributions. In particular, they provide means to estimate location (they called it shift), scale, and shape parameters for the Weibull distribution to describe response time distributions in an absolute identification task. The Weibull distribution is attractive among reaction time modelers for various reasons. Its shape can be made to resemble typical response time distributions and its parameters are subject to psychological interpretation. For instance, the shape parameter, β, is related to structural differences of central processes of different participant groups or experimental conditions; speed difference of execution of different groups is reflected in the scale parameter, θ; and differences in peripheral processes are manifested in the location parameter, ψ (Rouder et al., 2003, 2005).

The response times, such as y_{ij} of participant i on trial j ($1 \le i \le I$; $1 \le j \le J_i$), are independent and identically distributed random variables from a three-parameter Weibull distribution with density

$$p(y_{ij}|\psi_i, \theta_i, \beta_i) = \frac{\beta_i}{\theta_i} \left(\frac{y_{ij} - \psi_i}{\theta_i} \right)^{\beta_i - 1} \exp\left\{ -\left(\frac{y_{ij} - \psi_i}{\theta_i} \right)^{\beta_i} \right\}, \quad (6.27)$$

where, $y_{ij} \ge \psi_i$, $\theta_i \ge 0$, and ψ_i, θ_i, and β_i are the location, scale, and shape (or slope) parameters, respectively. Figure 6.3 shows the change in one parameter while holding the remaining two fixed.

We proceed according to the hierarchical Bayesian approach where modeling is done in two (or more) stages.

In the first stage, prior distributions are assigned to the parameters of the Weibull distribution. Rouder et al. (2003) chose a noninformative prior

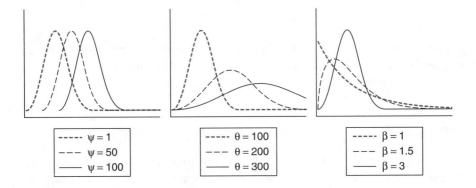

$\psi = 1$	$\theta = 100$	$\beta = 1$
$\psi = 50$	$\theta = 200$	$\beta = 1.5$
$\psi = 100$	$\theta = 300$	$\beta = 3$

Figure 6.3   The Weibull Distribution of Location ($\theta = 100$, $\beta = 3$), Scale ($\psi = 1$, $\beta = 3$), and Shape ($\psi = 1$, $\theta = 100$)

distribution over a finite range ψ_i, that is, a uniform distribution over the interval (a, b):

$$\psi_i \sim U(a, b) \tag{6.28}$$

and Gamma distributions for θ_i and β_i, that is,

$$\beta_i \,|\, \eta_1, \eta_2 \sim \text{Gamma}\,(\eta_1, \eta_2) \tag{6.29}$$

$$\theta_i^{-\beta_i} | \xi_1, \xi_2 \sim \text{Gamma}(\xi_1, \xi_2). \tag{6.30}$$

The structural information of the first stage pertains to all priors—that is, the parameters are iid of the specified kind. For technical reason, β_i is restricted to $\beta_i > 0.01$. In the second stage, hyperprior distributions are defined for β_i and $\theta_i^{-\beta_i}$, but not for ψ. In particular,

$$\xi_k \sim \text{Gamma}(a_k, b_k), \quad k = 1, 2 \tag{6.31}$$

$$\eta_k \sim \text{Gamma}(c_k, d_k), \quad k = 1, 2. \tag{6.32}$$

The Gamma distribution was chosen because of its tractability and convenience. The parameters a, b of the uniform, and a_1, a_2, b_1, b_2, c_1, c_2, d_1, d_2 were set to constants.

The posterior distribution is

$$\begin{aligned} p(\psi, \theta, \beta, \xi, \eta | y) \propto {}&\times p(y|\psi, \theta, \beta, \xi, \eta) p(\beta|\eta) \\ & p(\theta|\xi, \beta) p(\psi) p(\xi|a, b) p(\eta|c, d) \end{aligned} \tag{6.33}$$

and already complex; a DAG is helpful for showing the dependencies of each variable (see Figure 6.4). For the specific distributions, see Rouder et al. (2003, p. 594f).

Reaction Times Analysis for Word Recognition

Peruggia et al. (2002) analyzed reaction time data to investigate word recognition memory. Four participants performed two recognition memory tests over a period of 10 days. On each test, the participant saw a study list of 32 words (at a rate of 400 ms per word), and immediately following the study a sequence of 40 test words (20 new and 20 old from the study list)

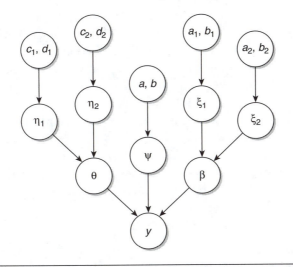

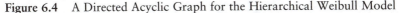

Figure 6.4   A Directed Acyclic Graph for the Hierarchical Weibull Model

was presented. The participants had to identify the word in the test list as new or old. The accuracy of the response (correct or incorrect) and the reaction time was recorded. Peruggia et al. used a Weibull distribution for analyzing their data and incorporated participant-specific effects and covariate effects through a regression with autoregressive normal errors for the logarithm of the scale parameter of the Weibull distribution. Before we present the model in more detail, we will briefly discuss the hierarchical approach to repeated measures and autoregression. For simplicity, we assume a linear model and mean response time as data.

Digression: Repeated Measures Within Subjects

The study of changes is essential for a variety of areas, most notable when learning or growth is involved. Measures are taken repeatedly for the same individual or organism and analyzed as a function of the measurement occasion. These repeated measures data can be viewed as hierarchical data with repeated measurements nested within individual entities. That is, the measurements are on Level 1 and the individual entities are on Level 2. For instance, in language acquisition, vocabulary expands rapidly in a nonlinear fashion while the rate of all kinds of errors decreases as a function of time (age). However, there are considerable individual differences (see McDonald, 1997, for a review). Similarly, acquisition of intellectual and perceptual-motor skills learning occurs nonlinearly (see Rosenbaum, Carlson, & Gilmore, 2001, for a review).

Hierarchical linear models are used for analyzing those data and other longitudinal data of all kinds. They appear under a variety of terms, including random effect models for longitudinal data (e.g., Laird & Ware, 1982); growth curve models, latent curve models, and longitudinal models (e.g., Hox, 2002); models for individual change and growth models (e.g., Raudenbush & Bryk, 2002); mixed linear models and models for repeated measures data (e.g., Goldstein, 2003). For longitudinal studies in education, age is often an explanatory variable, whereas in many experiments and in particular in clinical studies, the measurement occasion itself is the explanatory variable.

For illustration, let us assume that we observe mean reaction time in the experimental study by Peruggia et al. (2002).

With y_{ti} denoting the observed mean response time at measurement occasion x_t for individual i, the model at Level 1 is given by

$$y_{ti} = \beta_{0i} + \beta_{1i} x_{ti} + e_{ti},$$ (6.34)

with $e_{ti} \sim N(0, \sigma_e^2)$. More complex structures of the residual are discussed later in the chapter. The βs are often called *change* or growth parameters, in particular, when x_{ti} indicates the age of person i at time t. Both the intercept and the coefficient can vary at Level 2 as a function of measured characteristics of the individual. Such characteristics are called *time invariant* covariates. The Level 2 model is defined as

$$\beta_{0i} = \gamma_{00} + \gamma_{01} z_i + u_{0i}$$ (6.35)

and

$$\beta_{1i} = \gamma_{10} + \gamma_{11} z_i + u_{1i},$$ (6.36)

where z_i is the explanatory variable of Level 2 and

$$\begin{pmatrix} u_{0i} \\ u_{1i} \end{pmatrix} \sim N \left[\begin{pmatrix} 0 \\ 0 \end{pmatrix}, \begin{pmatrix} \tau_{00} & \tau_{01} \\ \tau_{10} & \tau_{11} \end{pmatrix} \right].$$

Note that the Level 1 parameters of individualchange, β_{0i} and β_{1i}, are correlated outcomes predicted by person characteristic z_i. Substituting Equations 6.35 and 6.36 into Equation 6.34, we get the combined model

$$y_{ti} = \gamma_{00} + \gamma_{10} x_{ti} + \gamma_{01} z_i + \gamma_{11} z_i x_{ti} + u_{1i} x_{ti} + u_{0i} + e_{ti}.$$ (6.37)

The model in Equation 6.37 assumes a so-called linear change function, that is, growth or decay occurs linearly as a function of time.[5] Often, however, in particular when practice or learning is involved and many measurement points are taken, the change curve may be better represented by a more complex function, for example, by a polynomial of degree P. For this case, the Level 1 model presented in Equation 6.34 can be extended to

$$y_{ti} = \beta_{0i} + \beta_{1i}x_{ti} + \beta_{2i}x_{ti}^2 + \cdots + \beta_{pi}x_{ti}^p + e_{ti}. \tag{6.38}$$

Note that Equation 6.38 is still a linear model, as the word linear refers to the linearity in the βs in the model—that is, $E(\beta_i)$ is a linear function of the βs. The xs may occur in a nonlinear way.

With the same rationale as before, each growth parameter can be expressed as a Level 2 model, that is,

$$\beta_{pi} = \gamma_{p0} + \gamma_{p1}z_i + u_{pi}, \tag{6.39}$$

with $p = 1, \ldots, P$. The symmetric covariance matrix $\mathbf{T}$ is a $(P + 1) \times (P + 1)$ matrix. One can use functions other than polynomials. For example, Snijders and Bosker (1999) give detailed examples for piecewise linear functions and spline functions. See also Raudenbush and Bryk (2002) for piecewise linear functions and Goldstein (2003) for spline functions. For the mean response time of Peruggia et al. (2002), we may want to apply a decreasing function of measurement occasions, for example, $1/x_{ti}$ or $1/(1+\log(x_{ti}))$.

Both, the Level 1 model and the Level 2 model can be extended to include more explanatory variables. On Level 1, for example, we could include another time-varying covariate such as the task administered. Imagine that the participants had to remember different list length on different days. Incorporating this idea, the linear model becomes

$$y_{ti} = \beta_{0i} + \beta_{1i}x_{ti} + \beta_{2i}w_{ti} + e_{ti}, \tag{6.40}$$

where x_{ti} indicates the measurement occasion and w_{ti} refers to the specific task. Note that experimental conditions in general can also be specified on Level 2 as fixed or as nonrandomly varying variable.

So far we have assumed that the residuals at Level 1 are mutually independent. However, this may not be the case, in particular when the measurements are obtained in relatively short time and when memory is involved. To account for this situation, autocorrelation among the Level 1 residuals is built into the model.

Autoregression

Goldstein, Healy, and Rashbash (1994) propose a time series model that consists of a multilevel model for repeated measurement augmented by an autocorrelation for Level 1 residuals. They consider first- and second-order autoregressive models for discrete and continuous time. For example, the discrete time first-order autoregressive model AR(1) with a single residual term at Level 1 has the following structure (Goldstein & McDonald, 1988):

$$e_t = \rho e_{(t-1)} + v_t, \tag{6.41}$$

Where e_t is the residual at occasion t with $\text{Var}(e_t) = \sigma_e^2$, ρ is the autocorrelation, and v_t is a residual error with $\text{Var}(v_t) = \sigma_v^2$, and $E(v_t) = 0$.

The Level 1 covariance matrix with n_i observations for participant i becomes

$$V_{1i} = \sigma_e^2 I + \rho \sigma_e^2 R, \tag{6.42}$$

where the $(k, 1)$th element of the $n_i \times n_i$ matrix $\mathbf{R}$ is defined as

$$R(k, l) = \left\{ \begin{matrix} 0 & \text{if } k = 1, \\ \rho^{(|k-l|-1)} & \text{if } k = 1. \end{matrix} \right\} \tag{6.43}$$

The discrete time case has some restrictions as it requires equally spaced time points. This can be dropped for the continuous time case.

Following Goldstein (2003), the general model for the Level 1 residuals can be defined as

$$\text{cov}(e_t e_{t-s}) = \sigma_e^2 f(s), \tag{6.44}$$

where s and t are points in time. The Level 1 subscript i has been dropped for convenience. The covariance between two measurements depends on the variance σ_e^2 and the time difference between two measurements. Goldstein (2003) defines the function $f(s)$ as a negative exponential of the following form:

$$f(s) = \alpha + \exp(-g(\beta, x, s)), \tag{6.45}$$

where α is a constant, and β a vector of parameters for the explanatory variables x. Goldstein proposes several choices for the g function. For example, $g = \beta_0 s$ gives a first-order autoregressive series for equal intervals; $g = \beta_0 s + \beta_1(t_1 + t_2) + \beta_2(t_1^2 + t_2^2)$ implies that the variance is a quadratic function of time for time points t_1 and t_2. For more examples of g functions, see Goldstein (2003, p. 132).

Advantages

Repeated measures data can also be analyzed by full multivariate models. In this case, each vector of responses, y_i, has a multivariate normal distribution with mean μ_i $(n_i \times 1)$ and a $n_i \times n_i$ covariance matrix Σ. n_i is the number of observations for the ith individual.

There are several advantages for using a multilevel model instead of a multivariate model. Laird and Ware (1982) point out that the latter approach becomes unattractive when individuals are measured at arbitrary or unique times, or when the dimension of the covariance matrix is large, because of the increasing number of variance parameters, and many of them will be poorly estimated. Furthermore, the full multivariate model cannot incorporate individual characteristics. Multilevel models, on the other hand, can handle unbalanced designs without any problem and are explicitly built to include explanatory variables on all levels.

Another advantage is that multilevel models account for individual change. That is, the change curve can be different for each individual, since the Level 1 model represents specific change parameters (the βs) within each individual. Change characteristics across a population of individuals are described at Level 2 (see also Hox, 2002; Raudenbush & Bryk, 2002).

Reaction Time Analysis for Word Recognition (continued)

We return to the study by Peruggia et al. (2002), in which they analyzed response time *distributions* rather than mean response time.

Let y be the random variable for the reaction time. A single reaction time measurement is indexed by the particular participant, i, $1 \le i \le 4$, the day of the study, d, $1 \le d \le 10$, the word lists, l, $1 \le l \le 2$, and the position of the word in the list, w, $1 \le w \le 40$, that is, y_{idlw}. Furthermore, two indicator variables are introduced, one indicating whether the response was given to an old word $(I_{\text{Old}(idlw)} \equiv I_O = 1)$ or to a new word $(I_{\text{Old}(idlw)} \equiv I_O = 0)$ and one for whether the response was correct $(I_{\text{Right}(idlw)} \equiv I_R = 1)$ or incorrect $(I_{\text{Right}(idlw)} \equiv I_R = 0)$. The response time y_{idlw} of participant i on day d with list l to word position w is a random variable from a two-parameter Weibull distribution with density

$$p(y_{idlw}|\theta_{idlw}, \beta_i) = \frac{\beta_i}{\theta_{idlw}} \left(\frac{y_{idlw}}{\theta_{idlw}}\right)^{\beta_i - 1} \exp\left\{-\left(\frac{y_{idlw}}{\theta_{idlw}}\right)^{\beta_i}\right\}. \quad (6.46)$$

Note that the two-parameter Weibull distribution is obtained by setting the location parameter $\psi = 0$ in Equation 6.27.

The prior distributions for the shape parameter is set to

$$\beta_i \sim \text{Exponential}(\lambda). \quad (6.47)$$

Note that this parameter is person-specific and does not depend on stimuli, the experimental condition, or the day on which the task is performed. This was done because it was apparent from the data that the four participants' mean response time as a function of performing days were quite different, and therefore, applying the same power law transformation to each participant was not advisable.

The transformed scale parameter, θ, is defined as a linear model with normally distributed residuals, that is,

$$\ln(\theta_{idlw}) = \alpha_{idl} + \gamma_1 I_O + \gamma_2 I_R + \gamma_3(I_O \cdot I_R) + \eta_{idlw}, \qquad (6.48)$$

with

$$\eta_{idl1} \sim N(0, \tau_1) \quad \text{for } w = 1$$

and

$$\eta_{idlw} \sim N(\phi_i \eta_{idlw-1}, \tau) \quad \text{for } 2 \leq w \leq 40.$$

The prior distribution is a Level 1 model with autoregressive covariance structure of order 1 to capture serial dependences in the response times.

For the Level 2 model, it is assumed that the coefficients α_{idl}, γ_1, γ_2, γ_3 are random variables with normal distributions, that is,

$$\alpha_{idl} \sim N(\alpha_d, \tau_\alpha)$$

and

$$\gamma_1, \gamma_2, \gamma_3 \sim N(0, 10^{-3}).$$

The linear model for the scale parameter incorporates a random effect (α) and fixed effects (γs).

Further hyperprior distributions are added. In particular, the Level 2 residual gets a distribution for the mean for $2 \leq w \leq 40$, that is,

$$\phi_i \sim N(\phi_0, \tau_\phi),$$

which in turn receives a prior distribution for the mean and the variance, that is,

$$\phi_0 \sim N(0, 1), \text{ and } \tau_\phi \sim \text{Gamma}(10^{-1}, 10^{-1}),$$

respectively.

Furthermore, the mean and the variance of the intercepts receive a prior distribution, that is,

$$\alpha_d \sim N(0, 10^{-3}) \text{ and } \tau_\alpha \sim \text{Gamma}(10^{-1}, 10^{-1}).$$

The remaining hyperprior distributions for the variances and for λ are $\tau, \tau_1, \lambda \sim \text{Gamma}(10^{-1}, 10^{-1})$. The Gamma distribution was chosen because of its tractability and convenience. Figure 6.5 shows a DAG, which is very useful for showing all the dependencies among the parameters of this complex model.

A Hierarchical Process-Dissociation Model

Rouder et al. (2008) propose a hierarchical version of Jacoby's (1991) process-dissociation model. The goal of the process-dissociation model is to separately measure conscious recollection and automatic activation in memory. Stem-completion tasks are among the experimental paradigms to test this model. In a first step, participants study a list of words, and in a second step, a stem is provided, e.g., br_, which is to be completed to form a word. Two testing conditions are distinguished—an *include* and an *exclude* condition. In the include condition, participants are instructed to complete the

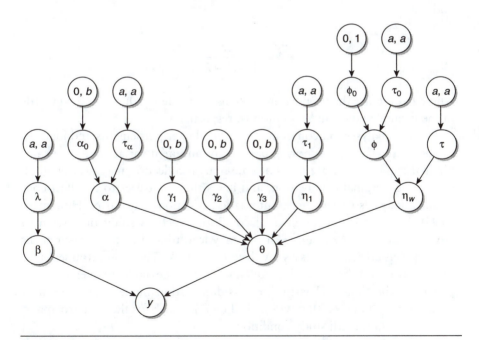

Figure 6.5   Directed Acyclic Graph (DAG) for the Peruggia et al. (2002) Model

stem with a word from the study list. In the exclude condition, participants are instructed to complete the stem with a word that was not in the study list. The model makes specific assumption of successful stem completion, depending on the experimental condition, and thereby, provides an estimate of conscious recollection and automatic activation. Let I and E be the probabilities of completing a stem with a word from the study list in the include and exclude conditions, respectively. Let R and A be the probability of conscious recollection and automatic activation, respectively, with recollection and automatic activation as binary processes. The Jacoby process-dissociation model is defined as

$$I = R + (1 - R)A \tag{6.49}$$

and

$$E = (1 - R)A. \tag{6.50}$$

Estimates for the two processes are given by

$$\hat{R} = \hat{I} - \hat{E}, \tag{6.51}$$

and

$$\hat{A} = \frac{\hat{E}}{1 - (\hat{I} - \hat{E})}, \tag{6.52}$$

where $\hat{I}$ and $\hat{E}$ are the proportion of stems completed with the studied words in the include and exclude conditions, respectively.

In most analyses, outcomes are aggregated over participants and items to obtain these estimates, ignoring participant and item variability. For example, participants who are good at conscious recollection may also be good at eliciting automatic activation, and items that are easier to recollect consciously may also elicit more automatic activation (Curran & Hintzman, 1995). Furthermore, experimental conditions such as study time seem to have an effect on the results. All this may lead to a distorted measurement of the psychological processes involved in the task. Therefore, Rouder et al. (2008) propose a three-level hierarchal version of the model to overcome this problem. The first level is the process-dissociation model as proposed in Equations 6.49 and 6.50, now indexed by i, j, and k for the ith participant, the jth item in the kth study condition,

$$I_{ijk} = R_{ijk} + (1 - R_{ijk})A_{ijk}, \tag{6.53}$$

and

$$E_{ijk} = (1 - R_{ijk})A_{ijk}. \tag{6.54}$$

The second level models the main effects of participants, items, and study conditions.

The parameters for R_{ijk} and E_{ijk} are restricted to [0, 1]. To span the real numbers, Rouder et al. (2008) put a linear model, specifically a probit model, on the parameters.[6] Let a_{ijk} and r_{ijk} denote the transformed parameters, that is $A_{ijk} = \Phi(a_{ijk})$ and $R_{ijk} = \Phi(r_{ijk})$, where Φ is a cumulative distribution function. The second level of the model is then defined as

$$r_{ijk} = \alpha_i^{(r)} + \beta_j^{(r)} + \mu_k^{(r)}, \tag{6.55}$$

and

$$a_{ijk} = \alpha_i^{(a)} + \beta_j^{(a)} + \mu_k^{(a)}, \tag{6.56}$$

where $\alpha_i^{(r)}$ and $\alpha_i^{(a)}$ denote the parameters for the ith participant's conscious recollection and automatic activation ability, respectively; $\beta_j^{(r)}$ and $\beta_j^{(a)}$ denote the parameters for the jth item's propensity to elicit conscious recollection and automatic activation, respectively; and $\mu_k^{(r)}$ and $\mu_k^{(a)}$ denote the parameters for the overall level of conscious recollection and automatic activation in the kth study condition, respectively.

In the current context, participants and items are not meant as factors in the experimental design, and variability of participants and items are merely random effects and should be modeled as such. Therefore, the αs and βs are random variables with a bivariate distribution, here bivariate normal distributions,

$$\begin{pmatrix} \alpha_i^{(r)} \\ \alpha_i^{(a)} \end{pmatrix} \sim N(0, \Sigma_\alpha), \quad i = 1, \dots, I$$

and

$$\begin{pmatrix} \beta_j^{(r)} \\ \beta_j^{(a)} \end{pmatrix} \sim N(0, \Sigma_\beta), \quad j = 1, \dots, J.$$

The Inverse-Wishart[7] is the conjugate prior distribution for the multivariate normal covariance matrix. Its density is always finite, and the integral is also always finite. In this application, the parameters were set to $m = 2$ and, Ω, a 2×2 scale matrix, to the identity matrix $\begin{pmatrix} 1 & 0 \\ 0 & 1 \end{pmatrix}$.

The parameters for the study conditions are also assumed to be normally distributed with

$$\mu_k^{(r)} = \mu_k^{(a)} \sim N(0, \sigma^2), \quad k = 1, \ldots, K.$$

The hyperparameter is set to $\sigma^2 = 1,000$.

Rouder et al. (2008) provide a full computer implementation of the analysis at http://pcl.missouri.edu. They apply the MCMC techniques for estimating the parameters. We turn to these methods next.

Parameter Estimation

In Bayesian analysis, each unknown parameter is associated with a probability distribution. As we have seen, posterior distributions can become very complex and most of them are mathematically not tractable for standard estimation procedures. This is seen as one reason why Bayesian methods were not attractive to practitioners. With the advent of statistical computing techniques, however, Bayesian methods experienced a renaissance and are now a fast-growing data analysis approach. The intimate link between modern Bayesian statistical practice and stochastic simulation techniques becomes apparent in the fast-growing literature of this field.

Markov chain simulations or MCMC methods provide a solution for multidimensional probability distributions that cannot be analytically calculated. MCMC techniques are a class of methods or algorithms for sampling values of the parameters from probability distributions. The basic idea is to construct an iterative Markov chain of consecutive values that, after a large number of steps, has the desired distribution as its equilibrium distribution. That is, the unknown parameters σ are drawn from the distributions—the prior distributions—and then adjusted in each iterative step to approximate the posterior distribution $p(\theta \mid y)$. Since the newly drawn values depend on the last values drawn, they build a Markov chain (see Chapter 4 appendix). From that distribution of simulated values, summary statistics such as mean, variance, and quantiles, and so on can be obtained as well.

There are several algorithms to produce the Markov chain, such as the Gibbs sampler and the Metropolis Hasting algorithm (MH), which are described in numerous publications, including codes for various programs.

We illustrate the basic ideas of a Gibbs sampler with an example provided by Casella and George (1992). Assume that we have a pair of random variables (X, Y). The Gibbs sampler samples from the condition distributions $p(x|y)$ and $p(y|x)$ to receive some information about the marginal, say $p(x)$. This is done by generating a Gibbs sequence of random variables

$$Y_0, X_0, Y_1, X_1, Y_2, X_2, \ldots, Y_k, X_k. \tag{6.57}$$

The initial value $Y_0 = y_0$ is set and the remaining values of 6.57 are obtained iteratively by alternately generating values from

$$X_j \sim p(x|Y_j = y_j)$$
$$Y_{j+1} \sim p(y|X_j = x_j). \tag{6.58}$$

For large enough k, X_k, converges to $p(x)$. Suppose we have the joint distribution

$$p(x, y) \propto \binom{n}{x} y^{x+\alpha-1} (1-y)^{n-x+\beta-1}, \tag{6.59}$$

$$x = 0, 1, \ldots, n \quad 0 \leq y \leq 1$$

From Equations 6.8, 6.12, and 6.13, we know that this can be expressed as conditional distributions, one is a Binomial and the other is a Beta, that is,

$$p(x|y) = \text{Bin}(n, y) \text{ and } p(y|x) = \text{Beta}(\alpha + x, \beta + n - x). \tag{6.60}$$

Assume that we are interested in the marginal $p(x)$ The Gibbs sampler allows us to generate a sample from it by applying Equation 6.58 to 6.60. Figure 6.6 shows histograms for $k = 100, 500,$ and $5,000$ with $n = 20, \alpha = 2, \beta = 4$ using MATLAB. The program can be found in Figure 6.8, left column. Note that for this example the Gibbs sampler is not needed, since the marginal can be obtained analytically, that is,

$$p(x) = \binom{n}{x} \frac{\Gamma(\alpha+\beta)}{\Gamma(\alpha)\Gamma(\beta)} \frac{\Gamma(n-x+\beta)}{\Gamma(\alpha+\beta+n)}, \quad x = 0, 1, \ldots, n, \tag{6.61}$$

and shown in the graph. The histograms are produced by Gibbs sampling with a sampling length of $k = 100, 500,$ and $5,000$. With increasing k, the simulated distribution produced by the Gibbs sampler resembles the beta-binomial distribution (Equation 6.61).

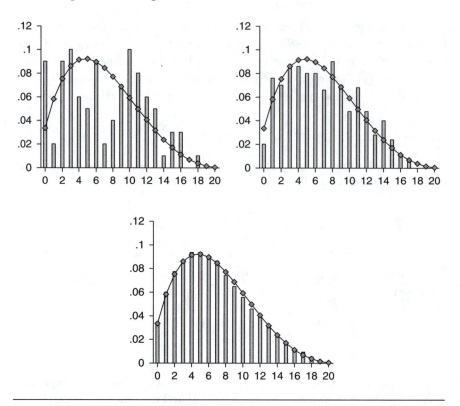

Figure 6.6   Beta-Binomial Distribution With $n = 20$, $\alpha = 2$, $\beta = 4$

Now assume that we have three random variables (X, Y, Z). The Gibbs sampler samples iteratively from $p(x \mid y, z)$, $p(y \mid x, z)$, and $p(z \mid x, y)$. The jth iteration is

$$
\begin{aligned}
X_j &\sim p(x|Y_j = y_j, Z_j = z_j), \\
Y_{j+1} &\sim p(y|X_j = x_j, Z_j = z_j), \\
Z_{j+1} &\sim p(z|X_j = x_j, Y_j = y_j)
\end{aligned}
\tag{6.62}
$$

and the Gibbs sequence of random variables produced by 6.62 is

$$
Y_0, Z_0, X_0, Y_1, Z_1, X_1, Y_2, Z_2, X_2, \ldots Y_k, Z_k, X_k.
\tag{6.63}
$$

As an example, we take again the joint distribution in Equation 6.59, but now we assume that n is a realization of a Poisson random variable with mean λ. The joint distribution becomes

$$p(x, y, n) \propto \binom{n}{x} y^{x+\alpha-1}(1-y)^{n-x+\beta-1} \exp(-\lambda)\frac{\lambda^n}{n!}, \qquad (6.64)$$

$$x = 0, 1, \ldots, n \quad 0 \leq y \leq 1, n = 1, 2, \ldots$$

As before, we want to receive some information about the marginal, $p(x)$, which cannot be calculated in closed form and, therefore, is determined by the Gibbs sampling. The conditional distributions are, as before,

$$p(x|y, n) = Bin(n, y)$$
$$p(y|x, n) = Beta(\alpha + x, \beta + n - x)$$

$$p(n|x, y) \propto \exp(-(1-y)\lambda)\frac{[(1-y)\lambda]^{n-x}}{(n-x)!}, \quad n = x, x+1, \ldots \ (6.65)$$

Applying the iteration scheme 6.62 to the distributions in Equation 6.65 generates a sequence $X_1, X_2, \ldots, X_m$ from $p(x)$. Figure 6.7 shows histograms

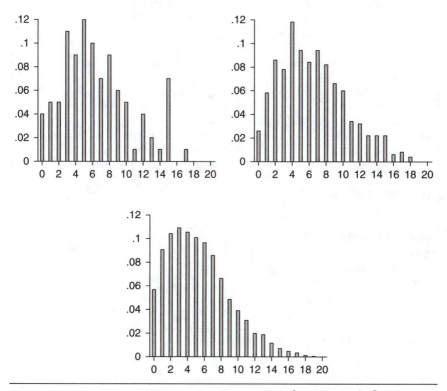

Figure 6.7   Beta-Binomial-Poisson Distribution With $\lambda = 16$, $\alpha = 2$, $\beta = 4$

NOTE: The histograms are produced by Gibbs sampling with a sampling length of $k = 100$, 500, and 5,000.

Beta-Binomial	Beta-Binomial-Poisson
| ```
n = 20;
a = 2;
b = 4;
% number of samples
m = 5000;
% create x,y vectors
x = zeros(m,1);
y = zeros(m,1);
% initial value
y(1) = rand;
% Gibbs sampling
for j = 2:m
  x(j) = binornd(n,y(j–1));
  % p(xly) is binomial
  y(j) = betarnd(x(j) + a, n – x(j) + b, 1, 1);
  % p(ylx) is beta
end

% Analytical beta-binomial
for i = 0:n;
  A = (factorial(n)/(factorial (n – i)*
  factorial(i)));
  B = gamma(a + b)/(gamma(a)*
  gamma(b));
  C = gamma(i + a)*gamma(n – i + b)/
  gamma(a + b + n);
  betanom(i + 1) = A * B * C;
end

% create figure
xx = 0:2:20;
yy = 0:.02:.12;

 [f, xout] = hist(x,100);
bar(xout,f./sum(f));
hold on;
plot([0:n], betanom, 'rd-');
hold off;
axis([–0.5 20.5 0.12]);
``` | ```
lambda = 16;
a = 2;
b = 4;
% number of samples
m = 5000;
% create x, y, z vectors
x = zeros(m,1);
y = zeros(m,1);
z = zeros(m,1);
% initial values
y(1) = rand;
za(1) = 4;
% Gibbs sampling
for j = 2:m
  x(j) = binornd(z(j – 1), y(j – 1));
  % p(xly,n) is binomial
  y(j) = betarnd(x(j)+a,z(j – 1) – x(j )+b, 1, 1);
  % p(ylx,n) is beta
  z(j) = poissrnd(lambda*(1 – y(j))) + x(j);
  % p(zlx,y) is Poisson
end

% create figure
xx = 0:2:20;
yy = 0:.02:.12;

fs = 16;
[f, xout] = hist(x,100);
bar(xout,f./sum(f));
axis([–0.5 20.5 0.12]);
``` |

Figure 6.8   MATLAB Program for Gibbs Sampler

for $k = 100$, 500, and $5,000$ with $\lambda = 16$, $\alpha = 2$, $\beta = 4$ using MATLAB. The program is in Figure 6.8, right column.

There are various programs providing routines for producing the Markov chains.

For example, WinBUGS and BUGS (Bayesian inference Using Gibbs Sampling) developed by the MRC Biostatistics Unit, Cambridge, UK, is an open source program and widely spread among Bayesian modelers (www .mrc-bsu.cam.ac.uk/bugs). Gill (2008) gives an introduction of Bayesian methods for social and behavioral sciences including R codes.

Concluding Remarks

Hierarchical Bayesian modeling becomes more and more attractive to cognitive psychologists. It is applied as a statistical tool (e.g., response time analysis) and more recently built into cognitive models such as Jacoby's (1991) process-dissociation model.

One advantage of hierarchical Bayesian modeling is that it can improve the estimation of the model parameters. It is a data-driven approach and allows inclusion of prior knowledge about the parameters. A possible drawback is that hierarchical modeling requires a great deal of computation, which, however, is facilitated by MCMC methods and user-friendly software. Furthermore, hierarchical Bayesian models do not substitute content models; they can be applied to them as structural/statistical means to support modeling in cognitive science.

Notes

1. To determine the parameters note that (Gelman et al., 2004, p. 582)

$$\alpha + \beta = \frac{E(\theta)(1 - E(\theta))}{\text{var}(\theta)} - 1, \alpha = (\alpha + \beta)E(\theta), \beta = (\alpha + \beta)(1 - E(\theta)).$$

2. The prior distribution is called the population distribution since the θ_js are viewed as samples from a common population distribution.

3. $\text{logit}(p) = \log\left(\dfrac{p}{1-p}\right).$

4. Recall that the Beta distribution is the posterior distribution of a binomial distribution with parameter θ after observing $\alpha - 1$ events with probability θ and $\beta - 1$ events with probability $1 - \theta$.

5. With few observations (three to four measurement occasions), it is convenient to employ a linear change function model (see Raudenbush & Bryk, 2002, p. 163).

6. Binary and binomial data are frequently obtained in many areas of cognitive psychology ranging from basic decisions in perception to memory to complex decision making to categorization. The standard assumption is that the observed responses—proportions y_{ij}—have a binomial distribution. The generalized linear model for it is (see McCullagh & Nelder, 1989, for details):

Random component:

With π_{ij} denoting the probability of "success" in n_{ij} trials,

$y_{ij}|\pi_{ij} \sim B(n_{ij}, \pi_{ij})$ with $E(y_{ij}|\pi_{ij})$, $= n_{ij}\pi_{ij}$, and $Var(y_{ij}|\pi_{ij}) = n_{ij}\pi_{ij}(1 - \pi_{ij})$.

Obviously, "success" refers to the predefined answer category such as "yes, detected," "yes, recalled."

Systematic component:

$$\eta_{ij} = \beta_{0j} + \beta_{1j}x_{i1j} + \beta_{2j}x_{i2j} + \cdots + \beta_{Kj}x_{iKj}$$

The model is linear in its parameters.

Link function:

The binomial distribution requires $0 < \pi_{ij} < 1$ and, therefore, the link function should be such that it maps the interval $(0, 1)$ onto the whole real line. This condition can be met by several possible link functions (see, e.g., Goldstein, 2003; McCullagh & Nelder, 1989):

a. Logit $\eta_{ij} = \log\left(\dfrac{\pi_{ij}}{1 - \pi_{ij}}\right)$;

b. Probit $\eta_{ij} = \Phi^{-1}(\pi_{ij})$, where $\Phi(\cdot)$ is the normal cumulative distribution function;

c. Complementary log-log $\eta_{ij} = \log(-\log(1 - \pi_{ij}))$.
    Note that η_{ij} can take on any real value while π_{ij} is restricted to the interval $[0, 1]$.

7. The Inverse-Wishart distribution is given by

$$p(s|m, \Omega) = \frac{|\Omega|^{m/2}|S|^{-(m+3/2)}}{2^m\Gamma_2(m/2)}\exp\left(-\frac{1}{2}\text{tr}(\Omega S^{-1})\right),$$

where S is a positive definite matrix and Γ_p is the multivariate gamma function.

References

Allenby, G., & Rossi, P. (2006). Hierarchical Bayes models: A practitioner's guide. In R. Grover & M. Vriens (Eds.), *The handbook of marketing research* (pp. 418–440). Thousand Oaks, CA: Sage.

Anderson, J. R., & Lebiere, C. (1998). *The atomic components of thought*. Mahwah, NJ: Erlbaum.

Anderson, T. W. (1971). *The statistical analysis of time series*. New York: Wiley.

Andrieu, C. (2003). An introduction to MCMC for machine learning. *Machine Learning, 50,* 5–43.

Ashby, F. G. (2000). A stochastic version of general recognition theory. *Journal of Mathematical Psychology, 44,* 310–329.

Ashby, G., & Maddox, W. T. (1993). Relations between prototype, exemplar, and decision bound models of categorization. *Journal of Mathematical Psychology, 37,* 372–400.

Batchelder, W. H. (1998). Multinomial processing tree models and psychological assessment. *Psychological Assessment, 10,* 331–344.

Bechara, A., & Damasio, A. R. (2005). The somatic marker hypothesis: A neural theory of economic decision. *Games and Economic Behavior, 52,* 336–372.

Bechara, A., Damasio, H., Tranel, D., & Damasio, A. R. (1997). Deciding advantageously before knowing the advantageous strategy. *Science, 275,* 1293–1295.

Berger, J. O. (1985). *Statistical decision theory and Bayesian analysis* (2nd ed.). New York: Springer-Verlag.

Bhattacharya, R. N., & Waymire, E. C. (1990). *Stochastic processes with applications*. New York: Wiley.

Bozdogan, H. (2000). On the information based measure of covariance complexity in its application to the evaluation of multivariate linear models. *Journal of Mathematical Psychology, 44,* 62–91.

Brown, M. W. (2000). Cross validation methods. *Journal of Mathematical Psychology, 44,* 108–132.

Busemeyer, J. R., & Stout, J. C. (2002). A contribution of cognitive decision models to clinical assessment: Decomposing performance on the Bechara Gambling Task. *Psychological Assessment, 14(3),* 253–262.

Busemeyer, J. R., & Townsend, J. T. (1993). Decision field theory: A dynamic cognition approach to decision making. *Psychological Review, 100,* 432–459.

Busemeyer, J. R., & Wang, Y. (2000). Model comparisons and model selections based on the generalization criterion methodology. *Journal of Mathematical Psychology, 44,* 171–189.

Casella, G. (1985). An introduction to empirical Bayes data analysis. *The American Statistician, 39*(2), 83–87.

Casella, G., & George, E. I. (1992). Explaining the Gibbs sampler. *The American Statistician, 46*(3), 167–174.

Cohen, A. L., Sanborn, A. N., & Shiffrin, R. M. (in press). Model evaluation using grouped or individual data. *Psychonomic Bulletin and Review, 15,* 692–712.

Collins, L. M. (2006). Analysis of longitudinal data: The integration of theoretical model, temporal model, and statistical model. *Annual Review of Psychology, 57,* 505–528.

Craik, F. I., & Lockhart, R. S. (1972). Levels of processing: A framework for memory research. *Journal of Verbal Learning and Verbal Behavior, 11*(6), 671–684.

Cudeck, R., & Harring, J. R. (2007). Analysis of nonlinear patterns of change with random coefficient models. *Annual Review of Psychology, 58,* 21.1–21.23.

Curran, T., & Hintzman, D. L. (1995). Violations of the independence assumption in process dissociation. *Journal of Experimental Psychology: Learning, Memory, and Cognition, 21,* 531–547.

Diederich, A. (1997). Dynamic stochastic models for decision making under time constraints. *Journal of Mathematical Psychology, 41,* 260–274.

Diederich, A., & Busemeyer, J. R. (2003). Simple matrix methods for analyzing diffusion models of choice probability, choice response time and simple response time. *Journal of Mathematical Psychology, 47*(3), 304–322.

Efron, B. (2003). Robbins, Empirical Bayes and microarrays. *The Annals of Statistics, 31*(2), 366–378.

Estes, W. K., & Maddox, T. (2005). The risk of drawing inferences about cognitive processes from model fits to individual versus average data. *Psychonomic Bulletin and Review, 53,* 134–140.

Feller, W. (1968). *An introduction to probability theory and its applications.* New York: Wiley.

Fletcher, R. (1987). *Practical methods of optimization.* New York: Wiley.

Forster, M. R. (2000). Key concepts in model selection: Performance and generalizability. *Journal of Mathematical Psychology, 44*(1), 205–231.

Gallant, A. R. (1986). *Nonlinear statistical models.* New York: Wiley.

Garner, W. R., Hake, H. W., & Eriksen, C. W. (1956). Operationism and the concept of perception. *Psychological Review, 63*(3), 149–159.

Gelman, A. (2006). Multilevel (hierarchical) modeling: What it can and can't do. *Technometrics, 48*(4), 432–435.

Gelman, A., Carlin, J. B., Stern, H. S., & Rubin, D. B. (2004). *Bayesian data analysis* (2nd ed.). Boca Raton, FL: Chapman & Hall.

Gilden, D. L. (2001). Cognitive emissions of $1/f$ noise. *Psychological Review, 108*(1), 33–56.

Gill, J. (2008). Bayesian methods: Asocial and behavioral sciences approach (2nd ed.). London: Chapman & Hall.

Gluck, M. A., & Bower, G. H. (1988) From conditioning to category learning: An adaptive network model. *Journal of Experimental Psychology: General, 128,* 309–331.

Goldstein, H. (2003). *Multilevel statistical models. Kendall's Library of Statistics 3.* (3rd ed.). London: Arnold.

Goldstein, H., Healy, M. J. R., & Rashbash, J. (1994). Multilevel time series models with applications to repeated measures data. *Statistics in Medicine, 11,* 1643–1655.

Goldstein, H., & McDonald, R. P. (1988). A general model for the analysis of multilevel data. *Psychometrica, 53*(4), 455–467.

Green, D. M., & Swets, J. A. (1966). *Signal detection theory and psychophysics.* New York: Wiley.

Griffiths, T. L., Kemp, C., & Tenenbaum, J. B. (2008). Bayesian models of cognition. In R. Sun (Ed.), *Cambridge handbook of computational cognitive modeling* (pp. 59–100). Cambridge, UK: Cambridge University Press.

Grossberg, S. (1982). *Studies of mind and brain: Neural principles of learning, perception, development, cognition, and motor control.* Hingham, MA: D. Reidel.

Grunwald, P. (2000). Model selection based on minimum descriptive length. *Journal of Mathematical Psychology, 44,* 133–152.

Heathcote, A. J., & Brown, S. D. (2002). Quantile maximum likelihood estimation of response time distributions. *Psychonomic Bulletin and Review, 9,* 394–401.

Hoffman, L., & Rovine, M. J. (2007). Multilevel models for the experimental psychologist: Foundations and illustrative examples. *Behavior Research Methods, 39*(1), 101–117.

Holland, J. H. (1975). *Adaptation in natural and artificial systems.* Ann Arbor: University of Michigan Press.

Hox, J. (2002). *Multilevel analysis: Techniques and applications.* Mahwah, NJ: Lawrence Erlbaum.

Ingber, L. (1993). Simulated annealing: Practice versus theory. *Mathematical Computer Modelling, 18*(11), 29–57.

Jacoby, L. L. (1991). A process dissociation framework: Separating automatic from intentional uses of memory. *Journal of Memory and Language, 30,* 513–541.

Kirkpatrick, S., Gelatt, C. D., & Vecchi, M. P. (1983). Optimization by simulated annealing. *Science, 220,* 671–680.

Knowlton, B. J., & Squire, L. (1993). The learning of categories: Parallel brain systems for item memory and category knowledge. *Science, 262,* 1747–1749.

Krantz, D. H., Luce, R. D., Suppes, P., & Tversky, A. (1972). *Foundations of measurement* (Vol. 1). San Diego, CA: Academic Press.

Kruschke, J. K. (1992). ALCOVE: An exemplar based connectionist model of category learning. *Psychological Review, 99,* 22–44.

Laird, N. M., & Ware, J. H. (1982). Random-effects models for longitudinal data. *Biometrics, 38,* 963–974.

Laming, D. R. (1968). *Information theory of choice-reaction times.* New York: Academic Press.

Lee, M. D. (2006). A hierarchical Bayesian model of human decision-making on an optimal stopping problem. *Cognitive Science, 30,* 555–580.

Lee, M. D. (2008). Three case studies in the Bayesian analysis of cognitive models. *Psychonomic Bulletin & Review, 15*, 1–15.

Lee, M. D., Fuss, I. G., & Navarro, D. J. (2007). A Bayesian approach to diffusion models of decision-making and response time. In B. Schölkopf, J. C. Platt, & T. Hofmann (Eds.), *Advances in Neural Information Processing Systems 19* (pp. 809–816). Cambridge, MA: MIT Press.

Link, S. W., & Heath, R. A. (1975). A sequential theory of psychological discrimination. *Psychometrika, 40*, 77–111.

Logan, G. (1988). Toward an instance theory of automatization. *Psychological Review, 95*, 492–527.

Luce, D., & Suppes, P. (1965). Preference, utility, and subjective probability. In R. D. Luce, R. R. Bush, & E. Galanter (Eds.), *Handbook of mathematical psychology* (Vol. 3, pp. 249–410).

Luce, R. D. (2000). *Utility of gains and losses: Measurement-theoretic and experimental approaches.* Mahwah, NJ: Lawrence Erlbaum.

Luenberger, D. G. (1979). *Introduction to dynamic systems: Theory models and applications.* New York: Wiley.

Maddox, W. T., & Filoteo, J. V. (2001). Striatal contributions to category learning: Quantitative modeling of simple linear and complex non-linear rule learning in patients with Parkinson's disease. *Journal of the International Neuropsychological Society, 7*, 710–727.

Malmberg, K. J., & Xu, J. (2006). The influence of averaging and noisy decision strategies on the recognition memory ROC. *Psychonomic Bulletin & Review, 13*, 99–105.

Marr, D. (1982). *Vision.* New York: W. H. Freeman.

McCullagh, P., & Nelder, J. A. (1989). Generalized linear models. (2nd ed.). New York: Chapman & Hall.

McDonald, J. L. (1997). Language acquisition: The acquisition of linguistic structure in normal and special populations. *Annual Review of Psychology, 48*, 215–241.

Medin, D. L., & Schaffer, M. M. (1978). Context theory of classification. *Psychological Review, 85*, 207–238.

Murdock, B. B. (1993). TODAM 2: A model for the storage and retrieval of item, associative, and serial order information. *Psychological Review, 100*, 183–203.

Myung, I. J. (2000). The importance of complexity in model selection. *Journal of Mathematical Psychology, 44*, 190–204.

Myung, I. J., Kim, C., & Pitt, M. A. (2000). Toward an explanation of the power law artifact: Insights from response surface analysis. *Memory and Cognition, 28*, 832–840.

Nelder, J. A., & Mead, R. (1965). A simplex method for function minimization. *Computer Journal, 7*, 308–313.

Newell, A. (1990). *Unified theories of cognition.* Cambridge, MA: Harvard University Press.

Nosofsky, R. M. (1988). Exemplar-based accounts of relations between classification, recognition, and typicality. *Journal of Experimental Psychology: Learning, Memory, Cognition, 14*, 700–708.

Nosofsky, R. M., & Palmeri, T. J. (1997). An exemplar-based random walk model of speeded classification. *Psychological Review, 104,* 226–300.

Nosofsky, R. M., & Zaki, S. F. (1998). Dissociations between categorization and recognition in amnesic and normal individuals: An exemplar based interpretation. *Psychological Science, 9,* 247–255.

O'Reilly, R. C., & Munakata, Y. (2000). *Computational explorations in cognitive neuroscience: Understanding the mind by simulating the brain.* Cambridge, MA: MIT Press.

Payne, J. W., Bettman, J. R., & Johnson, E. J. (1993). *The adaptive decision maker.* New York: Cambridge University Press.

Peruggia, M., Van Zandt, T., & Chen, M. (2002). Was it a car or a cat I saw? An analysis of response times for word recognition. In C. Gatsonis, R. E. Kass, A. Carriquiry, A. Gelman, D. Higdon, D. K. Pauler, et al. (Eds.), *Case studies in Bayesian statistics* (Vol. 6, pp. 319–334). New York: Springer-Verlag.

Pike, A. R. (1966). Stochastic models of choice behavior: Response probabilities and latencies of finite Markov chain systems. *British Journal of Mathematical and Statistical Psychology, 19,* 15–32.

Rao, C. R. (1965). *Linear statistical inference and its applications.* New York: Wiley.

Ratcliff, R. (1978). A theory of memory retrieval. *Psychological Review, 85,* 59–108.

Ratcliff, R., & Smith, P. L. (2004). A comparison of sequential sampling models for two-choice reaction time. *Psychological Review, 111,* 333–367.

Ratcliff, R., Thaper, A., & McKoon, G. (2001). The effects of aging on reaction time in a signal detection task. *Psychology & Aging, 16,* 323–341.

Ratcliff, R., & Tuerlinckx, F. (2002). Estimating parameters of the diffusion model: Approaches to dealing with contaminant reaction times and parameter variability. *Psychonomic Bulletin and Review, 9,* 438–481.

Raudenbush, S. W. (2001). Comparing personal trajectories and drawing causal inferences from longitudinal data. *Annual Review of Psychology, 52,* 501–525.

Raudenbush, S. W., & Bryk, A. S. (2002). *Hierarchical linear models: Applications and data analysis methods* (2nd ed.). Thousand Oaks, CA: Sage.

Roberts, S., & Pashler, H. (2000). How persuasive is a good fit? A comment on theory testing. *Psychological Review, 107,* 358–367.

Rosenbaum, D. A., Carlson, R. A., & Gilmore, R. O. (2001). Acquisition of intellectual and perceptual-motor skills. *Annual Review of Psychology, 52,* 453–470.

Rouder, J. N., & Lu, J. (2005). An introduction to Bayesian hierarchical models with an application in the theory of signal detection. *Psychonomic Bulletin & Review, 12,* 573–604.

Rouder, J. N., Lu, J., Morey, R. D., Sun, D., & Speckman, P. L. (2008). A hierarchical process-dissociation model. *Journal of Experimental Psychology: General, 137*(2), 370–389.

Rouder, J. N., Lu, J., Speckman, P. L., Sun, D., & Jiang, Y. (2005). A hierarchical model for estimating response time distributions. *Psychonomic Bulletin & Review, 12,* 195–223.

Rouder, J. N., Lu, J., Sun, D., Speckman, P. L., Morey, R. D., & Naveh-Benjamin, M. (2007). Signal detection models with random participant and item effects [Online]. *Psychometrika, 72*(4).

Rouder, J. N., Morey, R. D., Speckman, P. L., & Pratte, M. S. (2007). Detecting chance: A solution to the null sensitivity problem in subliminal priming. *Psychonomic Bulletin & Review, 14*, 597–605.

Rouder, J. N., Sun, D., Speckman, P. L., Lu, J., & Zhou, D. (2003). A hierarchical Bayesian statistical framework for response time distributions. *Psychometrika, 68*(4), 589–606.

Ruben, D. C., & Wenzel, A. E. (1996). One hundred years of forgetting: A quantitative description of retention. *Psychological Review, 105*(4), 734–760.

Rumelhart, D., & McClelland, J. L. (1986). *Parallel distributed processing: Explorations in the microstructure of cognition.* Cambridge, MA: MIT Press.

Shiffrin, R., & Steyvers, M. (1997). A model for recognition memory: REM—retrieving effectively from memory. *Psychonomic Bulletin and Review, 4*, 145–166.

Sivia, D. S., & Skilling, J. (2006). *Data analysis: A Bayesian tutorial* (2nd ed.). Oxford, UK: Oxford University Press.

Smith, P. L. (2000). Stochastic dynamic models of response time and accuracy: A foundational primer. *Journal of Mathematical Psychology, 44*, 408–463.

Snijders, T. A. B., & Bosker, R. J. (1999). *Multilevel analysis: An introduction to basic and advanced multilevel modeling.* London: Sage.

Strang, G. (1988). *Linear algebra and its applications.* San Diego: Harcourt Brace Jovanovich.

Sutton, R. S., & Barto, A. G. (1998). *Reinforcement learning: An introduction.* Cambridge, MA: MIT Press.

Tolman, E. C. (1948). Cognitive maps in rats and men. *Psychological Review, 55*(4), 189–208.

Townsend, J. T. (1990). Serial vs. parallel processing: Sometimes they look like Tweedledum and Tweedledee but they can (and should be) distinguished. *Psychological Science, 1*, 46–54.

Townsend, J. T., & Ashby, F. G. (1983). *Stochastic modeling of elementary psychological processes.* Cambridge, UK: Cambridge University Press.

Usher, M., & McClelland, J. L. (2001). The time course of perceptual choice: The leaky, competing accumulator model. *Psychological Review, 108*(3), 550–592.

Van Zandt, T. (2000). How to fit a response time distribution. *Psychonomic Bulletin and Review, 7*, 424–465.

Vandekerckhove, J., Tuerlinckx, F., & Lee, M. D. (2008). A Bayesian approach to diffusion process models of decision making. In V. Sloutsky, B. Love, & K. McRae (Eds.), *Proceedings of the 30th Annual Conference of the Cognitive Science Society* (pp. 1429–1434). Austin, TX: Cognitive Science Society.

Vickers, D. (1979). *Decision processes in visual perception.* New York: Academic Press.

Wasserman, L. (2000). Bayesian model selection and model averaging. *Journal of Mathematical Psychology, 44*, 92–107.

Index

Note: In page references, f indicates figures and t indicates tables.

About the Authors

Jerome R. Busemeyer is currently a professor of psychological and brain sciences and professor in cognitive science at Indiana University. He has served on several national grant-review panels. His research work has been federally funded by the U.S. government for the past 25 years. He has published more than 100 articles in various psychological and mathematical social science journals. Currently, he is the chief editor of *Journal of Mathematical Psychology*. During the past few years, he served as the manager of the Cognition and Decision Program at the Air Force Office of Scientific Research. His recent research explores mathematical models of decision making and learning. Perhaps his most important work so far is the development of a dynamic model of human decision making called decision field theory. He received his PhD degree from the University of South Carolina at Columbia.

Adele Diederich is currently a professor in psychology at Jacobs University, Germany. She has served on grant-review panels in the United States, and her research has been funded by the German government for the past 10 years. She has published more than 50 articles in various psychological and mathematical social science journals. She is now Editor of *Experimental Psychology* and Associate Editor of the *European Journal of Pure and Applied Mathematics*. She is also on the editorial board of *Journal of Mathematical Psychology*. Her current research focuses on developing mathematical models for sensory processing and decision making. Her multistage diffusion model for decision making is considered to be her most important work so far. She has been awarded the Heisenberg Fellowship. She received her PhD degree from the University of Hamburg, Germany.